"In a world prone to outrage, leaders must navigate with grace, resilience, and strategic insight. This book provides the tools for managing effectively amidst turmoil, ensuring your organization not only endures but thrives."

—**FRANCES FREI,** Professor, Harvard Business School;
former Senior Vice President, Uber; and coauthor, *Move Fast and Fix Things*

"*The Age of Outrage* is extremely helpful to leaders facing today's confrontations, prompting them to ask the right questions and presenting a toolbox not only for responding in a measured, de-escalating, and thereby effective manner, but also for enhancing resilience at many levels."

—**THOMAS BECKER,** Global Vice President of Sustainability and
Mobility Strategy, BMW Group

"We live in an era of outrage and outages, and Ramanna has masterfully created a very thoughtful and timely leadership playbook to deal with these complex but very relevant issues of today. A must-read for every leader and for aspiring future leaders."

—**KOUSHIK CHATTERJEE,** Executive Director and
Chief Financial Officer, Tata Steel

"Karthik Ramanna helps CEOs and other top leaders survive a crisis in the age of social media. His chapter on temperate leadership should be required reading for executives from Wall Street to Main Street who would otherwise be tempted to suppress dissent."

—**BROOKE MASTERS,** US Financial Editor, *Financial Times*

"*The Age of Outrage* offers a transformative read for anyone interested in understanding and navigating the complexities of leadership in turbulent times. His framework for managing outrage is particularly insightful, promising valuable strategies for leaders across various sectors. A must-read for those looking to lead effectively in an era where outrage seems omnipresent."

—**SIR SAJID JAVID,** former UK Chancellor of the Exchequer;
former UK Home Secretary; and former Conservative Party MP

"As Karthik Ramanna writes, we urgently need to update our leadership playbook for these tumultuous times. His framework for how to shape and live by your organization's values should be required reading for leaders making decisions that will determine our future."

—**CONGRESSMAN SETH MOULTON,** US House of Representatives (D-Massachusetts); former candidate, Democratic nomination for US President

"Reading *The Age of Outrage,* one wonders how many communications calamities might have been avoided with the benefit of these insights. Karthik Ramanna has produced a user's manual for the current context. Not taking sides, he helps leaders in both the private and public sectors understand the instability of this moment—and act accordingly."

—**DAVID RHODES,** Executive Chairman, Sky News Group; former President, CBS News; former Vice President, Fox News

The

Age

of

OUTRAGE

The

Age

of

OUTRAGE

How to Lead in a Polarized World

KARTHIK RAMANNA

HARVARD BUSINESS REVIEW PRESS
BOSTON, MASSACHUSETTS

Library of Congress Cataloging-in-Publication Data
Names: Ramanna, Karthik, author.
Title: The age of outrage : how to lead in a polarized world / Karthik Ramanna.
Description: Boston, Massachusetts : Harvard Business Review Press, [2024] | Includes index. |
Identifiers: LCCN 2024005625 (print) | LCCN 2024005626 (ebook) | ISBN 9781647826291 (hardcover) | ISBN 9781647826307 (epub)
Subjects: LCSH: Leadership. | Polarization (Social sciences) | Right and left (Political science) | Corporate image. | Customer relations.
Classification: LCC HD57.7 .R358 2024 (print) | LCC HD57.7 (ebook) | DDC 658.4/092—dc23/eng/20240327
LC record available at https://lccn.loc.gov/2024005625
LC ebook record available at https://lccn.loc.gov/2024005626

ISBN: 978-1-64782-629-1
eISBN: 978-1-64782-630-7

For Siddy and Sammy

Contents

Preface

As an academic leader at Oxford University's Blavatnik School of Government, I increasingly found myself confronting individuals who were angry with "the way the world works" and what they saw as my role in it. One student bluntly declared: "You *are* the system." As a brown, gay man, and an immigrant twice over, I was at once somewhat amused and astonished. Where, I wondered, did this kind of hostility against established institutions, such as Oxford, and those within them come from?

Oxford and its professors are not the only targets. These days almost every leader (and sometimes even rank-and-file employees) in the business, government, or not-for-profit sectors, from organizations of all sizes, must deal with their share of people with very short fuses. Witness the dilemma government leaders in Ottawa, Canada, faced in early 2022, when confronted with blockades of the city by truckers constituting a "Freedom Convoy;" or the associated challenges confronting businesses such as GoFundMe or TD Bank, which were then facing pressures to cut off donations to the protesting truckers. Even popular companies like Apple and acclaimed universities like Harvard, or once-iconic leaders like Angela Merkel, can find themselves suddenly managing outrage flashpoints, both with internal members of their teams and with external stakeholders.

Of course, dealing with angry stakeholders is as old as organizations themselves. But "managing outrage" is not "managing *in the age of* outrage." There is something distinctive about the zeitgeist of our times that makes the outrage that I and many other organizational leaders encounter different from a quite recent past in which civility was still a norm. Outrage is no longer an occasional phenomenon—it is a daily part of life, and managing outrage has moved from being an occasional leadership challenge (like PR handling of a crisis) to a necessary and critical capability (like financial acumen or strategic thinking). Which brings me to my motive in writing this book.

The Origin of the Book

About eight years ago, I decided to accept a role as professor and director of the Master of Public Policy (MPP) program at the University of Oxford's newly established Blavatnik School of Government. This decision entailed turning several dials, so to speak, including moving continents and countries from the United States to the UK and moving employers from Harvard to Oxford. Turning any one of these dials seemed at the time like a major undertaking, so doing all at once seemed downright daunting. But it was the thrill of what could be accomplished in this new setting that provoked me to take the plunge.

In an era of profound distrust in governments, I would have the ability to shape the leadership curriculum for those likely to be tomorrow's presidents and prime ministers, given Oxford's unparalleled ability to attract the world's best and brightest public-service students. (For instance, all but four of Britain's seventeen prime ministers since the Second World War have been Oxford graduates.)

My initial foray into leadership education, at Harvard Business School, had given me reassuring experience of the task ahead and potential pitfalls. I had come to teaching leadership from a career in quantitative economics, largely in the wake of the 2008–2009 financial crisis, when I realized that the world needed something more than MIT-trained economists (like me) teaching Harvard MBAs how to make more money. My HBS students had responded well to my pivot to leadership development, signaling the value of such a shift, but now the task at Oxford was more ambitious and potentially transformational. I settled into my role eager to fix the way we educated leaders for government.

As diverse as my HBS classroom was, it did not prepare me for the tremendous diversity I was to experience among my MPPs. For one, the MPPs ranged in age from twenty-one to fifty-one and, for another, have to date hailed from over 120 countries. But still more relevant: whereas one can safely assume that more than 95 percent of students at HBS see a career in business as a life well lived (why else would they be there?), I often joke that fewer than 50 percent of the Oxford MPPs are entirely convinced that universal adult suffrage is essential to a good society. Put differently, the scope and range for fundamental disagreement in my new program was tremendous, and from this diversity, I was expected to forge an educational experience that would be meaningful and last a lifetime. To boot, I went from being seen by my students as "one of the good guys" (the "ethics professor" at HBS) to becoming the suspicious American transplant from what is sometimes called the "West Point of capitalism."[1]

During my seven years as Oxford MPP director, I came to fully realize how arrogant and imperialistic I had been to imagine I would forge the leadership curriculum for a new generation of government leaders from scores of countries. Indeed, I have had a wonderful innings in the role, and I am very proud of my accomplishments and would do it all again in a heartbeat, but my job of "fixing public-leadership education" is incomplete and will *never* be complete. It is an ongoing task that future cohorts of educators must inherit, sometimes building on my success and more often correcting my mistakes.

The structural incompleteness of my task, and of many other leadership roles today, is a feature of this age of outrage and the deep disagreements it embodies. To some of my students, I *am* the problem—because in my role I represent Oxford's centuries-old history of Western expansionism, with a legacy of empire and baggage therein. With my personal history as a person of color, a sexual minority, and a somewhat incurable immigrant, I hardly saw myself as the "elite establishment" that so many fear and distrust (and even hate) today. I grew up in a working-class suburb of Mumbai in what was then a very much more impoverished India (where, for instance, homosexuality was still illegal, punishable by years of hard labor), later educated on merit scholarships from age eighteen all the way through a doctorate. And when I was once nominated for a senior oversight role in the UK, I was told, with perhaps chilling candor, that I "hadn't been in the country long enough." How did I then come to embody *the system*?

As I reflected further, I realized my detractors' point. I had not been educated at Eton or Oxford, of course, and was not myself the product of imperial privilege as India's founding father, Jawaharlal Nehru, had been (Harrow School and Cambridge University) but by playing within the rules of that game, I did now represent in many ways a version of that same system. And, as someone in an interracial same-sex marriage, I also embodied the modern cosmopolitan values that were out of keeping with the social conservatism of many of the places that are fearful of the future and feel they have been dealt a raw deal by the globalists. My institutional leadership is, in a sense, like all institutional leadership in this age of outrage, somewhat *othering*.

Therefore, in a spirit of self-reflection, I offer the system for managing in the age of outrage presented in this book. It is in part the fruit of study into both how organizations around the world have triggered an era of institutional distrust and how they have managed the fallout of outrage that may or may not be of their direct creation. I have also learned from the insights and reactions of the students who have studied these cases with me in the classroom. My contribution has been to relate, as I see relevant, those experiences—lived and studied—to the rich literature in the psychological, organizational, and political sciences on the causes and dynamics of outrage and its management at an individual, group, and systemic scale.

Perhaps what I most want to convey here is that this book is not just for straight, white, silver-haired men over the age of fifty. I developed the framework first for myself (an unlikely leader for a place like Oxford), and I submit that anyone—regardless of color, demographic background, income level, or origin story—can find such a framework helpful. After all, almost anyone can be blamed for something outside their control, and in fact, if you are a leader, you probably will be at some point. In the age of outrage, it is part of the job description. And, despite your leadership urge to fix the problem, you will not be able to do so fully. Modesty, I will argue, is an essential leadership ingredient for this age.

Managing in the Age of Outrage

I see this *age* of outrage as rooted in a perfect storm of the three main drivers of outrage, which have become especially salient in modern, economically developed countries. These drivers themselves are familiar—people's outrage at institutions and leaders typically stems from some combination of despair about the future (our institutions and leaders cannot make our lives better), a sense of past injustice or exclusion (our institutions and leaders have given us a raw deal), and a belief some hostile or alien "other" is to blame for our plight (because our institutions and leaders prefer them).

Throughout history, groups of people have felt and reacted to these emotions, sometimes with violent consequences, but for the most part, these expressions of outrage are localized and contained. Less often, we see large groups of people coming together with a sense of shared despair and exclusion looking to overthrow a status quo seen as distant, uncaring, and remote. I submit that in the modern, developed economies of the West, we are experiencing such a period. For many people in the United States and the Western world, more broadly, there is real fear of an uncertain future that will be worse than the present, deep resentment about governance decisions from the recent and distant pasts, and a nagging sense that traditional cultures are under siege, all amplified through social media platforms, which are enabling outraged people to find each other and feed off their shared sense of desperation, exclusion, and isolation.

The potential consequences of this dynamic are severe—in past times when such storms have raged, the result has often been global or civil war and widespread devastation, and today there are many reasons to fear similar outcomes, perhaps even more devastating than before.

Yet history is not destiny, and I do believe that leaders and institutions can work their way through this age of outrage. In this book, I offer a framework for those with organizational and institutional agency to move beyond the stalemate and to hopefully avoid catastrophic violence. With this framework, current and aspiring leaders can go beyond standard posturing and rhetorical approaches to buy time and, instead, create space for starting conversations between parties that are otherwise unproductively hostile to each other. More importantly, the framework offers a path to action for leaders to make a positive difference in a divided world.

I have built the framework inductively through a series of deep-dive case-studies on organizations from both public and private sectors, including IKEA, the London Metropolitan Police, Nestlé, and Oxford University Hospitals. Additional case studies draw on lessons from managing in these times of turmoil in hugely varied settings such as the Brazilian National Education Council as it tries to protect gender minorities in the age of political protagonists like President Bolsonaro, the US Attorney's Office for the Southern District of New York as it tries to source talent and retain prosecutorial independence in a politicized justice system, the Finance Ministry of Colombia as it tries to pass urgent tax reforms in the face of populist protests, the Kaduna State Peace Commission in Nigeria as it tries to build understanding in the face of rising ethnic killings, and even the Vatican as it tries to combat corruption at its highest ranks in the fallout from sexual-abuse scandals.[2]

What characterizes these cases is not simply the presence of an immediate crisis that needs good PR tactics, but more significantly the need for a sustained new approach to general management that acknowledges and addresses the breakdown in trust across societies and stakeholders. To learn from these case studies, I have drawn on analytical insights from disciplines as wide-ranging as the science of aggression and literary criticism, from managerial economics, organizational behavior, and political philosophy (although I caution readers that my intent is not to comprehensively survey these literatures, but to highlight scholarship that resonates with my work with managers).

The framework I have developed is not intended to be a replacement for essential conversations about organizational strategy or values, that is, questions of *what* to do over the long run. The framework's purpose, rather, is to create space for those conversations to emerge as part of its checklists, and its core focus is managerial; that is, it addresses issues of *how* to operate over the intermediate run. In this sense, what I say in the book may be a disappointment for those looking for revolutionary changes to the way the world works. I am not ruling those out, but such rapid, systemic changes in times of deep polarization often provoke violence, which we are all well served to avoid. Rather, I hope to suggest a more measured, sustainable path for personal and organizational effectiveness in this distinctive age.

This, therefore, is a book for leaders operating in organizational and systemic contexts. The leaders do not have to sit at the top of a hierarchy to find the messages here useful—leadership is a mindset about serving others to leave situations better than one finds them, one can lead from anywhere in an organization. The framework introduced here is *managerial* in nature, in that it involves steps and processes that can be systematically pursued: in effect, I argue that leading in the age of outrage requires a managerial mindset and discipline.

The book consists of seven chapters, including an introduction (chapter 1), five chapters each corresponding to a step in the framework, and a conclusion (chapter 7). In the introductory chapter, I present the framework as a whole and then take a dive into the socioeconomic drivers of the age of outrage with the aim of demonstrating why they have become more salient in many parts of the world and how they are reinforcing each other. I argue that outrage has become a structural problem for organizations, which necessitates that they develop a system of practices and principles for managing the problem. Understanding the drivers is essential to the framework itself, as knowledge of the roots of outrage is key to managing in its wake.

In the second chapter, my focus is on the level of the individual, as I describe first the general aggression model, a unified behavioral theory on how outrage develops at the human and neurobiological levels. The model draws on various research streams and offers guidance on what individuals can do to "turn down the temperature" in the face of anger and aggression. I then go on to discuss a set of basic practices and protocols that provide a foundation on which managers can act out the remainder of my age of outrage framework, illustrating with a description of how the Nigerian state of Kaduna addresses the endemic problem of religious and ethnic strife in a sharply divided region and how social media giant Meta (formerly Facebook) manages discussions around outrage-inducing content on its platform.

In the third chapter, I return to the drivers of outrage as I describe what a leader facing an immediate crisis must do to try make sense of its causes and to figure out how to manage conversations that can surface operational consensus. The focus of this chapter is at the group level. The goal is to identify possible avenues for leaders to create some kind of (intermediate) mitigation of the crisis so the organization can continue to function and grow. As an example, we'll look at the case of the London Metropolitan Police (the Met) when faced with outrage from minority communities over one of its key policing policies—stop-and-search. I'll show how the crisis evolved, and I'll consider the Met's response. By way of comparison, we'll also revisit the Kaduna case study. The key challenge at this step of the process is creating a platform for discussion, if none exists. This involves identifying the appropriate person to lead the process, airing the narratives and lived experience of the stakeholders involved, and figuring out the right channels through which to move forward. The process requires participation from carefully selected representatives of key stakeholders, which in turn requires careful moderation.

In chapter 4, we move from understanding the context and motivations for outrage toward formulating a response. This requires, beyond the individual and group analyses that precede, an awareness of the organization's limitations within a wider system. This step is a more focused exercise, often internal to the organization and its leadership team: the broad stakeholder group that we met in the previous chapter has done its job, and it is now up to a smaller group of executives to develop and recommend a specific course of action to the individual ultimately responsible for deciding what the organization will do. The members of this executive group may well include the decision-maker, and some, if not all, of the group should have participated in the first process and will thereby have heard the scripts of other stakeholders at firsthand. The group should consider two sets of questions. First, given the resources and know-how at its disposal, how well-placed is the organization to take actions that address the outrage at deeper levels, for example, to reduce people's fears for the future and their sense of past injustice? And second, if the organization is contemplating a new commitment, can it meet that commitment without affecting prior commitments? For instance, if stakeholder expectations around the organization's prior moral commitments have evolved, how do those changes affect the currently contemplated commitments? We'll look at how organizations can address these two sets of questions drawing on examples from companies such as Nestlé, Johnson & Johnson, and IKEA.

Chapter 5 moves to implementation. To do this in an age of outrage requires one to unpick the power dynamics of decision-making, focusing on identifying what kind of power an organizational leader can wield, internally and externally, and through what channels. I'll present an approach to help leaders do just that, illustrating from case studies of crisis leadership approaches adopted by the chief medical officer of the Oxford University Hospitals during the Covid-19 pandemic and the head of the Vatican's financial supervisory authority, responsible for fiscal and banking oversight of the Catholic Church.

I'll conclude by discussing what kind of considerations should influence the implementation approach and the risks that the decision-maker may incur—leaders in the age of outrage are never likely to completely fulfill their goals, and they may have to pay a price for making the best decision for their organizations. We'll also see that, in making their decisions, leaders should, in general, lean into the future they wish to see rather than treat the challenge they face as an exercise in short-term firefighting.

In the sixth chapter, I turn from communication, analysis, and decision-making to understand the culture and behaviors of the organization and people who can best survive (and perhaps even thrive) in an age of outrage. Coping with ongoing outrage is a draining experience for the organization as a whole and the people in it. Here, I explore what makes both resilient. At the organizational level, we examine the concept of relational contracts, exemplified by the workplace culture of the Japanese carmaker Toyota. We then move on to examine what qualities to look for in leaders of resilient organizations, focusing on the example of the Oxford University Hospitals leader Meghana Pandit, who understood that she could create a more resilient organization by letting other people in the organization make decisions. I'll also discuss the case of the US Attorney's Office for the Southern District of New York, an unusual organization that has learned how to ensure that it has leaders at the top who are both strongly imbued with their organization's values of prosecutorial independence but who have also had the benefit of a highly diverse and varied career. I conclude by looking at the stoic mindset and philosophy of many resilient leaders to understand what made them able to endure and recover from setbacks, drawing on the experience of Admiral James Stockdale, who survived captivity in Vietnam, and Chris Liddell, a senior corporate executive who navigated four tumultuous years near the top of the Trump White House.

In the concluding seventh chapter, I suggest that this framework, or something like it, may well represent a transformation in the way organizations build buy-in. The traditional approach to this challenge has usually required the leader to rally diverse people around a well-articulated common value or aspiration, usually one that is not easily defined or even realizable—which is why they are sometimes labeled the "noble lie." The concept of the American dream is an example of this. But in our age of outrage, it has become increasingly difficult for shared beliefs to build around even the most general values, especially if the leader's own interests are questioned. In this context, I argue that the framework may facilitate the necessary dialogue required for a new step-by-step consensus vision to evolve from the bottom up, effectively co-opting stakeholders in the construction of a shared but incremental aspiration or value, in lieu of a grand noble lie. A necessary part of this transition will be moving away from the traditional Aristotelian heroic leader of rousing rhetoric to a new model in which leadership is characterized by another, oft-overlooked classical virtue of *temperance.*

And with that, I invite you to begin chapter 1.

The

Age

of

OUTRAGE

Chapter 1

The Age of Outrage

Between February and March 2022, Florida's House, Senate, and governor passed into law a bill that prevented the state's public schools from hosting discussions on sexual orientation and gender identity "in a manner that is not age-appropriate." As the bill moved through the stages of passage, local media reported that the Walt Disney Company had made political contributions to the bill's key proponents.[1]

The matter immediately set off a firestorm of criticism within Disney, as numerous affiliated creators and employees noted that the company's support was at odds with its stated values and aspirations. They pointed out that Disney had attempted to profit from a progressive image, hosting, for example, unofficial "Gay Days" in its Orlando theme park, even as it tried to walk both sides of the fence across America's culture wars.

Disney's then CEO, Bob Chapek, at first reacted defensively, arguing that the company would neither support nor condemn Florida's new "Don't Say Gay" bill, as it came to be called. Then, he quickly relented and offered a $5 million donation to America's leading LGBT+ organization, the Human Rights Campaign. This donation was about twenty-five times the size of its original campaign contributions to the bill's supporters, but the Human Rights Campaign turned it down. The damage was done.

Disney, as a cultural force in modern America—a company that through its action (or inaction) shapes American values over the long run—seems especially vulnerable to this age of outrage. What Disney's make-believe princesses and princes do today shape societal norms for tomorrow. Parents, activists, and politicians across the spectrum understand this reality, and so the company is very much their target as a means to mold the country in their vision.

But as America, and a good bit of the rest of the world, seemingly tears itself apart over issues like climate change, demographic shifts, stagnating wages, intergenerational inequities, and racism—let alone LGBT+ rights—what is a company like Disney to do? How can it keep its image and attention focused on its core purpose—of delivering wholesome entertainment? When should it wear its values on its sleeve, and when should it defer to pragmatism? And where does pragmatism stop and hypocrisy begin? Whom can it trust for advice and input, internally and externally, as it navigates these questions? And how does it not deplete and exhaust its employees and leadership in what is apparently a never-ending litany of angry outpourings?

Disney is certainly not alone among companies in confronting these questions. And beyond companies, nonprofits and government agencies too must navigate the age of outrage. What are the lessons to learn from those who are successfully managing through these times and even from those who are arguably just muddling through?

A Practical Framework for Managing in the Age of Outrage

The framework that I present in this book offers an approach through which leaders faced with angry stakeholders can make sense of the outrage they are confronted with, work with relevant stakeholders to progress through it, and perhaps even emerge stronger for it. As figure 1-1 shows, at the framework's core is an approach to "turn down the temperature" in the moment, making discussion, analysis,

FIGURE 1-1

A framework for managing in the age of outrage

At the core of the book's framework for managing in the age of outrage is the platform to help leaders de-escalate an aggressive situation. Thereafter, the framework involves four steps, each that informs and is informed by the platform. Depending on their situation, leaders can adopt the framework at any step, but once in the system, progress is achieved by cycling through the steps until the situation is brought under control so that the organization can sustain its mission or even thrive going forward.

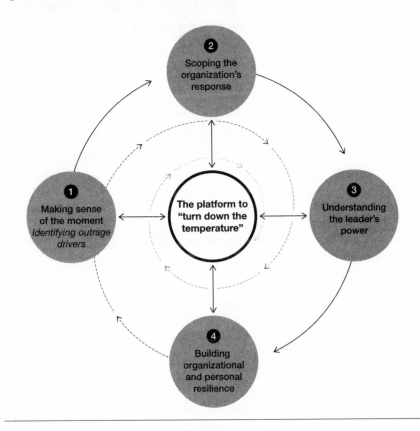

and better decision-making possible. That approach is based on a behavioral theory (known as the general aggression model) and an associated set of managerial protocols, which then support four further processes that, I argue, leaders should engage in as they seek to reconcile the organization's decisions with the age of outrage they encounter: (1) an analysis of the root causes and catalysts of the proximate crisis (i.e., making sense of the outrage); (2) the scoping and bounding of organizational responses; (3) identifying tactics for progress and getting things done (i.e., the art of implementation); and (4) building and renewing individual and organizational resilience.

To bring this framework to life, consider again the case of Disney. Foremost, as CEO Chapek tried to manage the fallout from "Don't Say Gay," was the need to cool emotions—his own, and those of activists, politicians, employees, customers, and investors on the left, right, and center. Without a protocol for calming the environment, any stakeholder engagement would likely make things worse. Then, he needed to understand what was driving the outrage at Disney— with a view to know what he could and could not control. Next, he could formulate a response—one that was both authentic to the company and sustainable over the intermediate run. For both preceding steps, he needed a trusted team of insiders and outsiders. Thereafter, he had to decide how to put his decisions into action in a way that helped him at least retain, if not build, goodwill for the next (inevitable) crisis. And finally, recognizing how exhausting all this was for himself and his team, he needed to create conditions for ongoing emotional renewal.

As indicated through the arrows in figure 1-1, an organization and its stakeholders can enter the age of outrage framework through any one of the stages or processes, but once in the system, progress is usually sequential and may well require multiple iterations of all the activities involved. The core platform to turn down the temperature both informs and is informed by the results of the four processes, and its primary function is to maintain a temperate emotional context around the four processes as people engage in them to work through outrage events.

To apply the age of outrage framework effectively, leaders must first understand just what is driving and intensifying the palpable aggression that they experience. Knowledge and acknowledgment of the socioeconomic and technological underpinnings of people's outrage in general will be very helpful in that endeavor. So, although the bulk of this book presents a managerial guide to the concepts, processes, and capabilities required for leading in an age of outrage, I discuss in the remainder of this chapter the drivers of the outrage that we are now confronted with, and to which I will be referring throughout the book. Thereafter, in subsequent chapters, we will dive into the framework's components.

The Drivers of the Age of Outrage

Outrage can stem from multiple causes, and I have found it helpful to generalize these causes into three groups. In some cases, as noted in the preface, a decision affects a particular stakeholder's economic and social prospects—perhaps depriving them of a future they had taken for granted. In others, the outrage stems from a historical griev-ance that makes the stakeholder suspicious of the decision-maker's motives. A third factor is the perception that the decision-maker is in some sense removed or alien to the stakeholder in terms of values and interests, siding with some other inimical stakeholder group.

One can argue that outrage has always existed and generally derives from the same causes as it always has. For instance, in the early twentieth century, with the emergence of organized labor, business leaders had to confront similar outbreaks of outrage at decisions that previously had been easy for them to make. Going further back, the British East India Company, perhaps one of the most profitable firms in history, went out of business in the middle of the nineteenth cen-tury because it attracted popular condemnation that forced the British government to act. Given this historical context, leaders must under-stand what is so different about the outrage that they are experiencing today. I submit that the difference often stems from the fact that all three traditional sources of outrage are unusually salient. There is growing despair at prospects for the future across more people than perhaps at any time since before the Second World War. Meanwhile, anger among more and larger groups of people at perceived biases and the legacies of past decisions is spilling over. At the same time, increasing migration across borders is bringing inimical groups with different values together, while the legacy of education and social policies has (sometimes justly) encouraged new groups to emerge with values that offend traditional sensibilities. What's more, all these factors are being collectively amplified through modern communication technologies—notably the rise of social media, which enables people with shared ideas and goals to form information bubbles and reinforce each other's fear, grievance, and identities.

So, when confronted with a crisis, a leader must ask, Does it stem from fear for the future, an experience of prior injustice, or from innate hostility to some other stakeholders—or some combination of the three, and if so, what combination? Only after understanding which drivers are in play, and how they are interacting with each other, can the organizational leader identify what possible avenues for progress exist and whether those are realistic options for the organization.

Let's begin by looking at what's behind our fears for the future.

Fear for the future

In 1992, the celebrated political scientist Francis Fukuyama published a book entitled *The End of History and the Last Man*, which offered the argument that the triumph of democratic capitalism in the Cold War had introduced a stable equilibrium in the political economy, leaving behind the ideological conflicts that had dogged the twentieth century. With rapid technological innovation, the world's population would live longer, enjoy more freedom, and partake in ever more wealth created by human ingenuity.

By the beginning of the new millennium, his argument seemed to have been thoroughly vindicated; the world was, by and large, an optimistic place. The traditional bastions of democracy and capitalism—the United States and the countries of Western Europe, many of which had just entered a single currency zone—stood tall, and the world's fastest-growing large country, China, was about to enter a period of political liberalization to accompany its apparent acceptance of free markets.

But two decades on, alarm bells are ringing about the impact of consumerist lifestyles on the planet's climate. At the same time, global demographic shifts are already creating the conditions for an era of global migration from Africa and Asia to Europe and the United States, which will impose immense financial and social pressures on both sides. To cap all that, following a financial crisis in 2008–2009 to almost rival the Great Crash of 1929, confidence in democratic countries—that they will be able to successfully manage techno-logical leaps in artificial intelligence (AI) and still enjoy a healthier and more prosperous future—appears to be diminishing across large swathes of the population worldwide.

A hotter, dirtier planet. Concern about climate change has prompted some global response, with agreements reached at the COP23 and subsequent climate summits on targets for lowering carbon emissions. In Europe, investment in wind and solar energy has increased and, following the outbreak of war in Ukraine, in nuclear energy as well— but, to date, there has been far from sufficient progress made to con-tain the rise in temperature levels needed to prevent the planet from reaching a climate tipping point. Few countries that signed up to the COP23 targets look like they will be delivering anywhere near the required reductions in carbon emissions to limit global temperature increases to levels that will not trigger irreversible climate change.[2] Increasingly, people are becoming aware that we will be bequeath-ing a hotter, climatically more violent planet to our children—to the extent that it will impose radical changes to where we can live (current shorelines are expected to change, displacing the people that live there now) and how we feed ourselves.

Experts and activists have long predicted these developments, but public concerns have risen significantly in the wake of multiple extreme weather incidents—including major floods in Europe and high-intensity hurricanes in the United States. A recent study by the Pew Foundation found that on average, around three-quarters of people surveyed in nineteen countries saw climate change as one of the five biggest major global threats. For all the European countries surveyed, it was the biggest or second biggest concern, and only for three (the United States, Malaysia, and Singapore) was the environment considered to be the least serious threat of the five.[3]

Climate change is not the only potential environmental issue stoking fears for the future of the planet. There is growing concern, for example, around the impact of plastics pollution as well. The most visible manifestation is the Great Pacific Garbage Patch, an area of about 1.6 million square kilometers in size, comprising both tiny plastic particles and relatively large plastic items that have not degraded. Similar, if smaller patches are to be found in the Atlantic and Indian oceans. The patches are growing at an accelerating rate in both area and plastic content—by one estimate, the plastic-mass concentration (in kg/km²) in the Pacific patch increased over threefold in about forty years.[4]

Technology and its discontents. With computerization and robotics increasingly playing a role in both production and operations—and, recently, AI seemingly taking over ideation as well—many jobs are at risk, and people appear to grasp (and fear) this reality. A recent study by my colleagues at Oxford, Carl Frey, Craig Holmes, and Michael Osborne, found that about 47 percent of jobs in the US economy are vulnerable to computerization in the next decade or so. The equivalent number is higher in many developing economies—in China, for example, 77 percent of jobs are deemed to be at risk.[5]

Most of the tasks being automated to date are those that require the application of easily definable routines—such as factory-floor operations and formulaic service roles. But technology is moving automation up the knowledge chain. With a smartphone and mapping applications, anyone today can become a London taxi driver—the months of studying it took to pass the city's famed "Knowledge" to become a Black Cabbie seem as quaint today as celestial and chart-based flight navigators in cockpits are to a world of instant geo-location and ubiquitous AirTags. And, as many self-employed people already know, accounting and tax software can substitute very well for human bookkeepers and tax advisers.

Increasingly, AI machine learning technologies are also putting higher-order jobs at risk—most obviously, perhaps, in medicine, where computers can seemingly diagnose abnormalities in scans and other medical observations more accurately than human radiographers with years of specialized training. In 2023, school and university examinations worldwide were abruptly disrupted by the introduction of ChatGPT, which obviated overnight many "take home" assessment formats and forced a reintroduction of in-person supervised papers that had been phased out during the Covid-19 pandemic. The *Harvard Business Review* has even reported on AI assuming the role of a startup strategy adviser.[6] In short, roles traditionally requiring well-trained knowledge workers can now be carried out by machines. What does all that imply for the employment prospects of children going into high school or university today?

To be sure, no one expects humans to lose out completely to automation and AI. As tech evangelist and billionaire Elon Musk himself has observed, "humans are underrated."[7] The Frey et al. Oxford report notes also that machines are still far from capable of operating physically in unstructured and complex environments (such as driving cars in crowded cities or even cleaning a house). But there are other contexts where tech is proving highly effective. Virtual shopping assistants, virtual bankers, and even virtual bloggers are already successfully interacting with humans, and their entry into the workforce will clearly complicate employment prospects for many.[8]

A backlash to these developments is already discernible. The world's licensed taxi drivers, for example, have not taken the threat of Uber and its ride-sharing competitors lying down: in 2015, drivers in cities across France staged violent protests that were captured by the world's press. Also in France, supermarket workers protested in 2019 against keeping big-box stores open past lunchtime on Sunday using automated checkout kiosks: French labor law, supported by many supermarket unions, prevents grocery workers from working those hours. "People don't need an extra half day shopping," noted one union representative.[9]

Meanwhile, in the United States, as McDonald's opened its first automated restaurant in late 2022, some irate customers took to social media complaining that the move would cost "millions of jobs"—and one user noted: "Honestly, if they go through with this, I'll just boycott McDonald's. Their food's mid at best anyway."[10]

Demography and its disconnects. By 2050, the African continent will be home to half of all young people in a world that overall will have rapidly aged.[11] That will completely change how the world looks, and some people are not happy about it. As my Oxford colleague Ian Goldin notes, this kind of statistic is a leading indicator of sharply falling workforces, not only in the developed world but also in the emerging economic superpowers of China, which is arguably on the edge of a demographic precipice, and India, where birth rates are now already below replacement levels.[12] The OECD forecasts an overall decline in the global workforce of around 25 percent over the next three decades.[13] This collapse will feed through into government revenues at a time when governments will be called on to provide more services to its elderly populations, not less.

For their part, many African nations today have little to offer the millions of young people coming down their demographic pipelines. Technology, as we've seen, is already automating the kinds of jobs that thirty years ago were exported to the emerging Asian economies. And, as more and more routine work is taken over by machines, it's almost certain that any jobs for tomorrow's young people will require a higher degree of cognitive adaptability, emotional sophistication, and communication skills. Preparing them for this future will require a reimagining of, and massive investment in, basic education. And that's before you get to figuring out how to provide the nutrition, housing, and health care that a fast-growing population needs—all in the context of growing environmental challenges. The record of African nations is not encouraging: In 2022, two-thirds of the countries identified in the top thirty of the global Fragile States Index were in Africa, and only one country from the continental mainland (Botswana) did not register a "warning" or "alert" on that list.[14]

The obvious response, at least for the younger generation in many less-developed countries, is migration to wealthier nations because they perceive that will be where essential public services are provided and the few good jobs will remain. As a long-term solution to the demographic challenges, migration makes some sense: the developed world has the infrastructure and capital to invest in educating migrants, and their aging populations will need increased service support. But the adjustments needed as societies transform with the new arrivals and their cultural practices will be keenly felt. As I will discuss later in this chapter, many groups of working-age Europeans already feel both threatened and concerned in the face of migrants with different values prepared to work for less money in a diminishing pool of unskilled jobs.

This brings me to the second driver of outrage: at the same time as fears about the future are rising, so too is the sense in many quarters that the world's leaders cannot be trusted to safeguard that future.

The raw deal

In 2013, French economist Thomas Piketty published a six-hundred-page book containing an extraordinary amount of data. It became a surprise bestseller, made its author a household name, and generated a debate that has continued ever since. The book, entitled *Capital in the 21st Century*, was ostensibly a play on and seemingly an update to Karl Marx's eponymous *Das Kapital*. Piketty's book advanced the proposition that in the increasingly liberal economic environment of the late twentieth and early twenty-first centuries, inequalities of wealth were steadily increasing and, absent reforms, would continue to increase.

It was an idea that resonated in the wake of the 2008–2009 financial crisis, which was widely portrayed as governance failure: the political establishment had become captured by greed and self-enrichment at the expense of average workers and voters.

While it is almost certainly true that liberal economics has fueled growth and given unparalleled access to goods and services for consumers rich and poor alike, a look at the data suggests that this rising tide of global wealth creation is no longer lifting all the boats. To begin with, levels of household debt have reached record highs and now represent a potential drag on economies traditionally driven by consumer spending.[15] To some extent, relief was provided by low interest rates during the Great Recession and the Covid-19 pandemic, but with the return of inflation and growing geopolitical uncertainty, the outlook for consumer-led growth is questionable at least in the medium term. Debt and inflation, however, may not be the most serious concerns, nor do they necessarily fuel existential discontent with a free-market system—debt levels are, in many cases, a product of personal choices, and people usually don't blame the Hilary Clintons and Mark Zuckerbergs of this world for their indebtedness. To understand the resentment against those who have most conspicuously benefited from free markets, we need to look elsewhere.

The left behind. In 2020, I wrote an essay for the *American Interest* in which I presented evidence, based on scholarship undertaken with my then research assistant Timon Forster, that offers a possible explanation. The essay, which in part forms the core of this chapter, focused on changes in wage-market returns to human capital in America.[16] Even as financial capital is highly unequally divided, all most people across the world have (and really cherish) is their human capital—it is their primary source of earning potential and self-worth. If people believe that a system is, over time, improving returns to their human capital, they are more likely to have confidence in it. If they feel that the system undervalues their human capital and structurally favors others at their expense, they will lose confidence in the system and seek redress elsewhere, such as through political outsiders and radi-cals. The US system, it turns out, does indeed appear to be favoring some sections of society at the expense of others.

The data for measuring returns to human capital in the United States comes from two sources. First, the US Census, which provides detailed information on who is engaged in what job at a given time. Censuses (a US constitutional requirement) are carried out every ten years, offering a series of snapshots of what people are doing over time. Measuring the human capital requirement of people's various job categories was a more challenging proposition: it is considerably easier and less controversial to measure financial capital than human capital, perhaps why the debate on inequality has largely focused on the former. So, second, I based our measurements of human capital on assessments of the cognitive intensity of each occupation in the US workforce as reported by the US Labor Department.

Combining this data, we created cognitive-skill percentiles for the US working population. Occupations in the first percentile have among the lowest cognitive-skill demands, according to the Labor Department (e.g., domestic cleaners), and those in the ninety-ninth percentile have among the highest cognitive-skill demands (e.g., aero-nautical engineers). Of course, using occupational cognitive skills to measure human capital has its limitations. Human capital manifests in ways other than cognitive skills, perhaps most distinctively, physical skills—for instance, the skills that allow someone to be a professional tennis player. But occupational physical skills, as assessed by the US Labor Department data, are on average inversely related to cognitive skills, and with few exceptions such as niche sportspersons, physical skills are in less in demand than cognitive skills in an industrialized economy. This conclusion is corroborated using additional data from the University of Chicago on the "social prestige" of occupations: our research suggests that social prestige is strongly associated with cognitive skills and inversely related to physical skills.

Having established our distribution of cognitive skills across US workers, we then charted the trends in inflation-adjusted wages for each percentile, as shown in figure 1-2, which compares wage returns in 1980 and 2017. The result is not reassuring. Although earners in the upper two-thirds (in more cognitively demanding jobs) have seen some improvements in inflation-adjusted wages, those in the lower third of the cognitive distribution have seen returns stagnate or even decline since 1980. Besides, most of the wage improvements come at the very high end of cognitive skills. And these trends do not account for nonwage benefits, such as health insurance or other perquisites, where such benefits, to the extent that they have grown with time, tend to have accrued more generously further up the distribution.

In effect, those who win the human-capital game, determined largely by how cognitively demanding their occupations are, have done well over time in America; those in less cognitively demanding occupations are worse off than they would have been nearly four decades ago.

FIGURE 1-2

US wage returns to human capital

This chart presents the average hourly wages, adjusted to 2017 dollars, for the US workforce arranged into percentiles by the cognitive intensity of their jobs (as reported by the US Labor Department). The data is presented for two years—1980 and 2017—to show how the wage returns to human capital in the US have changed over time. The data suggests that much of the first forty percentiles of the US working population were better off in 1980 than in 2017.

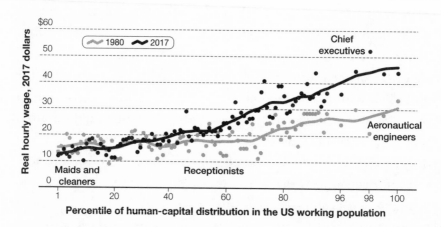

Source: US Current Population Survey, CEPR ORG Extract 2.3, 2017; O*NET, 2017

Consider Joe, a typical freight handler in 1980, in the middle of his career. At the time, Joe's occupation would have put him in the ninth percentile of cognitive skills in the US population, and he could have expected to earn $17.27 an hour in 2017 dollars. Joe's 1980 wages were about 60 percent of those in the ninety-fifth percentile of skills in the United States, such as physicists and astronomers. Were Joe the freight handler instead to find himself in the middle of his career in 2017, he would be in a less favorable position. While his occupation would still place him in the ninth percentile of US skills, his real wages would have fallen to $14.57 per hour and would represent only about 40 percent of those in the ninety-fifth percentile.

And it's not just Joe's earnings that are in question—Joe's life expectancy has declined relative to those above him in the skills hierarchy. In 2020, economists Anne Case and Angus Deaton, the latter a Nobel laureate, published a book, partly based on their seminal analysis of US death rates in the working-age population. Entitled *The Deaths of Despair and the Future of Capitalism*, it painted a very different picture from the one implied by Fukuyama's *The End of History*. Among Case and Deaton's findings was the chilling realization that "if the white mortality rate for ages 45–54 had held at their 1998 value, 96,000 deaths would have been avoided from 1999–2013. . . . If it had continued to decline at its previous (1979-1998) rate, half a million deaths would have been avoided."[17] This trend was closely linked to educational levels: while the racial divide in terms of death rates "had narrowed by 70% between 1990 and 2018," educational divides had "more than doubled" the death rates for both Black and white people.[18] In other words, while having a college degree makes an increasingly big difference to your life expectancy, this is now largely because life expectancy is falling for degree have-nots like Joe, our hypothetical freight handler.

Put bluntly, Americans have experienced an economic system that, over a fairly long period, has left at least one-third of the population worse off. I suspect even Milton Friedman, the arch-evangelist of liberal economics, who was not worried about inequality so long as

Optimism in Unequal India

Not all countries share the US experience in returns to human capital stagnating for large sections of society. As part of my research in this area, our team looked at a few other countries, and I was struck by one case in particular: India.

On a crisp sunny late morning in the November before the Covid-19 crisis hit, I was picked up from the airport of a small Indian city in the Punjab, near the border with Pakistan (population about one million). I was there, as a paid adviser, to visit Lovely Professional University (LPU), what is ostensibly the largest private university campus in the world. Set amid the chaos and bustle that is characteristic of Indian urban sprawl, the somewhat curiously named university campus is a stunning contrast to its surroundings. An oasis of calm, neatly manicured lawns and wide roads with broad sidewalks surrounds impressive buildings that school and house thousands of students.

LPU's campus is purposefully aspirational to those both inside and outside its walls. Its students are mostly from the emerging professional class in India, children of those who just broke the cycle of economic precarity in the wake of India's liberalizing reforms starting in the 1990s. LPU's alumni seek to be the country's new upper-middle class and wealthy. Not all will succeed, of course, but the fact that so many are willing to make the investment in LPU's substantial tuition fees—a small fortune by local standards, where much of higher education is essentially heavily state-subsidized—is itself testimony to their optimism in India's future.

It is rare to match the vibrancy of campuses like LPU anywhere in the West's rustbelts—the entrepreneurial hustle that is palpable broadly across universities and business parks in China, India, and other high-growth economies breeds its own infectious energy and economic opportunities.

What's interesting about India is that while income inequalities are much greater than in the United States, the rising tide in India has, in fact, lifted most boats, as figure 1-3 shows. At the same time, Indians are broadly more hopeful for the future than are people in the United States, as suggested by surveys from the Edelman Trust Barometer. In effect, people in India feel that the social contract is broadly working for them. This may explain why, despite a torrent of negative press on life in India in the Western media, economic liberalization has, in fact, proved quite popular.

FIGURE 1-3

India wage returns to human capital

This chart presents the average weekly wages, adjusted to 2017 dollars, for the Indian workforce (excluding farming jobs) arranged into percentiles by the cognitive intensity of their roles. The data is presented for two years—1983 and 2012—to show how the wage returns to human capital in India have changed over time. The data suggests that much of the Indian working population was better off in 2012 relative to 1983.

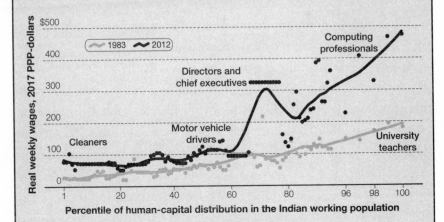

Note: Working population excludes cultivators, crop growers, and agricultural laborers.

Source: IPUMS, 2017; National Sample Survey, 2017

growth was lifting all or most boats, would find this scenario disturbing. Those left behind have little motivation to support political leaders associated with the free-market policies delivering such unequal growth. (Our research into the spread of returns to human capital was not confined to the United States; see the sidebar "Optimism in Unequal India.")

Free markets—or cheating the working class? The celebrated physicist Stanislaw Ulam is said to have challenged Paul Samuelson—perhaps the twentieth century's most widely regarded economist—to name one theory in all of the social sciences that is both nontrivial and true.[19] Samuelson took his time to construct a response (years, by his own account), but when he did, he offered up David Ricardo's theory of comparative advantage in international trade. Put simply, the theory argues that trade benefits all countries because it promotes efficiency by driving countries to focus on their relative advantages rather than their absolute advantages. This nonintuitive result has been the intellectual backbone of public policy driving globalization, which in turn encouraged many Western companies to offshore large parts of the supply chain to low labor-cost countries.

As I pointed out in the *American Interest* essay, the trouble is that the jobs in 1980 most vulnerable to offshoring were, in general, below the fiftieth percentile of the US workforce's human-capital distribution, precisely those that have been left behind by free-market-led growth. But the story doesn't end there. The offshoring of manufacturing jobs meant greater demand, and a wage premium, for service skills that enable offshoring—skills in IT, back-office finance, logistics, and so on. The wage premium on these jobs helped drive the service boom of the late 1990s. But it also incentivized the creation of new business processes that would allow those jobs to be themselves offshored. Again, free-trade policy carried the day. Since the late 1990s, globalization has gradually displaced white-collar workers, especially those whose skills can be easily catalogued and replicated elsewhere for lower wages (i.e., skills where tacit or implicit knowledge is less relevant).

The bottom line is that the benefits to free-market policy, to which the Western political establishment was wedded until only very recently, appear to have largely accrued to very high-skill workers, investors, and business owners, which serves only to widen their divide with their middle-class populations. From the perspective of those workers, free-market policies around offshoring (and lower-skill immigration) can plausibly be, as presented by populists such as Donald Trump, the product of collusion between political leaders and other elites to benefit themselves. This perception is polarizing the country's politics, to the extent that it is becoming increasingly difficult to find consensus, which brings me to my next point: in the absence of trust in the political system, the social and economic progress that might benefit those left behind becomes virtually impossible to achieve.

Broken trust and broken systems. The United States is not the only country characterized by a growing distrust of the political establishment, and the recent experience of Colombia's president Iván Duque and his finance ministry provides an instructive example in a very different kind of country of how a widespread sense of exclusion mires even well-meaning attempts at reform. In 2021, Duque's country was in the grips of the Covid-19 pandemic and facing the imminent prospect of fiscal collapse as a result of the scale of public-sector spending created by that crisis. Duque realized if Colombia were to retain its hard-won investment-grade debt status, he would have to reform the country's tax rules. I supervised a case study for the Blavatnik School on this experience (coauthored by my colleagues İrem Güçeri, Clare Leaver, and Oenone Kubie) on which the following is based.[20]

The problem with Colombia was that, even more than most Latin American countries, its tax revenues are largely the result of indirect taxation—principally sales taxes such as VAT—rather than of direct taxes (such as income, corporate, or property taxes). This means that the system is already regressive—indirect consumption taxes generally hit poor consumers more than wealthy ones. In Colombia, the situation was further aggravated by the extraordinary degree to which special interests had managed to obtain loopholes. For instance, imports of Scottish smoked salmon, hardly a food staple, were exempted from VAT.

In figuring out where to begin, Duque consulted broadly with economists of all political persuasions within Colombia as well as economists at the International Monetary Fund and World Bank. They all advised him to begin by fixing the VAT system, which had no fewer than four distinct tax brackets: fully taxable items, on which a rate of 19 percent was levied; preferential items, taxed at 5 percent; exempt items on which a 0 percent rate was applied and which even allowed the sellers of the items to reclaim benefits for VAT paid to suppliers; and excluded items, on which no VAT was levied but for which sellers could not claim benefits for VAT paid. Over time, more and more categories of goods had been grouped into the exempt and excluded items, mostly through political compromises struck by successive governments. Beyond Scottish salmon, chocolates, tourism, and even adult magazines were also included as exempt items. Airfares also got off lightly, classified as they were in the preferential category. Meanwhile the excluded category included iPhones, cosmetic surgery, football tickets, and movie rentals. Fixing VAT clearly offered plenty of low-hanging fiscal fruit for the government's taking, besides addressing the perverse regressive taxation.

Duque duly put together a sensible reform proposal: the preferential category would include only essential items such as staple foodstuffs; the exempt category would be reserved for exports only, with the excluded category reserved for items that provided value for society in general, such as education and health-care-related goods and services. He presented his new package for consideration by the legislature in May 2021. It met with howls of protest, because, in this genuine effort to clean up the system, he was undoing decades of political compromises, and importantly, people had already lost trust in government to do the right thing. Tax reform had been a plank in almost every government's platform for decades, and a running joke in the media was that according to the country's politicians, Colombia needed a generational tax reset every two years. But, with many previous administrations, fixing the tax system had never been a goal: it was simply a piece of political theater whose real purpose was to reward the power base of whichever politicians had won the last election. Duque found that introducing genuine reform meant treading on the toes of strongly entrenched vested interests, and that would in turn require first winning the trust of a whole segment of disaffected society.

The many and varied groups that stood to lose from the reform responded by claiming that Duque was simply the front man for a technocratic elite that wanted to put more money in their own hands at the expense of the various groups of people who stood to lose out in cash terms as a result. And the argument was all too believable because that is what almost every other tax reform had turned into. Colombian politicians simply did not have the credibility to sell a genuine reform. In the wake of street protests, Duque's finance ministry was obliged to go back to the drawing board and come up with something that he could credibly sell. A reform was eventually passed, but it was sadly inferior to Duque's original vision.

Colombia's experience illustrates an important weakness in the current state of many democracies: the political process for change all too often reduces to barter between special interests. Although negotiation and compromise are always essential for political progress, if citizens come to see elected politicians as proxies for elite interests, they inevitably lose faith in the system.

And this brings me to the third major driver of outrage.

Ideologies of othering

The "othering" term I use to describe the third driver of outrage seeks to capture the growing degree to which different social groupings increasingly blame each other both for a decline in their economic and social prospects and for perceived historical injustices. The growing intensity of this blame game reflects several major shifts.

First, as I've already noted, recent technological advances, particularly around computerization and artificial intelligence, may very well be weakening the link that the establishment has long taken for granted between the Enlightenment values of the West and broad-based economic progress. In many ways, Enlightenment values, which supported scientific enquiry, had chimed with industrialization, which was the fruit of that enquiry, bringing jobs and prosperity for many members of society. An enlightened society, therefore, was an industrial and prosperous one. But as technology weakens that link, trust in Enlightenment values seems to be breaking down both within the West, which is seeing a backlash against the social liberalism inherent in those values, and outside the West, as other countries, notably China, close the economic gap and develop a confidence in their cultural distinctiveness. Increasingly, therefore, many people—for many different reasons—have come to see the social liberalism that has held sway in Western democracies as unrelated or even inimical to empowerment and prosperity.

This emerging discontent is being amplified through shifts in how people obtain and share information, as subscription-based social media channels replace mass television networks and newspapers, traditionally controlled by paid-up members of the establishment. The new media enable groups of people with shared issues and beliefs to build shared identities, in many cases reinforcing their sense of grievance and facilitating their mobilization into active protest against the perceived elitism of Enlightenment values.

To unpick the sources of this anger, we have to go back to another book published in the 1990s.

History strikes back. Published in 1996, the book in question was *The Clash of Civilizations and the Remaking of the World Order.*[21] Its author, Samuel Huntington, was responding to the argument presented by his former student Francis Fukuyama that, with the economic failure of the communist experiment, Western demo-cratic capitalism had emerged as the dominant socioeconomic model. While flawed in many respects, Huntington's counterargument, at a macro, societal level was extraordinarily prescient.

For Huntington, the economic and social triumph of the Enlight-enment values of democratic capitalism did not herald an end of his-tory but rather a reversion to it. His argument is based on the theory that the world is incurably divided, on an essentially geographic basis, into several "civilizations." He defines a civilization as the broadest level of distinctive cultural identity that humans can have. An Italian living in Rome will have multiple cultural identities: she can identify as a native Roman, an Italian, a European, or a Catholic. These iden-tities can include different people (not all Roman natives are necessar-ily Italian or Catholic) and, importantly, different numbers of people. The broadest grouping, however, that she is likely to identify with is that of the Westerner—essentially all the people living in or who have roots in Western Europe, and therefore who broadly identify with a set of common values rooted in the region's religious, ethical, and philosophical history. Huntington identifies seven other clearly definable "civilizations": the Muslim world, the Christian Orthodox world (largely the Slavic nations), Confucian, Japanese, Hindu, Latin American, and (sub-Saharan) African.

Huntington proposed the idea that increasing economic engage-ment and cross-border migration from fast-growing populations in less-developed countries would prompt increasing conflict, partic-ularly between the Muslim and Western civilizations, whose reli-gions are both missionary faiths that claim to be uniquely true, and which share many uneasy geographic borders. He also argued that the economic development of Asian countries, which did not share the political and social values of the West, could also lead to geopolitical conflict, as China sought to displace the United States as the world's dominant superpower, bringing other Asian countries into its sphere of influence. Many of the conflicts that have broken out since the fall of the Berlin Wall can be explained by this theory. The war in

Ukraine, for example, can be seen as a predictable attempt by Ortho-dox Russia to reclaim Ukraine as part of its Orthodox, pan-Slavic *Russkiy Mir* (Russian World) from a culturally hostile West.

These cultural clashes, however, are not just a source of geopolitical conflicts over borders and territories; they are increasingly mirrored within countries. As we've also seen, the economic success of Western civilization's model of democratic capitalism has made Western coun-tries a magnet for migrants from the Muslim, Asian, Latin American, and African worlds, who often encounter an unfriendly reception from local inhabitants, who see the migrants not only as competition for jobs, but as alien in religious or social traditions. In this context, the cultural differences become a lightning rod for rage—both at the migrants themselves, but also against a liberal elite seen as promot-ing migration in the interests of lowering wage costs for large busi-nesses. For their part, migrants develop a growing resentment to their host countries, from which they feel excluded, which makes them amenable to fundamentalist movements at war with what they see as a hostile Christian world.

That all sounds depressing enough, and while it is not without its flaws, the Huntington theory certainly offers a plausible explanation for some of the anger and conflict we are witnessing. But not all con-flicts and resentment are rooted in such civilizational frictions. An unemployed Protestant dockworker from East Belfast is as Western and even as Irish as his Catholic counterpoint, yet their sectarian con-flict continues to define their shared island's history. The claim that "othering" is particularly salient today cannot depend entirely on the interaction of macro-level constructs. One further missing ingredi-ent is technology, particularly the highly accessible social media plat-forms that have come to dominate everyday life, which have greatly enabled the ability of individuals to build communities around their individual identities.

Social media. Humans are naturally social creatures. We are quick to form communities and find our identities in them. And, as Huntington observed, we all have multiple identities, enabling us to belong to all sorts of groups. What he did not mention, however, was that we appear to form new identities very quickly in response to a given social context.

Of course, we have known about identity building for decades, if not longer. In fact, a great quantity of marketing dollars is invested in helping people build identities that companies can exploit. The Harley-Davidson Owners Group (HOG) is a classic example.[22] The global consulting firm McKinsey has long been leveraging its network of former employees, who regularly bring in new business for the firm.[23] What's new since the turn of the millennium is that the new technologies of social media and search have greatly increased the potential for building and reinforcing social identities, without necessarily requiring frequent physical engagement. We can construct new identities for ourselves without ever leaving the house. All we need is an internet connection and a smartphone.

In fact, thanks to modern technology, we can even identify and target people with whom we think we can identify. In many ways, this has been a boon: people suffering from certain health conditions, for example, can find and join support groups online and receive moral support and practical advice. But the results are not always benign. Young men who feel rejected by women can also find common cause and advice from other men who have been rejected or at least claim to have been. And who knows what these other men might advise?

In part, this problem with social media stems from the nature of the recommendation algorithms used by internet platforms to generate page views on their sites. Looking up material generates recommendations for that material—and content like it. While internet surfers do, at some level, understand this dynamic, repeated exposure to angry material is likely to skew people toward believing uncritically, particularly if they are younger and vulnerable to such messaging, a phenomenon referred to as emotional contagion.[24] As a result, the proportion of biased, even mendacious information is likely to swamp contradictory and even-handed content, resulting in a hyper-spiral of confirmation bias.[25] Of course, as long as viewing the material doesn't lead anywhere, relatively little harm is done. Unfortunately, evidence suggests that repeated exposure to, for example, toxic masculinity may well result in someone acting out his fantasies in the real world, in an attempt to prove himself and win the approval of his toxic role model.[26]

The bottom line is that the technology of social media enables the rapid formation of social groups. Many of these groups are benign and even helpful, but they can just as easily be the opposite. When social grouping required a physical presence, it was harder for toxic groups to form, as people could not keep their identities concealed and travel to and from meetings. In order to socialize, they needed to make connections with others they might not agree with and find common ground. In online forums, they can remain incognito and check in from anywhere, which means that they can find and mix with people who closely mirror and reinforce their existing opinions, no matter how offensive. And people leave (or are shut out of) social media groups rather than negotiate across and live with disagreement.

The result of this dynamic is that people with toxic views can join, grow, and lead groups to take ever more extreme social and political positions for little or no reputational risk, while the algorithms of the social media companies bias the information flows ever further. This is a recipe for outraged conflict.

A Perfect Storm

As I hope the foregoing has made clear, the age of outrage is a complex interplay of many factors. What might, at first, seem to organizational managers as a short-term crisis needing a quick PR fix—recall Disney, and CEO Chapek's $5 million donation to the Human Rights Campaign following the passage of "Don't Say Gay"—is likely, instead, to be something far more deep-seated that will require the organization to develop new capabilities and processes over a sustained period.

Outrage, and its management, is not as clear-cut as one might have first considered it to be.

Many of the issues that trigger outbreaks of outrage are fundamental beliefs around, for example, the roles of men and women in society: What are the beliefs and principles that we should follow in educating our children? How do we define marriage or family? These are foundational questions around which different civilizations, and even communities therein, can have sharp differences. For most of the past half-century, these issues took somewhat of a back seat to the ideological debate between democratic capitalism and communism, focusing on political and economic rights as opposed to religious and moral ones.

But as it appears more likely to a large group of people not only that the democratic capitalist system and its proponents cannot deliver a prosperous future in the face of advances such as AI but that, in some sense, the proponents of the system have systematically sided with other interests, those people start looking to fundamental alternatives. For Francis Fukuyama's vision to be true, people must be in the roughly same place in terms of their narrative. But in Huntington's world, as experiences with the system diverge and people become more fearful, they look to explain their condition in terms of the differences that separate themselves and others.

The breakdown is more than a clash between the very crudely defined groups of people described by Huntington. Modern social media is tearing these "civilizations" apart into smaller groups that are often deeply hostile to other communities inside even national boundaries. According to this logic, dispossessed groups—like poor whites with declining life expectancy—blame a woke liberal elite that they believe sides with immigrants and overseas countries more than with their own fellow citizens. At the same time, they also find unlikely allies in other groups experiencing similar fears. A laid-off freight-handler in Ohio may find he has more in common with supporters of Vladimir Putin or Viktor Orbán than with the Harvard or Oxford graduates who occupy "deep state" positions of power in the

West. Indeed, at a recent Republican party rally in March 2022, in the wake of Russia's Ukraine invasion, attendees were heard chanting "Putin! Putin!"[27] This would have been unimaginable as recently as twenty years ago, anywhere in America, let alone at gatherings of the political party that had traditionally regarded Russia as *the* threat to the American way of life.

Let us turn now to look at how organizational leaders can navigate these rough waters, where a large proportion of the population has begun to feel like they are on the cusp of war.

Leading in a Polarized World

At present, most individuals and organizations manage hostility on an ad hoc basis, typically as an exercise in crisis management. If outrage were a relatively idiosyncratic occurrence, this approach would probably be sufficient. But if we accept the proposition that we are experiencing a period in which outrage is systematic, then individuals and organizations need to embrace a more structured approach. Just as governments have systems for managing regular adverse weather events—think blizzards, hurricanes, or tornadoes in the United States—so organizations and their leaders need an equivalent for managing the stakeholder hostilities that now contextualize nearly all their decisions.

The objective of any workable system for managing in an age of outrage must be to surface a way forward among participants that will, at best, form the basis for progress toward a mutually acceptable goal and, at the least, do no further harm to exacerbate the outrage. But for a leader to have any hope of realizing this objective, they must accept two basic axioms that, like all axioms, express truths that might seem self-evident on rendering. The first is that no matter what you do, you can never fully address the demands made of you. And the second: no matter what you do, you will be seen as part of the problem.

The first axiom is intuitive enough. We can all accept at some level the proposition that some problems are inherently complex and may never be resolved to everyone's satisfaction. It is also very likely that people's positions and agency powers may shift during a negotiation. A good example of this is provided by the process in the 2010s of defining a national core curriculum for Brazil's schools, on which I coauthored a case study at Oxford with my colleagues Anna Petherick and Oenone Kubie.[28] Negotiating the principles had been a long, drawn-out process that in many ways exemplifies the framework I will describe in this book.

Schooling in Brazil is highly decentralized across state and municipal governments, with varied standards and priorities for education, which have created, in turn, some variance in quality. In 2014, Brazil's Congress, after years of deliberation, authorized a working group to draft a nationwide common core for its schools that would, after approval by a designated civil authority—the National Council of Education—be considered adopted. Importantly, the core curriculum would not be subject to a vote in Congress. In 2017, the working group, which included a diverse set of academic experts and civil servants, issued their third (and what they hoped would be the final) draft of the common core. At the last minute, however, the cross-party Evangelical Caucus of Brazil's Congress declared its opposition to the draft, in particular to its clauses on respect for gender identity and sexuality, which had been agreed within the working group and had survived two drafts exposed to public comment (in 2015 and in 2016), including over nine thousand attempted amendments. The Evangelical Caucus had not been a particularly involved stakeholder at the time the process had begun, but when the final draft was presented for approval, it was in a position not only to take the project out of the hands of the working group altogether, returning the issue to Congress, but also to block the then government's entire legislative agenda, even beyond education.

The leader of the working group in 2017, Maria Helena Guimarães de Castro, eventually decided on her own authority—and in the face of opposition from many in the group, including those who had spent years carefully negotiating consensus—to shelve the offending clauses in the interests of saving the project and at least getting a draft that could legally be adopted without requiring an unraveling from Congress. Many teachers severely criticized the decision, which undermines the credibility of the reform. Yet partial though it is, the reform still represents to many a giant step forward for Brazil.

The second axiom—that you will be seen as part of the problem—is intended to give perspective to organizational leaders that you cannot and should not see yourself as the *whole* solution. At the very least, doing so is self-defeating, but it is also likely arrogant and imprudent. Even if certain organizational agents think of themselves as progressive champions of the marginalized, by virtue of being in a position of establishment power, they will be seen as part of the problem. This is a hard realization, but a useful one—as I learned through my own personal experience, described in the preface to this book.

Taken together, the two axioms enable one to move away from an ultimately self-defeating mindset in which the manager or leader figures as a heroic problem-solver toward a recognition that there will always be work unfinished and disagreement over certain critical issues. Matters around which outrage develops are often open-ended, and their scope may well evolve as circumstances and attitudes change as a result both of what happens in the system and of external influences and events. It is because of these properties that the matters do not lend themselves to being definitively fixed but rather require incremental and dynamic management. This, the axioms remind us, cannot be done through any single person's expertise and will alone, but rather through a collaborative exercise in which the leader serves as *one* enabler rather than the overall motor. Trying to be the latter is a surefire route to physical, mental, and emotional exhaustion, let alone failure.

I do recognize, however, that internalizing these truths can be a challenge for many leaders. It certainly was a challenge for me. It requires leaders to accept their limitations, and that goes against much of the training and the very gut instinct that many leaders have—and a lot of the aspirational messaging around what makes a leader. I will return to this point in the concluding chapter, but now let us turn to the framework for managing in the age of outrage, beginning in the next chapter with a focus on the individual. First, I will walk through some of the science that underpins the framework's core platform to turn down the temperature, and then I will discuss the basic practices and protocols that can effect that science into practice.

Chapter 2

Turning Down the Temperature

In March 2018, newspapers in Britain and the United States revealed via a whistleblower that Facebook (now Meta) had cooperated with a relatively unknown company called Cambridge Analytica, which had harvested social media data from millions of users to target voters in the 2016 US presidential elections. Cambridge Analytica, it was noted, had been retained by Donald Trump's campaign, among others. Of particular concern was how Cambridge Analytica had used "psychological profiling" to identify swing voters and then show them made-up advertisements accusing Trump's opponent, Hilary Clinton, of corruption, with a view to at least having them stay home on election day.[1] Facebook was implicated in "betraying" its users and trying to "manipulate" election outcomes for profit.

Even as the crisis accelerated, resulting in congressional hearings and a loss of over $100 billion in market capitalization for Facebook, the company's practices had defenders. For instance, Meghan McCain, daughter of former US presidential candidate John McCain (who had run against Barack Obama in 2008), argued that the practices were not too different from those of the Obama campaign in 2012: "It happened under Obama, and it was lauded by the media as being genius," she suggested.[2]

The cacophony of political and social responses to Facebook's role in the affair reflected America's deep divisions in the age of outrage. Facebook needed to respond, not least to stop its bleeding valuation, but Trump, the alleged beneficiary of its actions, was now America's president, so the company could not afford to overreact. But before it could do anything, the company had to turn down the temperature, both internally among its executives and sometimes shocked employees and externally at least among key stakeholders.

Doing that successfully requires two things: a theory about how outrage is triggered at the personal level, and a platform of capabilities and practices that enables leadership to put that theory into practice. Let's begin by looking at the theory.

The General Aggression Model

Sound management frameworks are based on academic theory—including what is perhaps the best-known framework for strategic decision-making: Michael Porter's five forces model, which is anchored in and inspired by industrial organization, the branch of economics that focuses on firm structure and the dynamics of markets and competition. The model leverages the intellectual investment of the many researchers who have contributed to the field. The framework also serves as a crucible for that work—as repeated applications of the model reveal avenues for new research and development.

The framework for managing in the age of outrage is similarly anchored in and inspired by theoretical work—in the first instance of turning down the temperature by work in behavioral psychology, in particular, research into the origins and dynamics of aggressive behavior. Before embarking on a description of the managerial practices that my framework proposes, I will lay out the basic intellectual foundation of the general aggression model (GAM), which synthesizes a number of specific hypotheses about what motivates aggression and how it plays out in people's behaviors. In some ways an analogue of the standard model in particle physics, the GAM was first proposed by professors Craig Anderson and Brad Bushman of Iowa State University, and their 2002 article in the *Annual Review of Psychology* provides an excellent overview on which the following discussion is based.[3]

As you would expect from a general model, the GAM offers a flexible definition of aggression that covers most of the aggressive behaviors we observe. According to this definition, aggression is "any behavior directed towards another individual with the proximate (immediate) intent to cause harm." In this definition, "harm" itself is not necessarily physical—it is broadly meant as something inflicted on a victim that is "not just" in the sense that it violates their humanity and civil rights. The perpetrator must also believe that the behavior will be harmful to the victim and that the victim will wish to avoid it. This definition not only excludes perverse (masochistic) situations in which perpetrator and victim collude but also allows for aggression to be seen not only as an immediate reaction to a situation (hostile aggression) but also as a behavioral tool (instrumental aggression) where the credible threat of harm is made in pursuit of some other goal. An armed robbery would be an example of the latter where a proximate goal of inflicting harm is used to ensure the underlying goal of taking the victim's possessions. Aggression can range from violent (causing physical trauma) to passive (making the victim psychologically uncomfortable).

Aggression, in the GAM, is usually a response to what is termed in behavioral psychology an "aversive situation," an event, social encounter, or condition that a person perceives as compromising their well-being. There are, therefore, two inputs to aggression: the person encountering the aversive situation and the circumstances of the situation. Let's begin with the person.

The person

Every person comes to an aversive situation with their own baggage, in the form of the physical and psychological characteristics driving their behaviors. These factors are not entirely independent of each other or of environmental factors—for example, physical characteristics may be reinforced (or mitigated) by environmental ones, and the boundaries between psychological and biological characteristics are blurred. Together, these characteristics combine to create "knowledge structures" or scripts encoded in the brain that determine, at least partially, a person's response to an aversive situation. For instance, if an event triggers access to a knowledge structure containing aggression, then aggressive behavior will likely result.

Physical characteristics include, perhaps most obviously, gender: many scientific studies suggest that men are more disposed to aggression than women, and that at least some of this is due to hormonal factors, which are also, in part, determined by genetic coding. There is evidence also that aversive events strike men and women differently: men react more violently to female infidelity, perhaps because female infidelity may compromise the survival of their genes. (This certainly has analogues in the natural world: when a lion pride's alpha male is deposed, for example, the incoming male is known to kill the former alpha's cubs.)

There are psychological factors at play as well. Recognized disorders such as narcissistic personality disorder (which itself has both environmental and biological origins) may directly trigger aggressive responses. A child used to parents who defer to the child's wishes is likely to have an inflated sense of self-esteem, which renders the child prone to reacting aggressively when their sense of self-esteem is threatened. Similarly, people suffering from a bipolar condition will react more or less aggressively depending on where they are in their mood cycle. Autism disorders can similarly help determine how a person perceives or reacts to a given situation.

Perhaps most importantly, a person's behavioral predispositions can be environmentally learned. These environmental factors are part of how a "situation" affects aggressive behavior, which I will discuss next. People come to aversive situations with a collection of beliefs, attitudes, and values about what behaviors are or are not acceptable, products often of the society they grew up in and their parents. People who have observed that aggressive behaviors produce positive results for the aggressor can come to believe that aggression is a successful strategy, which is more likely to occur in societies where there are few constraints on aggression.

Specific attitudes around such behavior may develop through upbringing: the child of a family in which the father has success- fully dominated the mother may come to believe that women are generally submissive. These beliefs and attitudes can be reinforced by social or religious values (in many conservative religious groups, for example, men are accorded superior status over women). People may also have long-term social goals that provide a motivation for aggression. People in gangs, for example, display violence in order to build their status and reputation in a group where violence is treated as a social good.

However, many, if not most social norms (which are themselves situational factors) inhibit aggression, because social groups need to work collaboratively to survive. And most people will choose not to act aggressively even if the opportunity presents itself, because their sense of value or self-worth depends in large part on conformity to the norms. When they do act aggressively, they will often try to seek a moral justification for the display of the aggression—they are, perhaps, teaching the victim a lesson. They may even claim that the victim is in some sense not completely human and therefore not pro- tected by social norms.[4]

The situation

Which script an aversive situation triggers in the person experienc- ing it will depend on the situation's specific features. Some situations discourage aggression. A church service, for example, where there are many witnesses and specified nonaggressive roles for participants in the situation is a context that discourages aggression. A country and western bar on a Saturday night is a context more conducive to an aggressive response to an aversive event. As Anderson and Bushman point out: "Many aggression facilitators are present: alcohol, aggressive cues, aggression-prone individuals, males competing for the attention of females, and relative anonymity." Research has also found that the perception that an aggressor is armed can trigger strong reactions in people who have been exposed to armed violence—whether real or artificial (as in video games). Cues for triggering aggressive scripts vary greatly and can be difficult to predict, but often they can include deliberate provocation, which is especially effective if the aggressor is familiar with the victim (in marital arguments, for example, one often talks about "knowing which buttons to press").

Situations that are perceived by a person as frustrating their goals or aspirations also trigger aggressive responses, even in situations where the cause for disruption is justified. For example, an airline might delay a flight to make a security check. Although this is reasonable, many passengers will react aggressively toward airline staff for fear that they might miss a connection or a meeting. In that example, the aggression is often displaced—the person going to an important meeting takes out their frustration on the airline gate staff for a decision that they were not responsible for and a situation they could not have avoided (although the aggressor could have taken an earlier flight).

The physical circumstances in which the aversive event occurs are also key factors in triggering an aggressive response. Plenty of research attests to the role of temperature, smell, noise, and space in triggering aggression. Hot, smelly rooms overcrowded with people talking loudly are very likely to trigger aggression from someone who's being told that they face a two-hour delay to their trip. The more acute the discomfort, the stronger the aggressive reaction (research shows that someone who experiences extreme pain is more likely to react aggressively). That's why creating positive "ambient" settings for discussing aversive situations—a cool, uncrowded odor-free room with good acoustics—can greatly help outraged stakeholders engage with the people or organization that outrages them.

Drugs also play a role in shaping a person's reaction to an aversive situation. If someone has taken a drug or stimulant (caffeine or alcohol), they may react differently than they would if the drug had not been involved.[5] In addition to providing a calming ambience for discussing questions of outrage, it may be advisable not to offer participants intoxicating substances. The influence of drugs appears to be indirect rather than direct—they don't increase aggression per se but rather amplify frustration and negative cues.

Finally, the circumstances of a situation may work on the incentives of a person entering that situation to respond with aggression. For example, a border guard who likes to collect "fees" for expediting entry might leave some cash on his desk to indicate to the person whose entry he is refusing that the payment of a bribe could resolve the situation. This both points to a solution and triggers some kind of cost-benefit analysis. Seeing the money, a frustrated but well-heeled traveler might well swallow their indignation at the refusal and instead fold a few dollar bills into their passport and proffer it again. Paying a small bribe would seem like a far less annoying and expensive outcome than catching a return flight.

Let's turn now to look at how the characteristics of the person and the aversive situation combine to produce an aggressive response, according to the GAM.

Routes to aggression

The personal and situational inputs to an individual facing an aversive situation lead to an aggressive response by shaping their internal state in three interconnected ways—through their mood or emotional response, through their more deliberate or cognitive decisions, and through ambient or "arousal" conditions. To see how this dynamic plays out, let's imagine a hypothetical aversive event.

Suppose that someone with a Confederate flag on their car drives into the rear of a Black person's car at a traffic light. This could affect the latter in a number of ways. Was it a hot day and was the victim's

air-conditioning broken? Was the Black driver returning home from
a workout at the gym, and after having downed a double espresso?
If so, they might be more prone to aggression (due to ambient conditions). These arousal factors predispose the victim to a heightened
aggressive response, as temperature, physical exercise, and caffeine are
known to do.[6]

The latter might have also assumed instinctively that the run–in
was an accident, until seeing the flag, which is a trigger to anger
(an emotional response). There is a particularly strong connection
between anger—an emotion—and aggression—the type of response.
In general, scholars observe that anger reduces the effect of inhibi-
tions set up by, say, social norms against aggression, causing people
to look for justification for aggression, and it may even bias a person's cognitive perception of an event. Anger also helps people who
respond aggressively to sustain their aggression by drawing attention
to provoking aspects of a situation (such as the presence of a Confederate flag on the car), which has the effect of keeping the person in
the internal state that led to an aggressive response. And "if anger is
triggered in an ambiguous social situation," it often offers a resolution of the ambiguities by pushing the angry participant to a hostile
interpretation of the aversive situation.[7]

The Confederate flag could further evoke an *analysis* (or cognitive response) in the Black driver that the crash was a deliberate act
of racial violence against a Black person, precipitating an aggressive
response script rather than a civil exchange of insurance details. This
is especially likely to happen if the victim has repeatedly experienced
race-based targeting, which conditions their knowledge structures.

In effect, human cognition is not necessarily an unbiased, logical
process of analysis. There are more nerves going from the brain to
the eye than from the eye to the brain, which implies that a lot of
what we perceive is in fact the product of what is going on in the
brain rather than in the real world, and the input from the eyes is less
the basis for what we see than corroboration for what we *think* we
see.[8] Human consciousness, therefore, is really a state of "controlled

hallucination" (as philosopher Andy Clark and neuroscientist Anil Seth describe), in which we confirm through our senses whether the hallucination seems to represent reality.[9] The hallucination itself, however, is largely the product of our lived experiences rather than some immediate clinical analysis of evidence. That is why knowledge structures or scripts are so important. They shape what we think of as cognition and what it means to be conscious. To be sure, humans are capable of rational analysis, but our capacity to perform it is easily overwhelmed. If a person's brain is distracted, processing a great deal of information at once—as in the case when a person is, say, driving in a crowded city or when an overworked manager is trying to resolve a crisis—our responses are more likely to be shaped by a combination of idiosyncratic scripts and emotions than by replicable logical analysis.

The outcomes

We have seen that personal and environmental features can result in an aggressive internal state in a person experiencing an aversive situation. But there are many possible scenarios that could plausibly play out in any given aversive situation. Let's look now at how a person ends up in a specific response, according to Anderson and Bushman's GAM.

The first reaction to any situation is an immediate, spontaneous appraisal of it, leading to a reflexive situational inference. If our Black motorist were thinking aggressive thoughts (perhaps ruminating on why he was unjustly stopped the night before by the police on his way home), he would probably take the bump as an act of aggression on the part of the white driver. On the other hand, if he was thinking about a good deed done to him earlier that day, he could likely perceive the same bump as an accident. In other words, the internal state *at the moment* of the aversive event "determines, to a great extent, which type of automatic inference is generated" and, consequently, what script will be triggered.[10]

An immediate appraisal will itself trigger emotions, identify possible responses, and propose an intention. If the Black driver has been reflecting on racial injustice, his immediate affective response might be anger, his objective could be redress, and he might confront the white driver in order to obtain some form of emotional compensation. If he has been thinking about the poor traffic conditions more generally, his response may be annoyance at the inconvenience, his objective likely will be to expedite the exchange of insurance details, and his actions may well be to put on his hazard lights and start the paperwork. These are very different scripts for what follows, and which script is triggered depends greatly on the driver's internal state.

What happens after the immediate appraisal further depends on the individual's resources and capabilities available. If the person has the resources and capabilities to immediately achieve their goal, they will usually act on the impulse of the immediate appraisal. So, if the Black driver's immediate appraisal is that the bump is racially motivated and he sees that the white driver is alone, he may well choose an angry confrontation.

But what if there are three or four large, muscled, tattooed white males in the car behind? In this situation, the Black driver is likely to reappraise the situation, if he determines that he does not have the resources and capabilities to achieve the objectives of his immediate appraisal—that of seeking redress for a racially motivated run-in. Or, as Bushman and Anderson put it, "the person will engage a more effortful set of reappraisals."

Reappraisal typically involves looking for more information about the cause of the event and previously unidentified features of it. The reappraisal can go through several iterations as various alternative interpretations are considered—for example, was that a baby he also saw in the other car? Does this event resemble previous experiences? If the reappraisal yields our Black driver to believe that the bump was a deliberate act, he might consciously choose to respond aggressively (now a thoughtful, rather than an emotive, course of action), perhaps to discourage the white driver from repeating the action in the future. Depending on the circumstances, the reappraisal could well increase the Black driver's level of anger as his mind connects the incident with other seemingly similar incidents.

Encoding the encounter

Once a response to an aversive situation is determined and acted on, the encounter is in some way encoded in the scripts of the parties involved, adding their personal inputs to the next similar situation. This is an important component of the model because the frequency at which people are exposed to certain aversive situations conditions the scripts that they are likely to seize on in perceiving a given situation. If the outcomes from the situations are frequently aggressive responses that, in some way, are perceived as successful in that they compel the other party to comply with the aggressor's preferences, aggression becomes more strongly encoded in the scripts that an aversive situation may trigger, making aggressive responses more likely.

Anderson and Bushman note that other studies of aggression seem to confirm this. As they point out, research demonstrates that a child's repeated exposure to physical abuse by parents predisposes them to inflicting abuse on their own children when the latter defy them (the aversive situation).[11] Similarly, boys who witness their fathers abusing their mothers can end up abusing their own spouses in turn. In other words, repeated exposure to violent behavior is itself a conditioning factor on individuals as they interact socially.

There are indirect effects as well. As a person displays aggression in aversive situations and becomes known for that behavior, the universe of people interacting with them can change. An aggressive child, for example, may be avoided by many other children and, increasingly, by adults as the child grows, and may well end up associating largely with people who are comfortable with and even value aggression, which in turn conditions the set of situations they will regularly encounter, all of which reinforces the direct effects from the outcomes.

The psychology of aggression is a large field, and the GAM synthesizes only a part of the valuable work produced by students of behavioral science and the brain, but it does suffice to provide a scientific foundation for this chapter. Having summarized the basic theory whereby aggression may arise in response to an aversive situation, I will now turn to what should make up the platform of a system for managing that aggression.

The Platform

The purpose of the platform, depicted in figure 2-1, is (metaphorically) turning down the temperature of the exchanges between an organization's leaders and outraged stakeholders (recall, for example, the question of de-escalation in the Facebook vignette introduced at

FIGURE 2-1

The platform to turn down the temperature

In an age of outrage, an organization needs a platform to turn down the temperature in crisis situations. This platform consists of a calming environment in which to hold discussions, rules of engagement, and a pre-agreed working group. All these components should be informed by a robust behavioral theory of aggression.

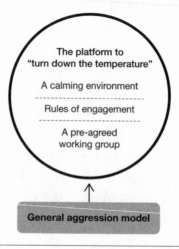

the beginning of this chapter). To achieve this reduction in temperature, it is important to ensure that the ambient conditions for dialogue are favorable, that the rules governing the dialogue are agreed, and that the participants have the authority and capability to speak for the stakeholders involved—the (potentially) offending organization on the one side and the outraged parties on the other.

A calming environment

Given the role of ambient conditions in creating negative affect, the physical environment in which any dialogue takes place should be conducive to calm conversation—the objective being to reduce as many triggers for negative scripts as possible and to provide the time and space needed for genuine reflective analysis. You should not have an important negotiation take place in an overcrowded, overheated room. You should give people water to drink, certainly, but keep coffee to break time rather than have people around the negotiating table fuel themselves with caffeine. Make sure that there is natural light in the room and that the colors are neutral. If you are all seated around a table, give some thought to the type of table. A rectangular table lends itself to the formation of hierarchies in the group, which may silence participants and allows the two sides to line up opposite each other, making it easier for the participants to imagine that they are in a confrontational situation, which itself could trigger negative scripts. Round tables might well serve better.

In many situations, it is also advisable to take the discussion to another location altogether—further impeding the accessibility of negative or aggressive scripts. That is why many peace negotiations take place on neutral ground. For a specific example, let's go back to the negotiations for Brazil's education reform that I introduced in the previous chapter.[12] When various civil society, educational, and governmental representatives first met to discuss the possibility of setting a national core curriculum, even before the Brazilian Congress approved the plan, the discussions took place, not in Brazil, but at

Yale University facilities in New Haven, Connecticut, in 2013. That made sense because education standards for schools in Brazil were a political hot potato.

Traditionally, educational standards had been set by local teachers, who determined whether their students had achieved satisfactory performance levels; the (left-wing) unions fiercely defended this prerogative. As a result, although common standards were mandated by the country's constitution, no government had succeeded in putting anything substantive on the statute books. At the same time, "despite spending around 4.2% of GDP on basic education (the OECD average was 3.3%), Brazil ranked in the bottom 20% of countries that participated in the OECD's [Program] for International Student Assessment in 2012 for all assessed subjects. According to domestic testing, in 2011 only 40% of students in the fifth year of schooling were at the 'adequate' level in Portuguese, and just 36% in mathematics."[13] These numbers fueled popular support (especially among business-friendly voters) for a national curriculum to ensure common standards and minimum levels of academic competence throughout the country.

If the first round of discussions had taken place in Brazil, militant advocates on all sides (including outraged teachers and voters) would have been able to make their presence felt by protesting outside the location where the talks were held. The presence of protestors could have directly posed a threat to participants, but even if that were not the case, the protestors provide stakeholder representatives with a gallery—which they could use to dig in, to amplify their message, or indeed to demonstrate to other stakeholders that they represent a powerful constituency, and refuse any concessions altogether. Playing in front of a gallery also could limit the degrees of freedom of stakeholder representatives: Out of a need to maintain their credibility with their constituencies, they might have been less willing to strike agreements with other parties or acknowledge the legitimacy of those other interests.

The chances that militant and conflicting protests would take place if the negotiators met somewhere in Brazil were high, given the volatile political conditions after 2010. The left-wing president first elected in 2011, Dilma Rousseff, was impeached shortly after winning reelection and forcibly removed from office in 2016, to be replaced by the right-wing vice president Michel Temer, who himself became embroiled in impeachment charges as part of a probe into political corruption. Brazil at the time was not an environment conducive to negotiating an issue on which people were so sharply divided along political lines. By taking the first-round discussions to a place outside Brazil—the neo-Gothic spires of Yale—the participants would have more space to feel and think differently, to consider and explore consensus positions (favoring more rational cognition), and the emotional temperature (and negative ambience) that inevitably comes with crowds of angry protestors would be mitigated.

Along with removing the participants from exposure to conflicts, it is also desirable to limit access to media. The venue in which the talks take place should not, therefore, sport prominently displayed televisions running live cable news channels. Nor should it be easy for participants to engage in social media transactions during discussions, as these channels of communication can prejudice the conversations and, again, push participants toward negative, aggressive scripts. For this reason, participants in consensus-building programs at the Oxford Blavatnik School of Government are sometimes required to leave their mobile phones in baskets at the front of the classroom—our objective is to get them to talk to each other, not people outside the room.

Admittedly, all this is the easy part: providing comfortable ambient conditions for dialogue and time for reflection on initial emotional impulses is relatively straightforward. But what can you do about differing scripts? Given that you have no control over the lived experiences that have shaped an individual's deep-seated script, it's best to avoid directly challenging it. You may not see it as legitimate, but you are unlikely to change it—certainly not in one sitting. You can, however, create a nonthreatening space where your stakeholders can feel free to share their scripts without feeling attacked for them, which brings me to the next element of the platform.

The rules of engagement

One of my responsibilities at Oxford's MPP program has been to convene current and aspiring public leaders from more than sixty jurisdictions (including China and the United States, India and Pakistan, Israel and Palestine, and Russia and Ukraine) to build coalitions on divisive issues such as climate change, migration, and inequality. Diverging scripts are endemic to our setting. To keep our community functioning and thriving, we have developed and agreed in advance on our rules of engagement. That is crucial, because you cannot contemporaneously seek legitimacy for a process that you are already using to address a contentious issue. As a manager, you should take the time to identify your key stakeholders and seek their commitment before you get into firefighting mode. (Indeed, this is what Facebook has done since the Cambridge Analytica scandal, as I will discuss later.)

Our community rules at the Blavatnik School are simple: First, *people must bring their authentic selves to the table*—they should not feel that they must self-censor in order to be heard. If a participant's religious beliefs make it difficult for them to accept homosexuality, for example, they should feel free to express that position, even though they are in a group whose moderator is in a gay marriage. But the corollary to this rule is our second rule—*no one may claim that a script is too offensive to be heard*. As a participant of the group, I am free to share my experience of being in a gay marriage, should this be relevant to the discussion. Equally, our participants should feel as free to express their reservations to me about gay marriage. And that brings me to the third, and perhaps most difficult rule: *all must be accountable for how their words land on others*. This third rule encourages all stakeholders to condition their communications, not in self-censorship, but with the hope of gradually helping others understand (even if not agree with) their worldview. In other words, I submit that what characterizes an effective manager in the age of outrage is their ability to take responsibility for the impact of their own words on the learning of others.

With this responsibility comes a heightened sense of self-awareness and a willingness to temper one's expression to be less misunderstood.

And that temperance, somewhat ironically, sometimes exposes the dogmatism (and fragilities) of one's own position on a divisive issue. Put differently, the accountability for how your words land on others helps surface and even encourages you to more freely acknowledge your biases when sharing your own scripts. This vulnerability, when held around the table, is in turn more likely to generate collective decisions that withstand the passage of time in a divided polity.

Properly applied, the rules set up members of the group to be leaders in the search for a solution rather than simply debaters. This is an important distinction, because the two are often confused in the political process. In the UK, for example, policy makers are typically not trained to engage in active listening and thoughtful consensus-building. The House of Commons is famous for the ferocity of its debate. Even the face-off layout of the government and opposition benches invites confrontation. While it can make for entertaining theater, the objective in these debates is generally to overwhelm the voice of the opposition through effective presentation of your point of view in the pursuit of votes—which, to the extent that any are not already spoken for, go to the more effective debater. In some respects, parliamentary debate in Britain is an exercise in machismo; debaters try to prove to their own side that they are more effective at confounding the opposition and, for that reason, deserve to be leaders. The famous weekly Prime Minister's Questions is more a test of the debating skills of the two parliamentary party leaders than a process of genuine enquiry, let alone learning.

The point is that people will easily adopt adversarial scripts when discussing difficult issues, unless the discussion is purposefully set up to avoid that happening, because the default structure of such discussions (which is more akin to "debate") makes it hard for people to see an issue in any way other than through their own lens.

A pre-agreed working group

In many cases, given our times, outrage and conflict between stakeholders are endemic. There may be a specific issue that triggers an

outbreak at any given time, but the potential is always present, because
the conditions that underpin outrage are long-standing. For instance,
many parts of the world are scarred by ethnic and sectarian divides
that may be reflected in economic outcomes. The State of Kaduna in
Nigeria, about which I wrote a case for the Blavatnik School with my
colleagues Thomas Simpson and Sarah McAra, provides an example.[14]
Straddling the country, it represents in microcosm many of the divisions characterizing one of the largest economies in sub-Saharan
Africa. The north of the state is largely made up of two ethnic groups,
the Hausa and the Fulani, who are both Muslim. The south of the
state is made up of multiple ethnic groups adhering to a wide variety
of Christian denominations. The latter are often farmers, tied to the
land, while the former tend to be pastoral herdsmen, whose cattle
graze the fallow farmlands, fertilizing them in exchange, but at times
causing damage, thereby creating the potential for conflict.

Antipathy between the Muslims and Christians runs deep and
goes back to precolonial times: the Hausa and Fulani often raided
the smaller southern ethnic groups and traded captives as slaves to
Arab traders in the north and to European merchants, who trans-
ported them to the Americas. After decolonization, the divisions
between the Muslim and Christian groups became increasingly violent, exacerbated by the emergence of crime syndicates, which the
state apparatus essentially proved unable to control. Many people
on both sides no longer regarded the state government as an honest
broker—Muslim and Christian officials were seen as favoring their
own groups—and the police and even military were overwhelmed by
the criminal gangs, who were frequently better armed. The violence
was often at its most acute during electoral campaigns, which were
generally highly partisan, typically resulting in uneasy compromises
over jobs between the ethno-political parties competing.

All told, it was estimated that in Kaduna alone, over twenty thousand people had died as a result of ethnic and sectarian violence
between 1980 and 2010. Kidnapping, extortion, sexual aggression,
and violent crime were routine, and the situation was compounded

by the ready availability of firearms—a by-product of an ongoing civil war in the northern states of Nigeria with Boko Haram, a fundamentalist Muslim group seeking to carve out an independent Islamic state.

It was in this context, that Priscilla Ankut accepted an invitation from the governor of Kaduna, a Muslim from the north, to head a peace commission to explore avenues for tackling the violence and division in the state. Prior to that appointment in 2017, Ankut's career had largely been spent with technocratic development institutions such as the British Council, the European Commission, and the UN Development Program. Born a Christian in southern Kaduna, but educated as a human rights lawyer in the north, she saw the post as an opportunity to give back to her home state what she had learned in her career in economic and social development. Many of her friends in the south, however, had advised her against taking the position out of their suspicion of any initiative on the part of the Muslim-led state government, which was generally perceived as hostile to Christians. But Ankut persisted.

One of the most important initiatives that she undertook as head of the peace commission was the creation of what she called the House of Kaduna Family, a cross-faith group of twenty-two senior, well-regarded religious leaders from all sides, drawn from across tribal lines. But rather than recruiting them from the traditional religious groupings—the Christian Association of Nigeria and the Jamaat al Islami—which are both strongly identified with specific political alliances, to the extent that each side would hold public prayer requesting divine support for their favored candidates at elections, she recruited members in an ad personam capacity based on her assessment of their leadership capabilities.

The name of the group itself carries some symbolism. Ankut saw the group as a kind of family council, an echo, perhaps, of a pre-colonial past in which tribal elders on all sides resolved intercommunity conflicts through discussion. And like a family, Kaduna is diverse and experiences internal conflicts and rivalries. Her idea was that such a group could serve as a unifying agent when crisis hit. Although she accepted that she would be able to do little in the foreseeable future to even reduce, let alone end, conflict and violence, she saw the group as a mechanism for healing divisions. As part of its mission, for example, the group conducted interfaith, politically neutral prayer meetings during elections, the idea being to counter the extent to which the traditional groupings stir people's emotions—and their propensity to violence—around those times.

It is unclear whether the group made much headway in lowering the violence in Kaduna, but it at least did supply a preexisting point of spiritual commonality and leadership, and a forum to turn down the temperature and in which to air grievances and discuss how to move through them. It is difficult to create a body for reconciliation in the immediate aftermath of violence, when passions are so high, so Ankut's brilliant move was to have one already in place to diffuse the aftermath of the seemingly inescapable violence.

The House of Kaduna Family is certainly not the only body of its kind. In South Africa, for example, Archbishop Desmond Tutu's Truth and Reconciliation Committee carried out a similar function in a similar context as part of the healing process following the end of apartheid.[15] Nor is the idea limited to the political domain. Many business organizations operating in a context of division and outrage have now put in place similar bodies. Issues around online abuse and privacy are common flashpoints of outrage, as the opening example on Facebook and the prior chapter's discussion on social media indicate.

Indeed, Meta, the parent company of Facebook and Instagram, now provides a case in point. In late 2018, at the suggestion of Harvard Law School professor Noah Feldman, Facebook founder Mark Zuckerberg announced the creation of an oversight board to monitor and adjudicate on content moderation for the company's social media platforms. The board provides an appeals process for content decisions, seeks to provide accountability for those decisions (which it has the authority to overturn), and provides guidelines for future decisions. Modeled to some extent on the US Supreme Court, the board plays a quasi-judicial role. At the time of writing this, it consisted of twenty members, who include former Danish prime minister Helle Thorning-Schmidt, the former European Court of Human Rights judge András Sajó, Internet Sans Frontières executive director Julie Owono, the Yemeni activist and Nobel Peace Prize winner Tawakkol Karman, and a former editor in chief of the *Guardian*, Alan Rusbridger. The operations of the board are directed by Thomas Hughes, the former CEO of Article 19, a human rights group focusing on freedom of expression, who also helped recruit the board's members.[16] Since its foundation, the board has made decisions on many contentious issues—including the suspension of former US president Donald Trump's account (upheld) and Facebook's removal of photographs of naked breasts as part of a breast cancer awareness program (reversed).[17]

Beyond the oversight board, Meta also launched in 2018, in collaboration with Harvard University, an initiative called Social Science One, to enable better understanding of the relation between social media and elections. This initiative was a direct result of the Cambridge Analytica scandal, and it has since supported academic research on an astonishingly comprehensive data set (about 1 million gigabytes) of "all public URLs shared and clicked by Facebook users globally" and their underlying metadata such as the users' ideological predispositions.[18]

Finally, organizational capabilities around conflict negotiation can also be developed with the help of educational institutions, such as my own Blavatnik School of Government (at the risk of sounding partial). Organizational leaders can take courses that increase their awareness of the psychodynamics of aggression, giving them the knowledge, vocabulary, and skills to initiate and participate in productive discussions. Organizations that have a cadre of managers with these capabilities can deploy them as needed to help manage outbreaks of outrage. What's more, as we saw earlier in the context of Brazil's education reform, the institutions can themselves at times offer a neutral place in which to host negotiations and discussions and may be able to deploy people with both practical and academic expertise in managing outrage.

• • •

Now that I have introduced the GAM theory and the platform to turning down the temperature, we can move to exploring the four processes that constitute the remainder of the age of outrage management framework. We'll look first, in chapter 3, at what's involved in building an understanding of the drivers of a specific crisis that a given leader or organization may face. This requires us to shift the conceptual focus from the individual to group dynamics.

Chapter 3

Making Sense of the Moment

Once you've started the process of turning down the temperature by creating a platform, the first step of our managerial framework is to make sense of the moment of crisis. Doing so requires that you have some idea of what's driving the outrage. Are all three drivers—fear of the future, past injustice, and othering—at play? One more than others? This chapter gives you the tools for drawing out people's "scripts" and listening and learning from them in order to identify the drivers in play. And, while you can't do much in the heat of a crisis to directly address the drivers—let alone remediate or eliminate them—you can publicly acknowledge them and work them into your organization's response.

Let's take a deep dive into how one organization responded to serious outrage—and what it might have done differently.

The London Metropolitan Police in Summer 2020

In June 2020, Britain's *Guardian* newspaper published an article revealing that in the prior month, the London Metropolitan Police, custodians of law and order in the UK's capital, had conducted

nearly 44,000 searches of pedestrians and vehicles using its powers
to "stop and search" individuals (i.e., without a warrant, but on the
basis of "reasonable grounds"). The number of such searches, the data
revealed, had hit an eight-year high, and, alarmingly, Black people
were searched at four times the rate of white people.

I coauthored a case study for Oxford on this situation, with my
colleagues Chris Stone and Sarah McAra.[1] Even as we grappled with
this shocking headline, I realized that it was not news. Concerns
about the long-standing stop-and-search policy had been raised since
at least the 1980s. Officers saw it as a valuable tool to confirm or allay
suspicions without having to first make arrests. Some citizens agreed
and felt that it discouraged people from carrying weapons or drugs.
But the data revealed that police had consistently searched individuals
from Black and minority ethnic (BAME) backgrounds, particularly
young Black men, at a disproportionately higher rate than their white
counterparts. While this troubled some citizens, others argued that
BAME communities were more likely to experience violence, and so
stop-and-search, as a preventative measure, was more likely to be conducted in those settings. The data had also suggested that the police
were not more likely to find any cause for arresting BAME individuals after having searched them than they were for white individuals.
Critics had long argued that these patterns, persisting over decades,
reflected racial discrimination, whereas supporters of stop-and-search
argued that the patterns actually indicated police fairness. The critics
were unpersuaded: They believed that officers were conducting many
of these stop-and-searches based on racial bias and stereotypes, rather
than on genuine suspicion of criminal activity. Not only was this
offensive to the individuals being searched, but—and some officers
themselves shared this concern—it also strained the Met's relationship with the very communities on which it relied for intelligence of
criminal activity.

Given this enduring debate, the outraged reaction of many Londoners to the *Guardian* article might have seemed surprising. Why was this
data, long in the public eye, now creating renewed crisis? Part of the
answer was that in June of 2020, the UK was just coming out of a three-

month lockdown that had initially been billed as a three-week lock-down. Nerves were strained. And the respite from lockdown was seen as a temporary lull consequent on the warmer summer weather. Most people fully anticipated, and indeed the government had warned of, a return to full Covid-19 restrictions in the fall.[2] Moreover, the effects of Covid-19 and the lockdown were being felt more so in minority communities. Another part of the answer was that sensitivity to race issues had been intensified by the very visible murder on May 25, 2020, of George Floyd in the United States by police officers on duty. Floyd's murder during his arrest (on suspicion of attempting to purchase goods with a counterfeit $20 bill), which was caught on video, had triggered widespread unrest in the United States that, in turn, had spread to the UK. Until the release of the stop-and-search data, however, the protests in London had not focused narrowly on the police, but on racism in society more generally: the general perception had been that practices at the Met—and in British policing generally—were substantially less problematic than, say, in the United States.

The release of the June 2020 stop-and-search data gave these protesters and activists an immediate focus. They demanded that the Met acknowledge that it was "institutionally racist" and accept the need for fundamental reform to police practice and culture. Of course, not everyone agreed. Many Londoners, who had been complying with the lockdown restrictions over the previous three months, deeply resented seeing people in blatant violation of social distancing standards at anti-policing and antiracism marches, which were still very much in place even after lockdown had been lifted, and they demanded that the police enforce the regulations. As these people pointed out, it was inconsistent at best to allow mass protests in the streets while limiting the number of people allowed at a funeral or visits to ailing parents and children in care.

Previous inquiries into institutional racism at the Met

In the past, analysis of similar outbreaks of public anger at perceived police racism and recommendations for change had been carried out through public inquiries of varying formality. In 1997, Britain's home secretary (a senior cabinet-level minister akin to the US attorney general), who, along with the mayor of London, appointed the Met's commissioner, had set up such an inquiry in the wake of public outrage at the handling of the investigation into the murder, in 1993, of Stephen Lawrence, a Black teenager. The inquiry, chaired by Sir William Macpherson, was completed in 1999 with the publication of the *Macpherson Report*, which concluded that the investigation "was marred by a combination of professional incompetence, institutional racism and a failure of leadership by senior officers."[3]

The report had pointed to the disproportionate use of stop-and-search against racial minorities: Black people were five times more likely to be stopped than white people at the time. And, as the inquiry pointed out, "[n]obody in the minority ethnic communities believes that the complex arguments which are sometimes used to explain the figures as to stop and search are valid."[4] While the report did not seek to eliminate stop-and-search, recognizing its "genuine usefulness," Macpherson called for greater monitoring and oversight as well as the publication of more comprehensive data.

Despite many changes in, amongst other things, police governance, training, and monitoring, the emotional depth of opposition to stop-and-search changed little following the *Macpherson Report,* and tensions around the practice reignited in the summer of 2011 in the wake of the fatal police shooting of Mark Duggan, a twenty-nine-year-old Black man. Research by the *Guardian* and the London School of Economics found that stop-and-search was one of the key factors the rioters, mostly young people, identified as the root of resentment of the police; they felt that the police targeted them unfairly and conducted searches aggressively.[5] Following these events, the Met prioritized improving the public's trust and confidence in stop-and-search, introducing a new approach that focused on enhancing the use of intelligence and focusing on tackling more serious crimes instead of petty misdemeanors.

The riots also prompted national conversations around stop-and-search, and then Home Secretary Theresa May, a Conservative, commissioned another report. The new inquiry found that across England and Wales, 27 percent of the nine thousand searches examined had not reported any "reasonable grounds," and yet many had still been approved by superior officers. Furthermore, disproportionality remained a concern: nationally, Black people were stopped seven times more often than white people. In 2014, May introduced a package of reforms, including the Best Use of Stop and Search (BUSS) scheme, a voluntary set of practices that expanded data-recording requirements, increased opportunities for public observation, and introduced stricter regulations for when stop-and-searches could be conducted. All forces, including the Met, signed up to the scheme.[6]

With the Met's efforts to better target its use of stop-and-search, along with the national BUSS scheme, the number of searches in London declined significantly: between 2011–2012 and 2017–2018, the total number of searches fell 74 percent, with searches per 1,000 Black people declining from 137 to 51, and from 44 to 11 for white people.[7]

How the accusation of institutional racism played out

Given this context (two public reports in a little over twenty years along with some recent reforms and evidence of consequent improvements), neither the Met leadership in the form of Commissioner Cressida Dick nor the political leaders with oversight of the Met (London's mayor and the UK home secretary) appeared to have much appetite for initiating another public inquiry. For her part, Dick, a highly regarded career police officer, was focused on reducing street violence in the capital, which had reportedly been increasing as the use of stop-and-search was curtailed during the 2010s. Dick herself publicly supported the professional use of stop-and-search (as did the home secretary and the mayor), noting that it saved lives, particularly the lives of young Black men. And while acknowledging that the police force needed to change, Dick's own view seemed to be that change was a long-term project. For instance, change would happen with better training, transparency, and oversight and as the demography of the force came to reflect the city's population more closely. At the time, in 2020, the Met was only 15 percent nonwhite in a city that was about 45 percent nonwhite. Finally, given the length of the public inquiry process (typically at least two years), there was a concern that announcing an inquiry, given that there had already been two in recent memory, would do little to lower the emotional temperature.

With an inquiry off the table, the debate on the future of London policing took place through the media, with both the police allies and self-identified victims of mis-policing transmitting through national and local media channels. A face-off resulted in which critics of the police demanded that Commissioner Dick declare that the Met was "institutionally racist." This Dick firmly refused to do, perhaps out of concern for the morale of her officers and a sense that the label ignored the progress that had been made in improving police practice and diversifying the force. (In 1999, only 3 percent of London's police officers were nonwhite, so the past two decades had seen a fivefold increase. And, at the time, the Met already had in place an intermediate-term strategy to enhance its "culture, behavior and internal processes" and to "reduce inequalities" in its "interactions with Londoners."[8]) Perhaps she felt that her own ability to further diversify and reform the force would be compromised if she were seen to embrace a politically loaded term that polarized people and implicated thousands of innocent police officers. At the same time, her critics pointed out that some twenty years previously, around the Macpherson Inquiry, she had herself conceded that the force was institutionally racist.[9]

Riding out the storm might have worked for Dick and the Met had the ambient conditions improved in the months following the *Guardian* article. They did not. Anti-policing sentiment and lockdown-related anxiety continued to fester in the British public, even as the country remained hopelessly divided over Brexit—the UK's shock decision to exit the European Union. Dick was, for no particular fault of her own, managing an outrage flashpoint in the metaphorical equivalent of a hot, crowded room, where everyone already felt jostled. Then, just as the dust appeared to be settling, the reputation of the Met took another body blow following the rape and murder of Londoner Sarah Everard by a serving police officer, Wayne Couzens, in March 2021. Police mishandling of a vigil in memory of Everard further inflamed public hostility to the Met—with the charge of institutional misogyny added to the charges against the force.[10]

This turn of events prompted Dick to institute an internal review of workplace culture and policing practices and intensified calls for her resignation as commissioner. She eventually left the post in April 2022 citing the mayor's loss of confidence in her leadership as the reason. Following her resignation, the reputation of the police took further hits, and a report into the Met under Baroness Louise Casey, a social-welfare official in the UK; (which Dick herself had initiated), concluded that "public respect has fallen to a low point. Londoners who do not have confidence in the Met outnumber those who do, and these measures have been lower amongst [Black] Londoners for years. The Met has yet to free itself of institutional racism. Public consent is broken. The Met has become unanchored from the Peelian principle of policing by consent set out when it was established."[11]

Could there have been a different way?

How to Make Sense of a Moment of Crisis

Even as we recognize the seeming impossibility of managing such a situation, let us consider what the Met and its commissioner might have done differently that could have helped them make sense of the moment—that is, understand what was driving the outrage directed at the force and perhaps identify possible avenues for the Met's leadership to progress toward some kind of mitigation. (For a summary graphic representation of the discussion that follows, see figure 3-1.)

FIGURE 3-1

Making sense of the moment

This chart summarizes the elements making up the first of the four framework processes (see figure 1-1).

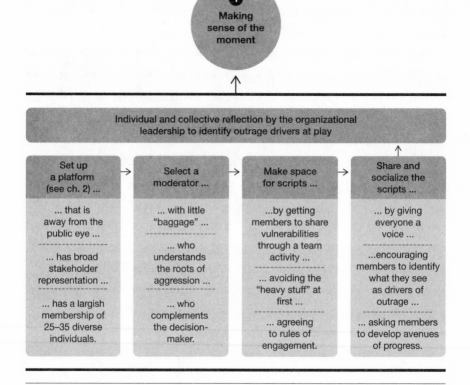

① **Making sense of the moment**

Individual and collective reflection by the organizational leadership to identify outrage drivers at play

| Set up a platform (see ch. 2) ... | → | Select a moderator ... | → | Make space for scripts ... | → | Share and socialize the scripts ... |

... that is away from the public eye ...

... has broad stakeholder representation ...

... has a largish membership of 25–35 diverse individuals.

... with little "baggage" ...

... who understands the roots of aggression ...

... who complements the decision-maker.

...by getting members to share vulnerabilities through a team activity ...

... avoiding the "heavy stuff" at first ...

... agreeing to rules of engagement.

... by giving everyone a voice ...

...encouraging members to identify what they see as drivers of outrage ...

... asking members to develop avenues of progress.

Set up a platform

As discussed in the previous chapter, having a platform in place to immediately help turn down the temperature of a crisis situation is critical to working toward positive outcomes over time. While the Met did indeed have numerous stakeholder groups—both internal and external—to advise it on sensitive matters (some created in the wake of the Macpherson Inquiry), none, to my eye, were of the sort that I will describe below. Indeed, this is often the case for organizations in the age of outrage, as we saw with the examples of both Disney and Facebook when they first confronted their crises. In our new angry, polarized reality, organizations need to have a "depolarization platform" already in place, such as that set up in Kaduna State by Priscilla Ankut. Ideally, such a platform is created before and independently of a particular outrage flashpoint because the creation can then focus on designing a discussion process and pre-agreeing on rules without a specific outrage issue getting in the way.

But absent that, a leader can try to convene an ad-hoc group in the crisis moment that could, in the event of a reasonably successful outcome, serve as the basis of a standing advisory group. Let me offer my take on how such a working group might be organized to get the job done.

The immediate priority would be to take the negotiation, at least in its initial phase, out of the public eye and into the care of a group of intermediaries who are each individually trusted by some material faction of the diverse public views at play. As I described in chapter 2, convening a group of stakeholder participants who agreed in advance to a multistakeholder process worked well in the case of Brazilian education reform, an issue that triggered high emotions to an extent comparable to those in the wake of the *Guardian* report on stop-and-search.

Who should the commissioner have invited? London is highly diverse, with a growing number of both old and young people, among the starkest rates of income inequality in the UK, and rising poverty levels, including high rates of child poverty. It is also one of the most ethnically diverse cities in Europe. According to the 2011 census, 60 percent of Londoners were white, 18.5 percent were Asian, 13 percent were Black, 5 percent were mixed, and 3.4 percent were "other" (i.e., Arab or any other ethnicity).[12]

And within these crudely defined groups, there was considerable variety in attitudes toward policing, immigration, and related issues. A policing expert told me that Asians of Pakistani descent, for example, have anecdotally different views on policing than do people of Indian origins, reflecting differences in the timing and circumstances of their or their forebears' arrival in Britain and their prevailing economic circumstances: Pakistani Britons, who were largely Muslim, were more likely to be critical of firmer policing than Indian, largely Hindu, Britons, who took a more favorable attitude. In fact, the two politicians with formal oversight of the Met at the time reflected this particular divide: Mayor Sadiq Khan, a Muslim of Pakistani heritage and a member of Britain's Labour Party, was sympathetic to protestors, while Home Secretary Priti Patel, a Hindu of Indian origin, was an advocate of firmer policing and a supporter of policies such as stop-and-search.

The London Met's reaction to the 2020 outrage flashpoint is a topic that I have regularly taught at Oxford. When I teach it, I typically assign roles to participants. One role is, of course, that of the commissioner. The other significant roles include the head of StopWatch, a community organization highly skeptical of the value of stop-and-search; the head of the Met's Black Police Officers Association; and a representative of the Met Superintendents Association, a largely white police officers' community of the Met's middle management. And then there are the roles of the mayor of London (the commissioner's immediate boss) and the home secretary, the political executive ultimately responsible for law and order in the UK (and the commissioner's dotted-line boss).

Note that some of these stakeholders have, as it were, a foot in both camps and may perform a catalytic role in identifying workable approaches. The head of the Black Police Officers Association is one such catalyst in the Met case. The association is not expressly opposed to accepting the charge that the Met is institutionally racist, partly because many Black officers have had personal experience of racism in the Met. No commissioner of police in this scenario can afford to have the Black Police Officers Association declare the Met to be, contrary to the commissioner's own instinct, institutionally racist. By the same token, having the association agree to work to diffuse the charge would both boost police morale and bolster the Met's standing in the Black community.

In inviting selected representatives, as described earlier, to form a discussion group to identify causes of disconcert and possible paths forward, Commissioner Dick could have begun to create a trusted platform for ongoing input to the Met's leadership in this age of ongoing outrage. My own experience in such active-listening contexts suggests starting with a group of twenty-five to thirty-five people, who can then be further divided into sufficiently diverse subgroups of five to seven. The key is to have differing lived experiences represented—here, by selecting several people from each of the various groups of Londoners concerned with stop-and-search, BAME officers, and Met middle management. To represent herself, the commissioner could have nominated her senior deputy executives, as it would have been difficult to have her in the room for discussions about what she should be doing differently.

This brings us to the next challenge.

Pick a moderator

The choice of the discussion leader or moderator in the process we are constructing is, of course, critical. In the Met's case, Dick herself could potentially have served as the discussion leader. The advantage of her involvement would have been that it made the exercise credible. But she was heavily compromised by her past: she was on the record as a strong supporter of stop-and-search. She had also accepted many years back that the Met was institutionally racist (but, importantly, at a time when the term was much less loaded than in 2020). And, she was experienced by others through her identity: she was both the first woman commissioner and the first openly gay one in the Met, with lots of unreasonable expectations from citizens on what she would therefore deliver operationally. For instance, given her background, many people could have expected her to be more sympathetic to the charges of institutional racism than a white male police commissioner.

What she needed, therefore, was a discussion leader who could win some trust from all stakeholders and who was not compromised by

prior positions or other factors. That person had to have experience in
negotiating and enough authority to command respect in a charged
situation. And, ideally, they could not be a person with directly relevant institutional power or any personal stake in the outcome. It is
precisely for this reason that in the UK, public inquiries are often led
by (retired) senior judges or academics with expertise in the field. In
the context of the Met case, a judge or academic would probably have
served equally well as the convenor or moderator of a working group.
The disadvantage of selecting a judge or academic (even a retired
one), though, was that their participation was likely to be limited to
the one event. Ideally, therefore, a moderator would have been someone in a position to turn the initial working group into something
more permanent.

A good example of such a person is someone like Priscilla Ankut, who
created the House of Kaduna Family. Ankut, in turn, was appointed by
the somewhat controversial and polarizing governor of Kaduna, whose
own position in the state was plausibly compromised as a moderator
in a way comparable to Dick's. A widely respected technocrat who
served with distinction for many years outside Nigeria, Ankut, on the
other hand, came with credibility and the advantage of distance from
immediate politics. She was also from a different ethnic group than the
governor appointing her. A moderator of this kind could also have been
tasked in London with helping to recruit a House of London Family,
with a particular focus on restoring London to its Peelian principle of
policing by consent. Of course, such a person might not have been
readily available, in which case Dick might have had to accept the
process as a one-off event and take the more traditional option.

Relatively neutral figures such as Ankut are often associated with
successful outcomes in conflict negotiation. A classic example is US
Senator George Mitchell, who played a key role in brokering peace
in Northern Ireland.[13] As a long-serving leader of one of the world's
most respected legislative bodies, he had both considerable experience
in forging agreements across multiple stakeholder groups and widely
recognized credibility. He also had no direct stake in the outcome,

beyond the general interest of helping to achieve peace in Northern Ireland, an issue of particular concern to Irish Americans, a powerful voting bloc in US politics. That said, the United States could influence both sides of the Irish conflict through its economic power—the US populace was both an important source of funding for the IRA and a potential investor in Northern Ireland, factors that enabled Mitchell to push both sides of the conflict to the table, with serious intent. In the case of the Met, however, there was no immediately apparent external agency that could have pushed stakeholders to the table, and the discussion leader would have to rely on their personal power and skillfulness.

Ideally, these capabilities would include experience with academic thinking about the drivers of aggression, such as the GAM outlined in chapter 2, because the discussion must begin by preparing people to share uncomfortable scripts, which the GAM identifies as an important driver of aggressive responses. Even removed from the locus of a conflict, the past can quickly overwhelm a discussion, which brings us to the next challenge facing the working group and its moderator.

The relationship between the moderator or discussion leader and the person appointing them is a critical factor, and the two, as we'll see at the end of this chapter, can have complementary roles. It is the responsibility of the moderator to manage a process of dialogue of which the desired outcomes are recommendations that all or most stakeholders can buy into. But, per the first axiom from chapter 1, that is a goal that may only be partly achieved. At the end of the process, therefore, we will see that executive leadership from an institutionally empowered leader, like Commissioner Dick, was required to realize some progress. The advantage of subcontracting management of the process of negotiation is that it takes enough heat out of an issue to allow for the varying scripts to be meaningfully heard.

Make space for the scripts

To uncover the drivers of outrage, you have to get people into a receptive state of mind for sharing and hearing diverse scripts. To that end, it helps to remind them that whatever their differences, there is still much that they have in common: in this case, they all want to live in a violence-free London. But before even having such difficult conversations, I suggest creating an experience of shared joy and accomplishment for the group. To this end, before teaching heavy case studies like that of the Met at Oxford, I begin the term by having my students compete in a mock team Olympics against each other, on rowing machines. Why rowing? Partly because it is a signature sport at Oxford (in other settings, different sports or activities might be more relevant). More importantly, rowing is a *team* sport, and for this exercise, students are randomly assigned into teams of eight and compete against the other teams. And, given the nature of the sport, they quickly realize that they cannot be rowing faster than their teammates—rather, they must learn to row at the pace of others in their boat (otherwise the boat will go around in circles).

This is certainly not what they're expecting in a cerebral policy management course at Oxford University—a student once remarked to me that I'd made the class smell like a gym. I told him that was the point. I wanted the experience to be a metaphor for the journey ahead in managing in the age of outrage—leaders should expect to sweat and work hard, and perhaps more importantly, to accept that they and other people might, from time to time, smell bad. It is, essentially, an exercise in exposing and sharing vulnerability. And, it is an activity where all participants got to experience, collectively, an instance of some shared accomplishment or victory. On that simulated success and happiness, more meaningful trust for the difficult (forthcoming) classroom conversations on race and policing and how to reform the Met can be built.

Sometimes my students do not understand why we are not diving right into the big problems: they ask why we are playing with make-believe rowboats and not talking about "the real stuff"—racism, police oppression, urban poverty, and the like. The answer is that if people work together first on trivial tasks (like a mock rowing Olympics) to experience what it is like to agree on differences in strategy and implementation, they will be better set up to collaborate on the big, wicked problems when we come to them. If they were to go straight into the big issues, there is a risk that people would very quickly get frustrated with each other because they would never have experienced vulnerability and success in the context of their diversity. Once people have sweat together and seen that they can work productively with people very different from themselves, they will be readier to come into a process of engaging with those people on the issues that really divide them.

With the rowing Olympics behind us, we are ready to reconvene for a plenary meeting in which I present the two general caveats from the preface: there is no perfect solution, and each actor, myself included, will be seen by someone else as part of the problem. I then introduce the basic elements of the GAM and ask participants to discuss and agree on basic rules of engagement along the lines set out in chapter 2—notably around personal authenticity, listening to the scripts of others, and being mindful of the impact of their own words on others. I also remind them that discussions should remain private and to keep phones and devices outside to reduce the chances of bringing external pressures into the room.

All these practices are easily replicable, with some practical modifications, in a real-world moderation setting. In fact, in the real world, this stage of "making space for the scripts" through some fun (ideally physical) activity is especially important, because, for the most part, the different stakeholders may not have had much experience working across a divide—and their whole experience of each other will have been on opposite sides of tables rather than acting as a team.

Now, we are ready for the discussions proper to open. They begin with an airing of experiences.

Share and socialize the scripts

In my course, after we have agreed on the basic rules of discussion, I invite students who may have personal experience of, for example, being stopped and searched by the police or who may have been involved in conducting such a procedure to speak to their narratives. (It is advisable to check in advance with participants on this.) In the initial sessions, the objective is to surface and share experiences so that everyone at least knows where everyone else is coming from. This can be a harrowing experience for some, especially when a student in the group has been at the receiving end of extreme aggression.

Some students have been reduced to tears as they've described their experiences with stop-and-search, and how they see policing as a force for subjugating certain peoples in society, rather than as a force for good. At the same time, there are often students from families with deep ties to law enforcement or who are law enforcement officers themselves. They sometimes feel shut down in these situations, afraid that if they present their different perspective, they will be viewed as racist. As a caution to fellow managers, there have been times when students have complained that I did not issue a warning about what to expect, telling me that they would not have come to class if they had known that that they would have to relive their experience, even if they were not talking.[14]

Painful though it can be, progress to solutions cannot be made unless people confront and are confronted by uncomfortable scripts. This is at least a requirement for leaders in a divided society, whom these students represent. For the group to find a solution they can buy into, each member needs to understand (even if not agree with) what motivates the others to take the positions they do. To my students, I point out that empathy—the ability to stand in someone else's shoes, no matter how different or even hostile those shoes may seem to you—is a key element in managing in the age of outrage. And all of the people in the room, in this simulated working group, are aspiring managers of some kind in the communities they represent.

Of course, the psychological dynamics of the classroom—for example, the professor-student relationship—may not translate easily to a real-world context. For one, in the real world, there is a risk that some participants will simply walk out of the talks—"I haven't come here to be accused of racism"—or, in an echo of my own experience in a classroom, "These people here are the problem." Some people just want to be heard for the injustice done to them; they do not want to (or are not ready to) move past that. This risk will, of course, be reduced if an organization has a preexisting platform along the lines set out in the House of Kaduna Family example in chapter 2. In the absence of that, careful framing by the moderator is required, notably a strong reminder that participants have not come to judge or be judged but rather to hear what stakeholders have to say in order to find a way forward. The moderator can also make sure that similar scripts do not follow one upon the other, to avoid piling up on one side.

Identify the drivers of outrage at play

After some participants have shared their experiences, I invite a discussion of what it tells us. Then, after all the scripts are aired, we can put them together to try and understand the causal drivers of outrage at stop-and-search. Specifically, we need to disentangle which of three drivers of outrage described in chapter 1 is at play, for which stakeholders, and to what extent: fear for the future, a sense of prior injustice, or ideologies of othering.

These discussions help us to separate what can and can't be done. As I noted in chapter 1, outrage fueled by ideologies of othering cannot easily be fixed. To the extent that some police officers stop and search Black people because they believe Black people to be inherently criminal, the only solution is to identify and remove those officers from the force. But to the extent that outrage is driven by fear for the future—that London's streets are becoming more dangerous for Black people due to police violence—then abandoning the policy, or reforming it, should address the concerns of stakeholders who share that fear. By the same token, if the outrage at stop-and-search is driven by a sense that police policy has unfairly targeted Black people in the past, then redressing that grievance will be essential if the policy is to be kept in place in some form. If, on the other

hand, hostile attitudes to stop-and-search spring solely from a sense
that police officers are inherently evil, then it is unlikely that progress
can be made with these stakeholders, at least not in the short term.

It can be difficult to disentangle othering from a sense of injustice,
because the former is often rooted in the latter. One way to help
people think about the difference is to ask people about their attitudes
to Black police officers. An interesting parallel could be drawn with
policing in Northern Ireland. Many Catholics saw the largely Protestant police force as an enemy rather than as a force of law and order.
It was not considered acceptable for people from republican, Catholic neighborhoods to cooperate with the police, let alone join them.
Catholics who did join not only faced discrimination in the workplace, but also risked being shunned by friends and family. They and
their families might even be targeted for assassination. How people
engage in such discussions can offer insight as to whether their per-
ceptions of the Met could be changed and what the levers for that
change might be.

I should reemphasize that everything I have described thus far is
difficult and painful for everyone involved, including the moderator,
or at least it should be if done well. It is important to create a space
for all involved, including the moderator, to recover both personally
and collectively from such an exercise. Such resilience-building is a
focus of chapter 6.

A Better Way Forward for the London Metropolitan Police?

After we've shared the scripts of the main stakeholders, and students have started to uncover how stop-and-search can be both
widely supported and highly criticized, I usually take the opportunity now to frame a challenge: "You, as Met commissioner, have a
policy that's popular with your ranks, but some people insist that it
doesn't work and does serious harm. The question is, what will you,

as commissioner, do now?" Typically, answering this question begins with making three strategic choices before proceeding to concrete recommendations. I identify these before breaking up the class into smaller groups to sketch a coherent action plan for the commissioner in answer to the challenge.

The basic choices are: (1) the commissioner could focus on initiatives that look internally, targeting the Met as an institution, or she could prioritize looking outward to the communities; (2) she could focus narrowly on stop-and-search or take a broader look at the Met and its policies overall; and (3) she can choose to either accept or resist the label of institutional racism.

Each of the choices has its pros and cons. Focusing on internal reform would give the commissioner greater control over the outcome: she can set the agenda and develop measurable targets. However, an internal focus might come at the expense of being directly engaged with affected communities. Similarly, a narrow focus on stop-and-search might improve the numbers, but it could mean that underlying causal issues are given short shrift. On the other hand, taking a broader look at the Met's policies might not yield sufficient short-term results for people to have confidence that something is being done. Finally, agreeing to own the label of institutional racism might serve as a temporary panacea, but it risks angering large segments of the population and the press who see the term as dangerously political. Moreover, it could alienate and demotivate the police ranks, making their job harder, and who may then be more hesitant to police people of color. (This last scenario played out recently in the UK: following investigation into cases of girls and young women being groomed for sexual abuse by gangs of Asian men in Rotherham and Rochdale, it turned out that local authorities had been reluctant to follow up on allegations, later proven, out of concern that they would be accused of racism if they did so.[15])

We can adapt this classroom approach to a real-world context as well. The Met stakeholders' group identified earlier could have been tasked to answer similar questions. Recall that we convened a group of between twenty-five and thirty-five participants, roughly from six different stakeholder communities. That provides enough diversity to allow for an airing of the scripts involved, especially if the larger group is divided into subgroups of five to seven where everyone can be heard.

Let's turn to look at how such breakout groups function.

The objective of the breakout groups is to identify avenues of progress in smaller, more-experimental settings, including the actions and actors that might bring all (or most) stakeholders together into a better place. The results from the breakout groups will not be definitive solutions, but they should be relatively concrete recommendations. As noted earlier, the breakout groups consist of one person representing each of the six stakeholders listed (the commissioner, the head of the Met's Black Police Officers Association, the head of StopWatch— a community organization skeptical of stop-and-search, the Met Superintendents Association, the mayor of London, and the home secretary). I usually designate the individual representing the commissioner as the breakout group's rapporteur, taking responsibility for presenting the group's solution to the full group. This has the added advantage of putting the commissioner's representative in listening mode more than in talking mode.

At the end of this process, the breakout group members should come up with recommendations for the Met that they feel comfortable presenting to the whole group. They may not succeed, but it should be the goal. If they fail, they can simply register the failure and note points of agreement, if any. Once all breakout groups have concluded their presentations to the whole group—either by reporting an impasse or by agreeing on a course of action for the Met—we give the floor to the commissioner's representatives to hear what they would like to take away. The goal is not to get them to definitively produce (and commit to) an action plan, but rather to identify what people can agree on—moving from emotional confrontation to pragmatic collaboration toward a shared goal of improving the quality of London's policing.

Processes such as the one I have described can play a key part in reducing the temperature and give space for a more reasoned reappraisal of aversive issues. Ideally, any carefully managed discussion of an aversive situation between alienated stakeholders would involve some "cooling" of this kind, directing people away from scripts that are triggered by emotions and ambient conditions. Work in breakout groups was a key element in the negotiation for education reform in Brazil, where the context was highly charged because everybody had an opinion on how (and what) to teach children. In sessions both in Yale and subsequently in Brazil, moderators from the not-for-profit Lemann Foundation essentially played the role of case-method facilitators. They took groups of people from opposing sides of the issue—say, two representatives of a left-wing teachers' union on one side and two people from an evangelical group on the other—and got the breakout groups to identify what they could agree on.

What Can the Leader Take Away?

At this stage, with scripts aired and, hopefully, some degree of empathy created through the process, we can, as organizational leaders, explicitly and rationally think about how much each of the three drivers of outrage described in chapter 1 are in play for each community— fears of the future, resentment at past injustice, and ideologies of othering—and identify what sort of changes and actions might serve to mitigate them.

Issues around past injustice are inevitably salient and may well dominate the discussion in the early stages. In the case of the Met, there is certainly plenty of evidence to substantiate claims of prior discrimination, a finding that has, as we've seen, been reached by numerous public inquiries. The demands for an acknowledgment that the Met remained institutionally racist stemmed in large measure from these grievances, and any cooling of the outrage almost certainly would have to acknowledge past wrongs on the part of the police. The question is not whether to right these wrongs in some way but how far to go in doing so, and to what extent your decision will affect or restrict your flexibility on other fronts.

What about attitudes toward the future? When I teach the Met case, I am struck by what has happened to the concept of community-based policing that has been at the heart of the Met's mission and purpose ever since its foundation nearly two hundred years ago. The Peelian idea was that people don't want to see the police as a local military equivalent—which is why police ranks are different from military ones. British police forces have inspectors and superintendents, detectives and police constables, chief constables and commissioners. This contrasts with the practice in the United States and many other countries, where police officers are captains and lieutenants, which are also army ranks. The only rank common to the military and the police in Britain is that of sergeant, which has its roots in the word *servant*. These choices were deliberate: the founders of the Met saw policing not as an arm of government power but as part of the local community, reflecting the community, and thereby acquiring legitimacy within it.

In classroom discussions, we inevitably ask ourselves whether that notion of community-based policing will work in a multicultural and multiracial Britain ten or twenty years from now. Or will the police need to transform into something more like the US model, where heavily armed police forces mimic the ethos of the military in order to successfully maintain peace in a highly individualistic society? The forces of law and order in the United States play a major role in keeping the peace between communities that rarely talk to each other, and because the police are not (and can't really be) representative of such a divided polity, their power to keep the peace rests on their heavily armed status, often using armored vehicles and military-style weaponry. The British police forces are increasingly dealing with the same sort of social fissures, and they struggle to be seen as representing the community as a whole. For now, importantly, most police in Britain, including in London, remain unarmed, as a commitment to policing's Peelian heritage.

Fear of social fracturing is shared across communities, and that may indicate a direction in which reform to police practices must go. An obvious avenue, and one that Commissioner Dick prioritized (and to some extent embodied), is to make sure that the people working at the Met broadly represented London's population. The Met has made progress in this direction, but as noted earlier, BAME representation in its workforce is still relatively low compared to the overall proportion in London's population. Of course, it is not only a recruitment issue—tenure and promotion also have to be managed to ensure that, in due course, proportional BAME representation is seen as a matter of sheer merit in all levels of the Met's hierarchy. Other steps that the Met could embrace include creating its equivalent of the House of Kaduna Family—a cross-community body of stakeholders who could advise and perhaps mediate in future crises. This is separate from the elected citizen boards that oversee local policing in England and Wales, as such elected boards necessarily must respond to short-term political demands.

This brings us to othering, a driver clearly in play at the Met. To begin with, the Casey report (released after Commissioner Dick left office) found clear evidence of racism within the ranks of the Met, often disguised as hazing. There was, for example, an instance when the turban of a Sikh police officer was forcibly removed by colleagues. There was also a certain amount of othering in community attitudes toward the police—in Black and Pakistani communities, for example, white police officers were simply assumed to be racist and were treated as enemies. And othering is often amplified by the socioeconomic drivers, that is, when people feel aggrieved and fearful of the future. To put it crudely, as one politician explained to me, in most societies you might find, say, 10 percent of people harboring racist views. When fear of the future and resentment of prior injustice are salient, that number might rise to even 40 percent (to judge by votes attracted by extremist political parties in Europe seeking to propagate ideologies of othering). But, by the same token, in allaying grievances and fear of the future, you can reduce the othering as well—and bring attachment to such exclusionary ideologies down to 10 percent, levels at which they can remain politically marginal.

Finally, it's important to accept the essential limitations of the progress and the sacrifices that achieving any progress will involve. As the first of the two axioms I introduced in the preface posited, there never is complete resolution to outrage: one can only mitigate it. And, per the second axiom, the people looking for solutions are very often part of the problem, a reality that inevitably compromises their ability to make progress. The implications of these two realities are inevitably that someone, perhaps everyone, will need to make a sacrifice in order to achieve progress. The conclusion of the Brazilian education reform process, referred to in chapter 1, illustrates this point. There, the protagonist, Maria Helena Guimarães de Castro, had to remove language that affirmed LGBT+ inclusiveness to keep the reform process alive.

Was her decision fair? It's difficult to deny the injustice done, but my point is that an actor with institutional authority in this age of outrage will almost certainly need to make hard decisions of this kind. In the context of the Met, had some kind of road map for police reform emerged from going through the hypothetical exercise I've been describing, there could well have been some similar roadblock to realizing the outcome. In that situation, as I suggested earlier in this chapter, it would have been up to the commissioner, with her authority, to make the hard decision. Whichever way she tilted, the aggrieved stakeholders would certainly have expressed their outrage. It is the leader's job to know when to make that call, and there is only so much agreement that an advisory group moderated by an independent moderator can supply.

• • •

By applying a process such as I've described in this chapter, you can identify ways to make sense of the moment of outrage you confront as an organizational leader and, above all, come to accept the sacrifices that collective progress demands. The former president of Colombia, Iván Duque, captured the spirit of this in calling for a do-over during the crisis around the country's VAT reform described earlier. He called it "a moment for greatness, consensus, and solidarity." He chose the words carefully: by *greatness*, he meant that the stakeholders in the process needed to commit to a goal that was bigger than their interests. The word *consensus* implied that sacrifice by everyone in the pursuit of the goal was required. And finally, *solidarity* was the motivation for the goal and the sacrifice: a recognition that we are still united by some core ideals. It is a powerful framing of what all involved need to do. And even though Duque's second attempt at VAT reform was less ideal than his first, the greatness, consensus, and solidarity it embedded meant that associated collections from the new tax system were nevertheless an improvement over prior years.[16]

Chapter 4

Scoping the Organization's Response

In the next process, we move from understanding the context and motivations for outrage toward formulating a response to the crisis at hand. This exercise is more focused, internal to the organization: the broad stakeholder group in the previous chapter hands on the baton to a small group of executives charged with recommending a specific course of action to the individual responsible for deciding what the organization will do. The members of this group may well include the decision-maker, and most, if not all, of the group should have participated in the first process, thereby hearing the scripts of other stakeholders firsthand.

In the context of the London Met, Commissioner Cressida Dick could have requested that her senior executives participating in the first process, had the Met taken that route, go through this second process. It may not always be necessary, though, to do the exercise as a group. Had Dick herself participated in the consultative process, she could even have undertaken this next stage on her own—as the chief decision-maker of the Met, that would have been her prerogative. But Dick was known for working through teams, and given the need for buy-in from across her workforce, involving a group of senior executives would likely have been a better option.

In working to formulate a response to stakeholder outrage, the group needs to consider two sets of questions, as shown in figure 4-1. The first set relates to the organization's capabilities: given the resources and know-how at its disposal, how well-placed is the organization to take various kinds of actions to reduce people's fears for the future and their sense of past injustice? Answering this question both defines what responses are feasible for the organization and clarifies to what extent stakeholders can reasonably expect an organization to respond, in view of the capabilities and resources at its disposal relative to other

FIGURE 4-1

Scoping the organization's response

In working to formulate a response to stakeholder outrage, you must consider two sets of questions, as shown below. The first set relates to the organization's capabilities: answering them clarifies to what extent the organization can reasonably respond, in view of the capabilities and resources at its disposal relative to other organizations. Answers to the second set of questions help the organization understand how stakeholder expectations have been and will be affected by a company's prior and current moral commitments.

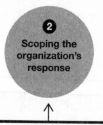

2
Scoping the organization's response

Assess asymmetries in capabilities	Analyze moral commitments
Am I directly responsible for the outrage?	When you make a moral commitment, what is your strategy for meeting that commitment authentically?
Will my inaction directly exacerbate the outrage?	What is your strategy for dealing with the shifting expectations around that commitment?
Is acting to alleviate the outrage part of my (implicit) contract with stakeholders?	What are the boundaries of that commitment and how have those been communicated to stakeholders?
Do I want it to be?	

organizations. It enables managers to figure out how far they should consider going in responding to outrage.

The second, complementary set of questions forces the company to clarify how its moral commitments meet stakeholder expectations. If it is contemplating a new commitment, can it meet that commitment without affecting prior ones? Have stakeholder expectations around the organization's moral commitments evolved and how do the changes affect current commitments? One of the factors limiting Cressida Dick's ability to respond to community outrage, for instance, was the expectation of the Met's police officers that she would protect their interests. Given this, it is difficult to imagine how she could accept the label of institutional racism. At the same time, she was also conscious that in responding too much to criticism of the stop-and-search policy, she would raise expectations to the point that the Met would not have been able to deliver.

In this chapter, we will take a deep dive into these two sets of questions. As is apparent from the questions, whereas the focus has hitherto been on understanding the individual (chapter 2) and group dynamics (chapter 3), now the organization has to consider its response in the context of systemic factors—that is, its capabilities and limitations given the structural drivers of outrage. This is a process that involves interweaving the framework for managing in the age of outrage with other frameworks that help organizations and leaders navigate questions of strategy and values. As I noted in the preface, my framework in this book is not intended to replace essential matters of ethics and business policy but rather to complement them, and the questions I raise in this chapter are an invitation to managers to do just that.

In what follows, we'll look at some case studies of business organizations, rather than the governmental settings we've seen thus far. We'll begin by looking at an outrage crisis faced by the Swiss food giant Nestlé, and the discussion that follows is based on a case study I coauthored while a professor at Harvard Business School.[1]

Nestlé in India: The Maggi Noodles Scandal

In 2015, food-safety regulators in India accused Nestlé of unsafe levels of the metal lead in its flagship local product, the instant noodle called Maggi, which enjoyed a near 80 percent domestic market share. Nestlé at first dismissed and then contested the reports of lead presence, convinced of its product's safety on the basis of its internal testing. But this approach came across as haughty and disdainful, and Nestlé quickly lost the support of its consumers. Bringing the situation under control was estimated to have cost Nestlé India about one-quarter of its 2014 revenues.

At the time of the crisis, Nestlé, a Swiss firm, had been operating in India for over a century. Part of its success was due to a strategy of customizing its products to uniquely Indian tastes. For instance, one of its signature products was packaged "Jeera Raita," a cumin-flavored yogurt traditional in many Indian cuisines.

Maggi Noodles had also been adopted to Indian tastes: one of the most popular variants was "Masala" flavored, giving the otherwise salty ramen a spicy kick. When Maggi was first introduced in India, in the 1980s, it was positioned as a quick-to-prepare meal for busy professionals; but this did not quite catch on in a market where many professionals still lived in extended families, with at least one family member a stay-at-home cook. It was then rebranded as a snack for hungry schoolchildren to tide them over from the end of lessons to dinnertime. This positioning was a success, and the product took off. Over time, as these schoolchildren grew up, Maggi followed them, broadening its reach to younger adults. In the early 2000s, when middle-class Indian consumers became more nutrition-conscious about packaged foods, Nestlé rebranded Maggi again as a health product, adopting the Hinglish tagline "taste bhi, health bhi" (tasty and healthy). By 2015 the product was deeply ensconced in consumer sentiment, winning advertising accolades such as "Most Powerful Brand in India" in a WPP–Millward Brown survey. By that year, Maggi Noodles accounted for about 30 percent of Nestlé India's sales.

All told, processed foods like Maggi Noodles constituted about a third of India's food retail industry in 2015, but about 75 percent of these processed foods were produced by a largely unorganized small-scale manufacturing sector. What's more, much of the processed-food retailing, including products made by Nestlé and other large global firms, happened through informal street vendors, of which there were an estimated 10 million.

One result of this fragmentation was the relative underdevelopment of the regulatory infrastructure around India's food industry in 2015—at least when compared to the standards of high-income countries. Although the federal government had promulgated a comprehensive reorganization of food-safety laws in 2006, establishing a Food Safety and Standards Authority of India, or FSSAI, with sweeping supervisory powers in theory, regulation was severely underfunded. In 2015, the FSSAI had received only 40 percent of requested funding from the government, which meant it was operating on a budget roughly one-twenty-fifth that of the US Food and Drug Administration, which served a population about a quarter of India's. Salaries were low, and there were many unfilled positions.

Possibly to compensate for its lack of resources, the FSSAI had taken a product-approval approach to food safety, rather than the ingredient-approval approach common in Western countries. The latter meant that products that only used approved ingredients were automatically approved, but it required the relevant food-standards regulator to pre-approve common ingredients, usually over 10,000 such ingredients. Without the capacity to do this, the FSSAI had only 377 approved ingredients in 2015, and so it tested finished products on an ad hoc basis. What this meant in practice was that the unorganized processed-food sector was largely unregulated, and established players such as Nestlé had to compete with products that used questionable ingredients and engaged in widespread mislabeling. In this setting, Nestlé's focus on quality was both a competitive advantage and a disadvantage, depending on whether the customer in question was sophisticated or uninformed.

In March 2014, routine testing in a food-safety lab in the Indian state of Uttar Pradesh, India's largest and most populous state, found monosodium glutamate or MSG in a sample of Maggi Noodles obtained off the shelf in a retail store. Since Nestlé advertised the Maggi Noodles product as having "No Added MSG," the regulator became concerned. When it raised the matter with Nestlé, the company denied that there was MSG in the product.

The Uttar Pradesh lab then sent the product sample to another government lab in the Indian city of Kolkata (formerly Calcutta) for further testing. Although the sample was sent there in July 2014, the results were substantially delayed. Perhaps this delay lulled Nestlé into believing that the matter was closed and put to rest. But in April 2015, the Kolkata lab finally announced its results: in addition to the MSG issue, the Kolkata lab announced that the sample contained lead at about 17.2 parts per million or ppm, which was well above the acceptable limit of 2.5 ppm. On April 30 of that year, the Uttar Pradesh government asked for a statewide recall of the particular batch of Maggi Noodles that it had tested, deeming the product unsafe for human consumption.

Upon hearing of the lab results, Nestlé CEO Paul Bulcke summoned the relevant product-safety managers to ask for absolute assurance on the quality and safety of Maggi Noodles, especially with regard to lead content. After being provided with internal evidence to that effect, Nestlé senior management decided to aggressively back the product. They pointed out to the regulator that the government's MSG test results were very likely due to naturally occurring glutamate in the product, since the company did not add any synthesized MSG in the Maggi production process. This meant that Nestlé's "No Added MSG" claim was still true in that Nestlé did not add artificial sources of monosodium glutamate to the product. They also argued that a recall was unnecessary since the government's own delays in testing meant that the tested product batch was unlikely to still be on retail shelves. Maggi was, after all, a popular, fast-moving product, and it was impossible for Nestlé to know for sure whether that batch was still being sold, given India's largely informal retail sector.

But by this point, government food labs in other Indian states were now beginning their own tests, and their results showed considerable variance, with some reporting above-acceptable levels of lead while others indicated the product was safe. Although none of these subsequent results reported lead levels as high as those in Kolkata, most suggested the presence of MSG. The variance in lead testing and the results on glutamates quickly became fodder for both India's populist politicians and its excitable media—both thrived on peddling stories of exploitation, often presenting themselves as saviors of the people against unscrupulous elites. News outlets led with stories such as "Maggi betrayal has broken our good Indian hearts" and "Maggi controversy shows how Indian consumers are taken for granted." Misinformation and rumormongering on social media amplified the confusion. In a matter of a few weeks, Nestlé India's stock price tumbled 15 percent.

Nestlé tried to fight back by arguing that other instant-noodle suppliers in the marketplace made similar claims about MSG—a version of the "everyone's doing it" excuse—but many of its consumers had already lost trust in the company. Nestlé also tried to provide rational explanations for why the government labs might have erroneously generated positive lead results. One of the most plausible of these was that lead was present in the water used by the labs to dilute reagents as part of the testing procedure. Ideally, such water would be highly distilled, but under-resourcing and poor training at the government labs could mean that ordinary tap water, with a lead presence, was being used instead. Naturally, the government labs rejected this explanation, and politicians, the media, and consumers were left unconvinced too.

Nestlé also noted that Maggi Noodles had two components—the dried ramen noodles and the flavoring packet, called the tastemaker, of which "Masala" was one of the most popular flavors. This tastemaker contained dried spices, which could have high lead content due to soil conditions in India. But, Nestlé noted, the concentrated tastemaker was not to be ingested on its own; rather it was to be combined with water and the ramen noodles prior to ingestion. Thus, Nestlé argued, the product should be tested "as consumed," and if this were done, the product would be deemed well within the acceptable levels of safety on lead. As with the arguments involving poor testing procedures at government labs, this explanation, even if technically correct, did not resonate with popular opinion.

Within weeks of the crisis first breaking out, Nestlé's instant noodles market share dropped to around 30 percent. And, at the peak of the crisis, instant noodles sales across the sector were reportedly down 90 percent nationwide. To restore confidence and trust in the market, Nestlé had to recall and destroy tens of millions of dollars' worth of perfectly edible inventory. It was a lose-lose situation.

The total dollar cost to Nestlé from a few weeks of poor management of public outrage amounted to hundreds of millions, given the logistics of tracking down what was essentially a one-year-old batch of a quick-moving product from thousands of unlicensed street vendors. And the notion that the company had to incinerate perfectly good food due to a public relations misunderstanding struck many within Nestlé as out-rageous. People were dying of hunger in India and elsewhere, several executives noted. Nestlé's local management was so aggrieved by the issue that they even sued the regulators over the lead test results. Predict-ably, the regulators countersued over the MSG issue, and no one really benefited from all this legal wrangling, except perhaps the lawyers.

It wasn't Nestlé alone that bore the costs of the Maggi fiasco. Thousands of its suppliers and resellers were hit hard, too. Maggi had been such a popular snack in India that street vendors set up dedicated cooking stations on pushcarts to prepare the ramen noodles and sell them to hungry pedestrians. These small businesses did not enjoy anything near the safety net that Nestlé was able to provide for itself through the crisis.

What should Nestlé have done instead?

Recognizing the asymmetry

The Nestlé story exposes the critical value of acting on one's asym-metric capabilities. Put simply, this is the imperative to act when you have positive-differential ability to address people's anger, whether or not you are directly responsible for it—not just because you can, but because if you don't, people will get angrier. People will get angrier because they will see you as cheating them of what they are due. Let me expand.

Nestlé, as a hundred-year resident of India, would have been aware from the get-go that both public enforcement of product-safety standards and lower consumer expectations of the informal sector relative to multinational corporations were hallmarks of doing business in emerging markets. In this scenario, companies, especially large and visible ones, cannot expect to get away with what might work for the average firm, let alone with blatant hypocrisy. On the one hand, Nestlé was drawing on its reputation for Swiss excellence to urge consumers to dismiss the regulators' lead allegations (which were indeed untrue, it eventually turned out). On the other hand, Nestlé was arguing that it should be afforded the same free pass as local companies on the "No Added MSG" claim.

To connect back to the drivers of outrage from the first chapter, what multinationals must contend with when doing business in emerging markets is the legacy of the "raw deal" that hangs over from colonialism. India is by and large a country optimistic about the future, and India today is perhaps even more optimistic than it was in 2015, at the time of this crisis. But the zeitgeist in the country (and in many former colonies) is nonetheless colored by a history of exploitation by foreign companies. And when a foreign company expects to be held to a double standard, it is accorded less trust and treated less kindly than a local one.

Nestlé in India enjoys an *asymmetry in capabilities* over its local competitors and other local stakeholders. Formally, "capability" is defined as being in a position to act in a given way, and Nestlé, as a big, successful, Swiss multinational, was seen as having a vastly greater capability to address the questions around lead content than the Indian regulators or its local competitors. And, in resolving the uncertainty about the product's safety, Nestlé also enjoyed an advantage over those potentially harmed by virtue of its technology and know-how. It was, therefore, in a position to lead and reassure. Yet, instead of approaching the situation with humility and sensitivity, it squandered its capability advantage through its dismissive treatment of regulators and its insistence that it be treated the same as its less capable competitors.

Nestlé's approach was probably conditioned to how it expected its regulators in Switzerland to engage—the company perhaps felt it was unacceptable for a regulator to make such a baseless charge about the product's lead content or to treat it differently from the competition on the no-MSG claim. Nestlé failed to adequately recognize the context of the historical raw deal and the growing sense of pride among Indians as their (still flawed) institutions come to assume greater global significance.

As Nestlé finally managed to get its Maggi Noodles crisis in India under control, I had the opportunity to sit down with the company's chief executive, Bulcke, in his sprawling office in Vevey, Switzerland. He said, quietly reflecting on the unfortunate episode: "In the end, I don't care who is right. You cannot force trust on consumers. We were totally right [about the absence of lead poisoning in Maggi Noodles], yet so wrong. We weren't engaging on the same premise as our stakeholders." This is the point: it doesn't matter that you are right if people don't trust you to be right. (We also learned this lesson from President Duque of Colombia and his VAT reforms in chapter 1.)

Assessing the exposure

There are many ways in which such an imperative to act on capability asymmetries can become a money pit for a for-profit business or, indeed, for any organization. After all, established organizations have technological and financial advantages on so many issues that provoke outrage—for instance, helping those left behind, mitigating income inequality, and addressing climate change. But, in practice, the responsibility to act on asymmetric capabilities can be bounded by your answers to the following four questions.

- Am I directly responsible for the outrage?

- Will my inaction directly exacerbate the outrage?

- Is acting to alleviate the outrage part of my (implicit) contract with stakeholders?

- Do I want it to be?

If the answer to any one of these questions is yes, then you must act.

The first question is self-evident, and there is usually no moral, legal, or even commercial dilemma about acting in response to a problem that is of your own making. We saw this with the Disney and Facebook examples earlier in the book. A trickier issue arises when the answer to the first question is no—here, the second question can help us find a way forward.

To answer the second question, consider two dimensions: the underlying harm provoking outrage, and your relative power over those being harmed in the situation. On the first dimension, the greater the expected underlying harm, the greater the imperative to act—on anyone's part, not just an organization's. This argument can be considered an extension of the "rule of rescue" from practical bio-ethics, which emphasizes "the powerful human proclivity to rescue" imminently endangered life, even if "at the expense of any nameless faces who will therefore be denied" opportunity.[2] The rule of rescue can explain why governments often spend vast sums of money searching for one sailor lost at sea, even as some of its own citizens continue to suffer from hunger or homelessness.

In the case of Maggi Noodles, the nature of the concerns about lead content was quite serious—nobody wants themselves or their children to be exposed to lead poisoning. It became imperative for Nestlé to address the concern with all care, even if the company itself found the concern ludicrous and the proposed solution (destroying perfectly good inventory) wasteful. Not doing so would simply make people angrier.

The second dimension relates to the (perceived) degree of your power over those being harmed—the greater this power, the stronger the case to act. "Power" is defined formally as your potential to mobilize the resources of others (here, those being harmed) to your ends. Why would such power catalyze you to act on your asymmetric capabilities? Quite simply because the more powerful you are over those being harmed, the more vulnerable they are to you (even if you are not responsible for their harm), and thus, the more your inaction will provoke further outrage. This observation is rooted in the notion of noblesse oblige (known also as "with great power comes great responsibility"), which is both an ethical and self-preserving principle among elites across civilizations and in sources as old as the *Iliad*.[3]

In Nestlé's case, at first blush, a company selling ramen noodles in a competitive market does not appear to enjoy much asymmetric power, no matter how wealthy the company or how superior its technology (that is, no matter how large the asymmetric capability). But in practice, the perceived power asymmetry in this situation was large. Maggi Noodles had become so successful and so deeply embedded in the lifestyles of consumers that it was no longer viewed as a discretionary purchase but as an essential one. Maggi's commanding market share and the few available substitutes further increased the company's perceived power. What's more, many consumers were unsophisticated (they were children). Add onto that the small businesses' substantial supply-chain dependency on Nestlé, and the Swiss giant found itself considerably more powerful than others involved and being harmed.

Given that Nestlé was exposed along both dimensions—underlying harm and relative power—its asymmetric capability to act to mitigate people's anxiety would have heightened in people's minds. Nestlé's answer to the second question would therefore have been yes. It should have acted even if it were not already directly responsible for at least part of the anger.

The third question—is acting to alleviate the anger part of my (implicit) contract with stakeholders?—addresses the implicit expectations of a company's stakeholders. What have you signaled through your deeds and words that might cause stakeholders to expect a response from you? For instance, do you have a brand identity as a responsible organizational entity? Have you engaged in a marketing campaign about your commitments on the issue at hand (for example, have you made unimpeachable commitments to product quality)? If so, then you may have already created a duty to respond.[4]

In the case of Maggi Noodles, recall that Nestlé was advertising the product as a health snack for children and young adults ("taste bhi, health bhi"), suggesting that the answer to this third question was yes. The company should also have asked itself which stakeholders had been influenced by its brand identity and marketing campaign—customers alone, or other stakeholders such as employees and the wider public? For instance, you might think you are only responsible to customers for product quality, but your marketing statements may have also opened up a commitment to your distributors and retailers.

The fourth and final question is quite simply about your aspirations. There is often no better moment than anger around a crisis to clarify organizational values and to shape corporate culture in ways that represent your best ambitions, as the following narrative demonstrates.

Leaning in to the Challenge: Johnson & Johnson

Perhaps one of the finest examples of an organization acting on its capability asymmetries comes from a time well before our current age of outrage. Johnson & Johnson CEO James Burke's management of the Tylenol crisis in the 1980s is now part of the canon of management teaching; as of a few years ago, a case study on this episode was one of the oldest continuously taught cases at the Harvard Business School, from which the following discussion draws.[5]

In 1982 in Chicago, an unidentified terrorist, with an as yet undetermined motive, chose to inject cyanide into caplets of the popular analgesic Tylenol. The act was apparently committed in a few randomly chosen retail outlets, but this very randomness provoked mass panic. Cyanide can kill at even the smallest of doses.

The company decided to pull all its nationwide inventory of Tylenol, at great cost. After months of redesigning, the company relaunched the product with tamper-evident packaging, so that consumers could discern if the product had been messed with. It is nearly impossible to actually prevent the malicious cyanide poisoning of caplets; one can only make such an attempt evident—and J&J's packaging innovation remains to this day the gold standard for over-the-counter pharmaceuticals and many other edibles.

Years after the episode, and shortly after Burke's passing in 2012, his son visited the classrooms at the Harvard Business School where my colleagues and I were teaching the case study. Burke Jr. told the story of how his father had agonized about the recall decision at first, because of the costs involved and because of how divided his leadership team was about the recall. This situation had led Burke into several sleepless nights early in the crisis. During one such episode, Burke climbed out of bed and walked to his bathroom's medicine cabinet to seek a cure for a throbbing headache. He instinctively reached for the Tylenol, but then he instinctively hesitated, second-guessing whether his own bottle of Tylenol had been poisoned. That hesitation was a moment of clarity for Burke, his son reported. To paraphrase the reflection: "If the CEO of Johnson & Johnson cannot implicitly trust Tylenol to be safe, how can he expect his customers to?"

What's remarkable about J&J's decision was that the company quickly recognized its capability asymmetry—its financial and technological capacity to solve a problem of great distress to its consumers—and chose to act on it. Importantly, recalling the product at great cost was not Burke's first instinct or indeed even his idea. His own admission was that he dithered in that moment of crisis. But when he heard from key stakeholders and experienced the emotions of those favoring the recall, he knew he had to act on J&J's capability asymmetries.

If we use the four questions framework to analyze J&J's response to the Tylenol scare, we get the following likely responses:

- Am I directly responsible for the outrage? *No*

- Will my inaction directly exacerbate the outrage? *Yes*

- Is acting to alleviate the outrage part of my (implicit) contract with stakeholders? *Yes*

- Do I want it to be? *Yes*

Obviously, the answer to the first question was no. J&J was not at fault, and the director of FBI, which was investigating the issue, even said as much. But the company felt a deep sense of responsibility to its consumers, noting that the nature of its product (caplets in easy-to-tamper boxes) made it particularly susceptible to hacking. What had happened with this terrorist incident in Chicago could be readily copied elsewhere (and, in fact, it was).

On the second question, the company's calculus considered both (1) its power asymmetry over its consumers—the product was popular, a market leader, and the consumers depended on it—and (2) the degree of harm that would be caused by inaction: cyanide kills! The latter was in fact one of Burke's own primary motives for the recall.

The answer to the final two questions is particularly noteworthy. J&J had a long-held value of putting its obligations to its consumers' health first, above profits or any other responsibilities—what the company called its "credo." As Burke and his team thought through the Tylenol crisis, they realized that their customers expected more of J&J than they would of other competitors, and J&J's senior management wanted it to stay that way. In fact, early in the crisis, the head of the FBI had even advised Burke not to pull Tylenol from retail shelves, in part because the FBI chief thought that pulling the product might encourage copy-cat poisoning attempts on other products. Some of Burke's lieutenants argued that the FBI's advice was a carte blanche for J&J to stand back from the crisis and thus save the company the enormous cost of a recall.

But others on Burke's team and Burke himself did not want to set the corporate response to a law-enforcement officer's hunch. They wanted the response to embody and further J&J's values and culture, its credo.

Which brings us to a punchline on the matter of acting on capability asymmetries: Great organizations should not set their behavior to the minimum standards expected of them (by the law, by their industry, or otherwise); instead, they should tread well above those rules. This is where Nestlé lost on "No Added MSG." Nor has J&J always been so true to its credo, as the company's ongoing baby powder scandal cruelly demonstrates. This product was one of the company's most iconic brands, dating back a century or more. Concerns, even within the company, that the talc-based product could sometimes contain asbestos (as asbestos and talc deposits are often found in the same place) dated back at least to the 1970s. And by the 2000s, the company was facing multiple (40,000 as of 2023) major lawsuits from consumers who claimed that use of the baby powder had resulted in deaths from a variety of conditions, including ovarian cancer and mesothelioma. Following a series of verdicts that found against the company and resulted in forcing it to make payouts running into billions of dollars, J&J closed that business line down, carving it out as a separate unit and filing, under Texas law, for Chapter 11 bankruptcy protection for the unit. As of 2023, J&J offered a blanket compensation award of $9 billion to settle all outstanding claims arising from use of talc-based baby powder.[6]

Amazon and Alibaba: Who Would You Rather Work For?

Both the Nestlé and J&J stories are chiefly about addressing anger and anxiety among customers or potential customers, but companies experience asymmetric capabilities not just with respect to customer angst. In Nestlé's case, the asymmetric capabilities also directly extended to its supply chain, particularly to its small farmers and retailers. And asymmetric capabilities can also apply to employees, to (minority) shareholders and creditors, and to the public at large. As discussed earlier, the extent to which an organization is expected to act on such capabilities is a function of factors such as power imbalances, the intensity of underlying harm, and expectations set from its own implicit commitments. The recent pandemic highlighted how very differently companies could respond with respect to their employees.

During the Covid-19 pandemic, there were several opportunities for major companies to act on their capability asymmetries, particularly given the outrage over rising income inequality and the sense that many employees were being left behind even as entrepreneurs and shareholders did very well. In the face of public-health lockdowns, online commerce experienced a windfall. Online platform retailers like Amazon and Alibaba, already flush with success and under public scrutiny for monopolistic practices, saw a new surge in business. Meeting this consumer demand required online retailers to put their already stretched workforces into overdrive. When those workers balked at the increased workload and risks of operating through a contagion, Amazon and Alibaba responded very differently.

Of course, neither company was directly responsible for the Covid-19 crisis, but both had high perceived power asymmetry relative to employees, and the harm was significant from any inaction over more stringent Covid-19 protections—a perfect situation for acting on capability asymmetries.

But Amazon initially refused to provide additional compensation to workers. It also did not stop the sales of nonessential items, with workers complaining that they were still packing wares such as dildos throughout the crisis. The company also refused to close its dispatching facilities for deep cleaning despite several employees testing positive for Covid-19. When some employees in New York protested, their convener was let go.[7] (In a wry coda, the same fate apparently later befell the Amazon executives who fired the convener.[8])

Alibaba, in contrast, faced criticism for going too far with preventative measures on employee safety. Concerned about workplace contagion from employees who attended large gatherings outside of work, the company started asking employees whether they were still attending religious services. Some of its employees in Southeast Asia saw this as invasive.[9] Privacy considerations aside, the company largely avoided negative publicity for labor practices during the Covid-19 pandemic. If anything, it worked with restaurant chains in China, whose own staff had been made redundant, to temporarily deploy those employees to fulfill online food orders at Alibaba.[10] The company even donated tens of thousands of testing kits and protective equipment to several overseas countries where it operated, perhaps a blatant act of reputation buying, but a win–win nonetheless.[11]

The financial costs to Alibaba from all these actions were likely negligible in terms of its long-term prospects, but the credit it earned for being seen as caring in a time of crisis was invaluable. Amazon, on the other hand, reinforced its stereotype of driving a hard bargain. The impact on its reputation will likely endure.

So far, the balance of the discussion suggests that firms with asymmetric capabilities often have a rationale for assuming more of the moral responsibility than is legally necessary for them. But the calculus requires a further step—a reassessment of how expectations of the organization's stakeholders are evolving and the implications of those changes for how effectively the firm can deliver on its moral commitments to stakeholders. Without such an assessment, an organization risks finding, in the near future, that expectations have overtaken the firm's strategies and capabilities for delivering on them. For an example, we'll look at a crisis at the iconic Scandinavian furniture retailer, IKEA, on which I coauthored a case study while on the faculty at Harvard Business School.[12]

In Shifting Sands: The Case of IKEA

On October 1, 2012, global furniture and lifestyle giant IKEA suddenly found itself in the spotlight for a policy that was neither new nor unique to the company. The Stockholm edition of the free city newspaper *Metro* had published a scoop—that IKEA had airbrushed out all images of women from the Saudi edition of its home-furnishings catalog. It went on to note that not only were female models removed from the catalog, but even a photo of one of IKEA's female designers had been purged.

An IKEA spokesperson had indicated to *Metro* that women had been airbrushed out of several Saudi catalogs since it first started operating there in the early 1980s. But the article contended that it was not forbidden to depict women in advertising in Saudi Arabia and that IKEA's decision was one of self-censorship rather than complying with local laws.

The reaction in Sweden was as swift as it was unsurprising. Sweden's minister for the European Union called the move "medieval," and the country's minister for gender equality stated: "For IKEA to remove an important part of Sweden's image and an important part of its values in a country that more than any other needs to know about IKEA's principles and values, that's completely wrong."[13] A customer in an IKEA store in Sweden, who happened to be an Arab Muslim woman, was quoted in the media saying, "I simply think it is silly. We exist in a society with women and men. You can't just remove women."[14]

The outrage quickly spread to IKEA's other Western markets, and soon pundits and activists on both sides of the Atlantic were weighing-in on the matter. IKEA was even accused of being "an active collaborator in official Saudi strategies to render women invisible and powerless." The company then faced calls for consumer boycotts across Europe and North America, which accounted for over 85 percent of its sales. What puzzled some in IKEA about this public storm was, "Why now?" Why, after all these years of doing business in Saudi Arabia with this advertising policy, had it become an issue? To answer that question, we must first assess IKEA's role in Swedish society.

The making of an icon

By 2012, the year of the *Metro* newspaper scoop, IKEA was the world's leading furniture manufacturer, with an estimated 5 percent global market share. The company was also noteworthy at the time as the only truly global furniture brand, as its nearest competitor in sales, Ashley Furniture Industries, was less than a quarter of its size and operated generally in the US and Canadian markets.

IKEA as a brand had always been associated with a lifestyle. Founder Ingvar Kamprad wanted "to create a better everyday life" for ordinary people by selling affordable but stylish furniture at mass-market scales. IKEA wore its Swedish egalitarian roots and identity on its sleeve—the company's stores, regardless of where they were located, often loudly displayed the Swedish national emblems. Given Sweden's neutrality in world affairs and the generally positive view of Scandinavian culture worldwide, this embrace of Swedish identity was a marketing coup. Customers often experienced a visit to IKEA as a visit to a smart Northern European city.

In keeping with its Scandinavian ethic, IKEA sought to be a responsible corporate citizen. In 2000, the company created IWAY, or the IKEA Way on purchasing products, materials, and services, to specify minimum acceptable standards for working conditions and environmental practices at its manufacturing suppliers. In 2004, the company became a participant in the United Nations Global Compact, an initiative for companies to commit publicly to upholding universal human rights, including on gender. In 2011, the company signed on to the UN Guiding Principles on Business and Human Rights, another affirmation of its social commitments. And in 2012, it outlined its values in its "People & Planet Positive" strategy, which focused again on its strong belief in supporting and respecting human rights in places where the company had influence through its business. Alongside these commitments, IKEA had cultivated, over the years, a very liberal-progressive image. As early as the 1990s, the company had featured a same-sex couple in one of its television advertisements. Through its IKEA Foundation, the company supported various charities and their activities to protect children from forced labor and to empower, in particular, girls and women.

Most of IKEA's business was in Northern Europe, Germany, and the Anglophone world, although, like every business of its scale, it coveted ambitious growth in Asia and other parts of the emerging world. By 2012, Inter IKEA Systems franchised 338 IKEA stores in 40 countries. Sales for the IKEA brand were dominated by Europe (70 percent), followed by North America (16 percent), Asia and Australia (8 percent), and Russia (6 percent). Germany was the company's largest single national market, with 14 percent of sales, while Sweden represented about 5 percent of global sales. Outside the IKEA Group, eleven independent franchise companies operated IKEA stores worldwide, and four of these eleven were in the Middle East. The Saudi franchisee was the Ghassan Ahmed Al Sulaiman Furniture Trading Company, with whom the company had done business since it first entered the kingdom in 1983.

IKEA's Saudi sensitivity

Saudi Arabia was IKEA's first foray in the Middle East; it established itself there well before going to more familiar destinations for Western brands such as Dubai and Israel. IKEA's long history in the Saudi peninsula meant that the brand was highly recognizable and well regarded there. In 2004, when the company reopened its flagship Jeddah store after a renovation, an estimated eight thousand customers waited in line to shop there on inauguration day, many even camping overnight to claim discounts.

For the most part, IKEA products in Saudi stores resembled Swedish equivalents, with the iconic Swedish furniture names like Karlstad and Ektorp simply rendered in Arabic script. But IKEA was also sensitive to avoid unnecessary trouble, for instance, by calling its wine glasses simply "glasses." The company likewise avoided Christmas-themed products and instead put out special collections during the Islamic holy season of Ramadan. Instead of displaying the Swedish national flag, which featured a Christian cross, IKEA displayed a faux flag with neutral horizontal stripes in the Swedish national colors. Further, the company's world-renowned meatballs in the country were halal, and the in-store restaurants were segregated into two areas: one for families and the other for single men. Local stores also designated special spaces for use as mosques for prayer, and during prayer time each day, the stores closed their doors to new customers for about twenty-five minutes. Also noteworthy, there was no music in the Saudi IKEA stores. All this helped to avoid offending the sensibilities of deeply conservative and powerful local Wahhabi clerics and the religious police.

IKEA's adaptation to Saudi values was by no means unique among Western companies. Recognizing the enormous market potential of the region, several Western brands had been accommodating with their image in the country. For instance, when Starbucks entered Saudi Arabia in 2011, it removed the long-haired woman from its logo, keeping solely her crown. British retailer Marks & Spencer hired exclusively female sales staff for its female lingerie store in Saudi Arabia. And Spanish clothier Zara also avoided music in its Saudi stores and at times blurred the images of female models featured on in-store fashion videos.

The country had not always been so conservative. Prior to 1979, women had regularly appeared on Saudi television and in newspaper ads. In November of that year, a group of extremists calling for the overthrow of the Saudi royal family seized the Grand Mosque of Mecca. After the insurgents were subdued, then monarch King Khalid decided he needed to appease religious hard-liners in the kingdom, giving religious conservatives more power over social norms. Representations of women in print and broadcast media were banned, gender segregation in public places become a requirement, and the religious police became more assertive and feared.

In the years that followed, Saudi Arabia remained highly conservative, and more restrictions on media images were introduced in 2003 in an attempt to placate hard-liners upset over Saudi Arabia's collaboration with the United States in the Iraq War. The results were visible: "offending" articles in imported publications were blackened, and local customers could expect to see pages in foreign magazines glued together if they were "unsuitable." Offenses ranged from news critical of the administration to pictures of bare legs and couples kissing or embracing. The laws, however, were not always very clear, and the religious judges in Saudi were not bound by past rulings. As a result, laws were not consistently applied and punishments for violations also varied considerably across judges and in different contexts. This situation contributed to a sense of fear and risk aversion among entrepreneurs.

The IKEA catalog

Each year, IKEA updated its catalog based on marketing and sales feedback from the previous year. In 2012, some 200 million catalogs were printed in 29 languages and 62 editions, featuring about 9,500 furnishing products. IKEA believed that the catalog had to strike the balance between being relevant in all of IKEA's markets and reflecting what the global brand stood for.

Usually the contents varied only slightly between markets and, according to the company, mostly due to differences in local market preferences. Reflecting its in-store practices of respecting Saudi norms, the company had for some years avoided portraying women in the Saudi catalog. An image in the Swedish catalog of a family seated at a dinner table—with a father, mother, and children—was rendered in the Saudi catalog as a father with children: the space where the mother was seated was simply an empty chair.

This workaround helped the company avoid local censorship laws that might otherwise require women to be dressed in veils, which its largely European female models were not. In 2010, a manager in IKEA's Jeddah store had commented: "We asked Inter IKEA Systems to replace the women with men in the catalog in order to be able to get the declaration from authorities to let the catalog enter the country," he said. "In our Riyadh store we have received some complaints from some customers asking us to replace or remove the pictures of the women who are without a full traditional dress and headscarf," he added.[15]

Interestingly, the policy of airbrushing women from the catalog was not entirely consistent with IKEA's messaging inside Saudi Arabia. In its locally produced advertising, IKEA did feature images of women, though in keeping with Saudi norms; adults in its ads were dressed in traditional gendered attire, including head coverings for women. On the other hand, customizing the representation of families for the Saudi catalog likely struck IKEA headquarters as an unnecessary expense— perhaps it was far simpler and cheaper to brush the women out.

What went wrong?

Given that the practice of airbrushing women out of the catalog was long established, it was somewhat understandable that IKEA headquarters was blindsided by the story. Had something changed about the rules of the game that invalidated IKEA's long-standing approach—and, if so, how did the company miss it? With hindsight, three factors came together to create a perfect storm for the company.

First, although the company's Saudi footprint was quite small— both by IKEA standards and by the standards of the local furniture market—this affluent region was a growth priority for the company, especially in light of its maturing Western markets. So, what was once an insignificant part of IKEA's business was suddenly attracting more scrutiny in the West.

Second, Saudi Arabia itself was changing—since the accession of a new king in 2005, the country had been flirting with liberalizing reforms, albeit in rather unpredictable fits and starts. Greater computer and internet freedoms also meant that what was once a largely paper-copy furniture catalog, in a country with very little contact with the outside world, was now easy to scan and email. And at least some local Saudis, women and men alike, felt that IKEA's airbrushing out female images was no longer appropriate. Saudi blogger Eman al-Nafjan, famous for defying traditions, such as by driving a car in June 2011, told CNN as the IKEA crisis broke in 2012: "We're beyond that right now in Saudi Arabia. . . . With Internet and satellite TV, there's really no such thing anymore as blacking-out women or airbrushing out women."[16]

Third, and perhaps most important, IKEA's increasingly salient global image as a force for progressive values—a company that stood up for gay rights when few would—was catching up to its actions. When you signal to the world that you will be a force for humanism, people take notice—especially if you are one of the world's largest lifestyle companies. But then they start to expect more of you, especially in an age when ideologies of othering are also taking root. If you are not prepared to meet those expectations, be prepared to face the bite back, as IKEA did. As marketing journalist Rob Gray explained, "This is the same company that in the 1990s ran one of the first TV commercials in the US to feature a gay couple—and received bomb threats in response. Obliterating women in an act of censorship certainly didn't look good to many IKEA customers in markets around the world more used to a liberal, inclusive stance from the brand."[17]

Those most upset with IKEA's actions in Saudi Arabia were its liberal consumers in the Western world—who had come to see IKEA as one of them. That, of course, was a moral commitment that IKEA had made willingly, and its commercial success had come in fair measure from marketing itself as a champion of the Scandinavian social ethic, including its inherent liberalism.

But embracing an identity also means owning responsibilities. If IKEA wasn't ready for the responsibilities that came with its identity, then it overcommitted itself by becoming a corporate icon for sexual rights. (Incidentally, this was also the case with Disney's scandal involving Florida's "Don't Say Gay" bill.) The real lesson here is to be prepared for the inevitable mission growth that comes from being a socially responsible organization in an age of outrage—and then to have a clear sense of boundaries, so one doesn't overcommit. While running a same-sex ad was edgy in the 1990s, by the 2010s a company with such an image was expected to be on the forefront of sexual progressivism, not simply still edgy.

Importantly, since IKEA is effectively privately held, the matter of fiduciary obligations to dispersed shareholders does not really factor in (as it does for Disney): as long as it has the support of the Kamprad family, the company's management can act decisively based on its own moral convictions. And given that the Saudi sales are a tiny fraction of IKEA's global sales and that the public outcry was in Western Europe (where a majority of IKEA's sales were located in 2012), it was entirely reasonable that Western stakeholders expected IKEA to take a more principled stand on Saudi censorship norms.

Eventually, IKEA chose to embrace its core identity and reissued the Saudi catalog with women—and, to its surprise, it experienced little backlash from local censors.

Anticipating the shifts

It is not unreasonable for an organization to hold different moral commitments—that is, its strategies for respecting stakeholders' norms—in different geographies at a given point in time. The scale of these commitments is a function of local expectations and the scale of the organization's capability asymmetries. But local expectations invariably change, as do capability imbalances, and the commitments made in one place at a previous time can come to jar significantly with (also evolving) commitments made elsewhere.

When IKEA first started in Saudi Arabia, the country was a deeply traditionalist society and the company had a very small presence there. But with time, both things changed: Saudis expected more freedom, and more was expected of IKEA in its core Scandi-progressive narrative. And variance in an organization's moral commitments across geographies or communities cannot sustain indefinitely, especially if that variance keeps growing. Eventually, the variance will look less like pragmatism and more like hypocrisy, and if the organization does not have a plan for convergence, it will simply invite outrage and, eventually, crisis. In this case, IKEA unwittingly found itself as a force *for* othering (by treating women so poorly) in stark contrast to its image of card-carrying Enlightenment humanism.

To avoid this happening, organizational leadership needs to ask itself three questions every time it is contemplating a moral commitment— and, moreover, it pays to revisit its existing commitments via these questions:

- When you make a moral commitment, what is your strategy for meeting that commitment authentically?

- What is your strategy for dealing with the shifting expectations around that commitment?

- What are the boundaries of that commitment and how have those been communicated to stakeholders?

Asking these questions focuses attention on how you or your organization will fulfill stakeholder expectations regarding a moral commitment, and how, as stakeholder expectations around that commitment (invariably) change, you and your organization plan to respond.

There were two moral commitments at play in the IKEA case: IKEA's moral commitment to exemplify Scandinavia's egalitarian and progressive ideals, and its commitment to respect local norms in Saudi Arabia. In respect to the first question, IKEA's authenticity was questionable on both commitments. There was a disconnect in presenting itself as a progressive icon in its major markets if it was airbrushing women out in Saudi Arabia, and with greater connectivity, the risks of being outed were rising. As regards respecting Saudi norms, the disconnect between policy for the catalog, IKEA's own TV advertising in Saudi Arabia, and liberalizing norms within the Kingdom had become almost glaring.

As for the second question, it was clear that IKEA had not reflected on the implications of changing expectations. It was prepared to use women in advertising on TV without reflecting on how attitude changes toward images of women on TV and the internet might also mean that it did not have to airbrush women out of print catalogs. It could, for example, have used the full original images (with women) on internet versions of its catalog and could, therefore, have simply made the Saudi catalog online only if it had been concerned that the Saudi Customs Authority would impound the print versions. By the same token, as regards the broader commitment, IKEA had come to lag the progressiveness of its mainstream customers and was less credible as a leading force in embodying Scandinavian attitudes. Moreover, US and European customers had become less comfortable with companies making local exceptions in their core values—and more alert to its possibility. (In effect, consumers have become more attuned to the rise of othering in this age of outrage, and they are willing to call out companies that participate in this, as Disney also learned.) Customers expected IKEA to advance its stated global values in Saudi Arabia, not adjust to cater to the sensitivities of the conservative elements in its society.

Finally, had IKEA addressed the third question explicitly, the company would quickly have realized that it had not communicated clearly, if at all, how far it was prepared to go in respecting either of the commitments involved. That might then have triggered some exploration as to what those boundaries should be.

The three questions can also be brought to bear on the decision about "institutional racism" that Commissioner Cressida Dick faced in the London Met Police case study we considered in the previous chapter. In determining whether to label her organization as racist, Dick had to recognize that it would signal to outraged opponents of stop-and-search a commitment from the Met that was beyond the capability of its current workforce to deliver. She knew, perhaps, that simply making that commitment without having the near-term organizational capabilities to authentically deliver on it would invite still more outrage (the first question). Besides, as I noted in chapter 3, the Met had already made another moral commitment, one dating to its foundation nearly two hundred years prior: the Peelian commitment to community-based policing. With London's shifting demographics and the low trust in policing among BAME Londoners, Dick already had a situation where she was unable to keep up with shifting expectations on current commitments (the second question). And, with that realization, perhaps Dick and other leaders of policing in the UK had now to consider whether new boundaries around the expectations of Peelian policing principles needed to be established in a new Britain.

Missing the Opportunity: The Case of "Dylan Pierce"

As with capabilities, in many cases the right approach to moral commitments is often to lean into them the way Johnson & Johnson did in respect of its commitment to put people first. More often when organizations do not push the boundaries of their already stated moral commitments, they run into trouble, as illustrated by a stylized case-study I wrote inspired by the experience of a gay employee at a Korean multinational.[18]

Dylan Pierce (name changed) was a star recruit at the San Francisco branch of a large Korean conglomerate with substantial operations and ambitions in the consumer tech sector. The company had hired Dylan, a consumer-interface developer, because it had a largely Korean male workforce and wanted more diverse perspectives when designing user interfaces. Dylan is gay, male, and an American of non-Korean ethnicity.

Dylan did so well at his job in the San Francisco office that within a year, he was asked if he might relocate to conglomerate headquarters in Seoul. The offer to move came with a substantial pay hike, and Dylan, who yearned for international work experience before applying to business school, accepted. But after some initial enthusiasm for Dylan's work on the part of his new Korean bosses, Dylan found he was being sidelined first from client meetings and then even from internal staff meetings. Perplexed and then furious, Dylan confronted his manager—to which he received the very frank feedback that he was "just too gay." A major client at the time was a Dubai-based entity, and beyond the Korean manager's own discomfort with Dylan, he felt Dylan's presence on the team would offend his client.

Humiliated and distressed about his isolation in a foreign country, Dylan took the concern to his company's human resources office. HR responded that the manager was acting within local norms and that Dylan had not appropriately adjusted to the move to Korea. When he threatened legal action, Dylan read between the lines of HR's response that the salary hike was intended to partially compensate him for any "cultural hardships." There was, at the time, no formal prohibition against sexual-orientation discrimination in the company's rulebooks as applied in Korea.

Importantly, Dylan had experienced no antigay discrimination while working for the Korean company in San Francisco. In fact, the branch office there had seemed very welcoming. Dylan expected this would continue in Korea, because being a diverse employer was the company's ambition. But, to the company, it was unreasonable for Dylan to expect (just yet) a gay-affirming workplace at headquarters—nobody else at headquarters could. However, in providing a gay-friendly environment in San Francisco, and in then bringing Dylan to Korea as part of its employee diversity strategy, the company had implicitly shifted expectations for Seoul as well. The organization just did not know that: it was too slow to lean into its aspirations.

Dylan promptly left and returned to another company in San Francisco. Later, he founded his own successful startup. Word of his treatment in Seoul got around Silicon Valley's highly fluid and politically aware workforce, to the Korean company's detriment. Since then, norms around expressing a gay identity in the workforce have changed dramatically, not just in the West, but globally. In Korea today, being out and proud in the workforce is better understood than it was just five years ago. What the Korean company had with

Dylan was an opportunity to live its ambition, to be seen as a pioneer in Korea acting on capability asymmetries (as IKEA once was), an opportunity that it unintentionally squandered, becoming (again like IKEA) an unwitting force for othering.

• • •

Once an organization's leadership has gone through the two exercises raised in this chapter—recognizing capability asymmetries and anticipating shifting expectations in the context of the dynamic drivers of outrage—it should have the makings of a strategy consistent with its values for managing and responding to stakeholder outrage. It will understand whether its capabilities make some action imperative and will reach a better understanding of how it is falling short on its (often already stated) moral obligations, given shifts in stakeholder expectations. We can now turn to the next step in the process—operationalizing the response.

Chapter 5

Understanding the Leader's Power

As a leader confronting crisis in an age of outrage starts to figure out where the crisis is coming from and what sort of response is both appropriate and sustainable, the challenge she now faces is how to get her organization behind that response. (Imagine, for instance, the challenges Disney CEO Chapek or Meta CEO Zuckerberg face as they try to get their very diverse organizations behind whatever response they deem appropriate to their respective outrage scandals—"Don't Say Gay" and Cambridge Analytica.) This requires the leader's cool and realistic assessment of her power within the organization and the system because it is not always obvious that the analytically preferred response to an outrage situation will win ground-level support in the organization or more widely. We saw this situation with the Colombia VAT reforms that President Duque proposed. And again, in the case of the London Met, we saw that the commissioner's capability to satisfy those outraged by the stop-and-search policy was, in fact, considerably limited by her need to maintain the morale of her officers, many of whom believed that the policy was an essential policing tool.

In this chapter, I'll explain how leaders can assess what kinds of power they have at their disposal and how they can best channel that power to drive preferred outcomes, illustrating the points with case studies of crisis leadership approaches adopted by the chief medical officer of the Oxford University Hospitals and the head of the Vatican's Supervisory and Financial Information Authority, responsible for oversight of the finances of the Catholic Church.[1] I'll conclude by discussing what kind of considerations should influence the decision to exercise power and the risks that the decision-maker may incur—leaders in the age of outrage may have to pay a price for making the best available (pragmatic) decisions for their organizations.

The Sources of Power

Management scholars, such as my Harvard colleague Kathleen McGinn, have defined power as the potential to mobilize the resources of others toward achieving a specific goal, and they traditionally identify three categories of power: positional, personal, and relational.[2]

A person's positional power derives from their official status in an organization. A military general, for example, can issue orders to junior officers to take certain actions, and those officers will, within the law, be expected to obey those orders without question. Leaders also derive power by virtue of their expertise, their moral authority, or other personal qualities. For example, a religious leader may have no formal power in a community but may well enjoy considerable spiritual hold over others, which may be used to convince them to agree to a certain course of action. This is personal power. Finally, a leader can have relational power through the strength of the networks that they have built. These networks may include former colleagues or school friends, people who may have a reason to help the leader achieve their goals—whether to repay a past favor or grant a favor to be repaid in the future.

Inspired by this classic definition of management power, I have developed a further categorization, one more layered and more applicable to power mapping in this age of outrage. As shown in figure 5-1,

FIGURE 5-1

Understanding the leader's power

This chart, inspired by work of organizational theorists such as Kathleen McGinn, shows how power and influence are distinct but related notions. It also introduces a new taxonomy for power that is especially suited to the age of outrage.

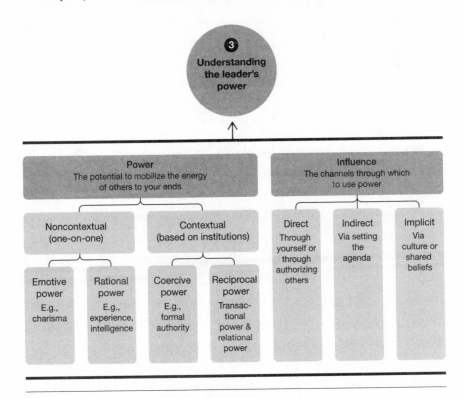

I distinguish the following four types of power: coercive, reciprocal, emotive, and rational. *Coercive power* is the ability to control others' actions through command. It can derive from the leader's hierarchal authority and her ability to control scarce resources, such as the ability to hire, promote, and fire individuals (especially when labor markets favor employers). It is the manager's most basic source of power, especially internal to an organization, but coercive power can also vary based on the type of organization and its inherent worker protections: managers in nonmilitary public-sector bodies generally have less coercive power than owner-managers in purely private organizations.

Reciprocal power derives from exchange-type settings. It can be purely transactional, as with a manager's power over an independent contractor in exchange for cash, but it does not have to be so: for example, in a social network, a quid pro quo is not expected from each instantiation of reciprocal power. However, even in these relational contexts, power accrues from the *perception* of reciprocity over the long run. The deeper your commitment to the exchange setting, the more your reciprocal power, as deep ties—such as those forged over many years, many interactions, and many types of interactions (e.g., commercial and recreational)—are more likely to mobilize others to your goals.

Whereas these first two types of power are situated in the empirical nuances of organizations and networks, the second two types— emotive power and rational power—derive from interactions of individuals even outside formal institutional arrangements. Philosophers separate these two settings, calling them "materialist" (of matter) and "idealist" (of the mind), respectively. *Emotive power* is a form of personal power that an individual can exercise over others, emanating, for example, from their charisma. Parents and children have emotive power over each other, as do those who share a common, deeply held faith. The kind of power Steve Jobs is thought to have held over hard-core Apple employees and customers can be characterized as emotive power. Finally, *rational power* is derived through reasoned (logical and evidentiary) explanation of one's goals and methods or through the perception of one's expertise and capabilities. Managers often use rational power when seeking to bring well-informed peers on board.

These four types of power can be roughly mapped onto the four *upāyas*, which are approaches to the "diplomatic" resolution of issues (i.e., outside of war) when nations have differing perspectives.[3] The *upāyas* were first mentioned in the ancient Sanskrit treatise the *Arthashastra*, which is considered the ultimate guidebook for international power politics—for those who think that even Machiavelli's *Prince* is too wishy-washy. Thought to have been penned some 2,300 years ago by Kautilya, a philosopher-teacher who helped establish ancient India's largest empire, the *upāyas* are now taught at the United States Military Academy West Point.[4] The *upāyas* are: *danda* (threats), *dāna* (compensation), *bhéda* (mind games), and *sāma* (reason), which I later realized are stylized manifestations of coercive power, reciprocal power, emotive power, and rational power, respectively, as contextualized to foreign policy.

To understand the value of this fourfold categorization of power, let's look at a case study I coauthored for the Blavatnik School about Meghana Pandit, chief medical officer of Oxford University Hospitals (OUH), who faced, and gracefully managed, a potential surgeons' revolt very early in the Covid-19 pandemic.[5]

Pandemic management at Oxford University Hospitals

The date was March 17, 2020, and governments across the world were only just starting to get a handle on pandemic priorities. There was still much scientific uncertainty about the virus and its effects, and governments were unwittingly creating further confusion by issuing sometimes contradictory and partial directives.

In this context, the UK government had announced via a press notice that elective surgeries must continue within the country's public network of hospitals, including OUH. The goal was to prevent a massive backlog of surgeries when the pandemic eased. But in that moment, with fear of shortages of surgical protective equipment and deep anxieties about the virus, all experienced within a general context of outrage (more later), some surgeons at OUH expressed strong concerns about complying with the government's order, arguing that it put them, their teams, and their families at risk. The surgeons' arguments, some emotively expressed in the heat of the uncertainty, noted that if entire teams became sick, this would itself be counterproductive to pandemic management. Pandit, as the head of all medical staff at the hospital, had to decide whether to enforce the

government's diktat or to risk her own role by siding with her surgeons in defying it.

OUH is one the world's leading research and teaching hospitals,
home to some of the profession's finest medical minds. But, like many
parts of Britain's National Health Service (NHS), it was entering the
pandemic in a somewhat compromised position, reeling from various drivers of outrage. Systemwide, public hospitals in Britain were
struggling to cope with the aftermath of Brexit. British hospitals had
substantially relied on European migrants to meet critical workforce
needs, and they had been deeply tied into EU-wide funding arrangements, especially for research. Post-Brexit, these spigots had abruptly
been turned down. The British government, somewhat fiscally adrift
after a Brexit-induced economic slowdown, had also not been able
to support its public health system as much as needed, which in turn
meant staff salaries for a highly mobile workforce were not keeping pace with internationally competitive levels. All this contributed
to the sense that both the NHS and the patients it served had been
handed a raw deal. Notwithstanding, the NHS was also expected to
lead in mitigating some of Britain's fears for the future—for instance,
by meeting ambitious decarbonization targets, given the health-care
sector's major role in climate change. And, if these systemic outrage
drivers were not enough to strain nerves at OUH, the hospital had its
fair share of idiosyncratic pressure points, too.

In 2018, for instance, the hospital had reported eight "never
events"—instances of critical safety failures, such as wrong-site surgery, that should *never* happen. The hospital's staff surveys had shown
great pride in individual performance but a lack of teamwork, a
perception that management did not support staff when mistakes
were made, and a tendency toward both risk aversion and disregard
of risk management processes. The UK's Care Quality Commission
had assessed the hospital as "requiring improvement."

In this context, the hospital's board, in early 2019, appointed Pandit
to lead. The decision involved many firsts: she was the first woman,
the first person of color, and the first non-native Briton to have the

role. As the former CMO at University Hospitals Coventry & War-
wickshire, she was also a relative outsider to the somewhat insular
medical professoriate in Oxford, an elite institution with a strong
tradition of building and sustaining talent from within, one that sees
itself as an exporter rather than an importer of leaders. For all these
reasons, Pandit was not the "predictable" choice to head the medical
staff at Oxford.

Her focus through 2019 had been to gradually reset OUH's culture
toward patient safety, patient satisfaction, learning from mistakes,
and building trust in management, while preserving and advancing
the hospital's culture of experimentation and pioneering research.
Although early results of these efforts from the beginning of 2020
suggested progress had been made ("never events" had dropped from
eight to two), the job was hardly done when the pandemic hit. OUH,
like the NHS more broadly, was very much experiencing what it
meant to operate in an age of outrage.

The Covid-19 crisis then hit OUH from all directions, requiring
Pandit and the team to make a multitude of decisions in short order
on issues ranging from canceling staff leave, managing shift rotations,
ensuring staff safety, fixing shortages in medical and safety equipment, allocating wards, testing and triaging patients (both Covid-19
infected and Covid-19-free), protecting patients not infected with
Covid-19, to developing partnerships with out-of-system hospitals.
At one point, her email inbox was receiving a hundred new messages every thirty minutes. It was into this maelstrom of competing
demands that the concerns from the worried surgeons landed.

How should she respond?

Pandit knew that she did have tremendous coercive power in this
situation: she was, after all, the "responsible officer" for all doctors
at OUH and so had final say over their licenses to practice. Besides,
she was the chair of the Covid Response Steering Group for Oxford
University Hospitals, giving her a broad decision-making mandate.
Effecting the government's order for elective surgeries to continue
was thus well within her command authority. She also enjoyed some

rational power: as a medical peer of the nervous surgeons, she could explain both the public health purpose of the government's elective-surgery order, the relative risks involved (although, these were unclear to everyone), as well the Hippocratic context in which the hospital was expected to function. But she lacked emotive power: being a relative newcomer and an outsider to the largely old-boys network of Oxford physicians, she was unlikely to be able to stir them to action through rousing rhetoric. She also lacked reciprocal power of the transactional kind: as a public hospital, OUH was unable to set salaries and bonuses, as these were largely determined by national pay scales that were themselves stagnating. Her relational reciprocal power was also weak. With just a year on the job, her efforts at cultural shift were still fledgling: if the pandemic had arrived three years later, and the cultural transformation had continued to succeed, Pandit would have likely had much more reciprocal power of the deep relational kind to draw on in confronting the threatened strike.

Pandit's obvious course of action, therefore, was to force her surgeon colleagues into complying with the government's requirements. Interestingly, when I teach this case study, particularly in executive education settings, some participants see the problem as a no-brainer. When I presented the case to a group of army doctors, for example, the participants could not understand why there was any debate. The government had issued an order, and it was, to their minds, clear in the context of the pandemic that it was Pandit's duty to order the surgeons to comply; the latter, arguably, were engaging in proto mutiny.

But Pandit was deeply reluctant to go down this route because she recognized that the costs of enforcement were considerable. To begin with, employing coercion to resolve this crisis risked compromising the cultural transformation that was her original mandate and that she had successfully initiated. The end goal of that transformation is an organization in which shared values and mutual trust between managers and staff drive decisions rather than orders from above—an organization where all members can draw on deep reservoirs of relationship-based reciprocal power.

What's more—and perhaps more critical in the context—Pandit realized that the pandemic would thrust many crises on her that could require her to exercise coercive power, and she knew that leaders who rely heavily on forcing through their agenda risk losing the trust of their people, which puts their entire leadership mandate at risk. What happens here is that each use of coercive power undermines both relational power (in this case, trust) and emotive power (i.e., forcing people to do things makes it harder to inspire them to do other things). At some point, the exercise of coercive power will prove misjudged or there may be an unintended consequence. For instance, a surgeon operating on a Covid-19-positive patient at OUH might contract the disease and unwittingly infect an elderly parent who dies in consequence. The surgeon could well blame Pandit for that outcome, very likely generating negative publicity, which might turn the very people whom Pandit needed to lead against her.

This calculus illustrates an important feature of coercive power, which is that in many organizations, it is a finite source of power, given the growing risks to its exercise. Other forms of power can be more easily renewed. If you draw on the support of your relationships, you can renew that reservoir by providing support to others when needed. You can also build your expertise, and you can even work on building your ability to connect emotionally. But, in most organizations, the people you coerce don't appreciate the experience, and for that reason, smart leaders treat their coercive power as a nonrenewable asset to be used sparingly. This is not universally true across all organizations, of course. In military or some religious organizations, coercive power is a norm and respected. Superiors in the hierarchy are expected to give orders. But even here, repeated errors of judgment in issuing orders create risks for a leader.

Pandit, of course, was not in a military or religious organization. She was in a learning and healing environment, one that had to advance both safety and innovation. Consequently, she knew she had to be sparing of her coercive power in a context where she might need it for a more serious crisis. But, as it was her main source of power, how could she avoid using it? This brings us to the next element going into her decision-making as a leader.

The Channels of Power

Beyond a spatial and temporal mapping of power, getting things done in an age of outrage requires managers to take stock of their influence. Referring again to figure 5-1, whereas power is defined as the potential to mobilize others' energy to your ends, influence is *how* you put such power to use.[6] Organizational psychologists have written extensively on influence, but for our purposes, we can frame the literature's insights into three questions for managers to ask themselves sequentially:

1. Can I exercise my power through shared beliefs?

2. Do I exercise my power through setting priorities?

3. Do I exercise my power through direct engagement (from myself or from my agents)?

The theory behind these questions is that managers have, broadly speaking, three modes of influence (including for decisions on hiring and promotions): getting things done implicitly through organizational culture; getting things done indirectly through the control of the agenda; and getting things done explicitly through direct engagement (by yourself or by others acting for you).

In general, the first approach is preferable to the second and the third, because effecting outcomes through shared beliefs can actually build up power, whereas the other options can erode power. Using the agenda (the second approach) as a way to signal decisions is a somewhat passive-aggressive tactic, because it signals to people lower on the agenda that their concerns matter less than others', thereby eroding (potential) emotive and reciprocal power. The exercise of coercive power (the third approach) implicitly denies agency to the people you are coercing, which, as I noted earlier reduces that power. Influencing through shared beliefs, on the other hand, reinforces those beliefs, thereby increasing both the leader's emotive power (she can appeal to colleagues again in the future with an even greater likelihood of success) and reciprocal power (by definition, relational power is increased when shared beliefs are reinforced).

In Pandit's case, if she had been further into her cultural transformation, she would have likely been able to answer affirmatively to the first question: probably, the surgeons would not have even threatened to revolt, as they would have had both a fuller trust in management to do right by them and a sharper focus on patient well-being. But we cannot choose when crises will hit, and so Pandit had to look further down the list of questions as "shared beliefs" were still a work in progress.

What about the second approach? As we've noted, Pandit had many issues on her plate in March 2020, beyond the surgeons' concerns. These included setting up quarantined Covid-19 wards separate from the general patient population, training medics to triage access to scarce ventilators and ICU beds for incoming patients, determining which hospital departments got access to scarce protective masks and Covid-19 testing, determining staff-leave policies to ensure a continuously refreshed team on-site to deal with the expected surge in patient volumes, and so on. By prioritizing these issues ahead of the surgeons' anxieties, she could have implicitly conveyed a decision to them. But doing that could well have alienated a key constituency, one whose buy-in was essential to managing through the pandemic and her longer-term project of cultural transformation.

That left the third option: explicitly exercising her power through direct engagement. But she chose to do it in a measured way, recognizing that she did not want to use her coercive power and that she had limited relational power. So, instead of engaging personally, she chose, much to the surprise of some around her, to act through the surgeons themselves. This she did by asking them to decide how to handle their situation, by empowering them to write their own policy guidance. In effect, she turned over her own power to the anxious surgeons and made them her agents. This was a big gamble, but it paid off: the surgeons quickly recognized, with the perspective of her substantial coercive power, that their worries were but one in a sea that was quickly swelling. Pandit's move also helped her increase her reciprocal power in the future. The surgeons appreciated the opportunity to be the decision-makers in a situation that they perceived as carrying high personal risks for themselves—they now were more comfortable seeing Pandit as their enabler and leader.

I'll return later to some further lessons that can be drawn from this case study, but let us briefly explore another example of how power can be put to use in the context of wider outrage factors.

Setting the Vatican's financial-reform agenda

A clever application of the second channel of power—that is, through control of the agenda or priorities—that I've encountered across the dozens of case studies that I have now written is the situation of René Brülhart, sometime director of the Autorità di Informazione Finanziaria, the Vatican's financial regulator, which oversees the operations of the Vatican Bank and much of the Vatican's finances. (I coauthored this case study for the Blavatnik School when it was known by the acronym AIF.[7] It has subsequently been redesignated ASIF, which I will use in this book.) As we will see later, Brülhart had very little ability to use the first channel and was somewhat restricted in the third channel, but he was still able to deploy his power to get the (immediate) job done.

In 2012, around the setting of this case study, the Vatican Bank provided financial services to individuals and institutions affiliated with the church in Vatican City and across the world, managing nearly €5 billion in assets for about 18,900 clients. The Vatican Bank has long been a focus of controversy for the Catholic Church, in recent memory perhaps taking second place only to the handling of child abuse by clerics. In the 1980s, for example, Roberto Calvi, a leading

Italian banker with close ties to the Vatican, was found dead, hanging from a girder under London's Blackfriars Bridge. He had until the day before been the chairman of Italy's Banco Ambrosiano, which had just collapsed in the wake of a political scandal. Correspondence later made public revealed that the Vatican Bank and Banco Ambrosiano had engaged in illegal transactions, and in 1984, the Vatican Bank paid out US$224 million to 120 of Banco Ambrosiano's creditors, acknowledging "moral involvement" in the bank's collapse.[8]

Despite the protracted fallout from that scandal, governance at the Institute for the Works of Religion (the Vatican Bank's formal name) remained questionable. In 2010, under threat of the bank's exclusion from the international financial system by US and EU regulators (because its poor governance made the bank a potential conduit for terrorist financing), Pope Benedict XVI created the Holy See's Financial Information Authority, now known as ASIF.

Even with the creation of this body, which was initially headed by a senior cleric, the Vatican Bank remained largely unsupervised in practice. Then, in July 2012, Moneyval, the Council of Europe's anti-money-laundering and anti-terrorism-financing committee, issued a report (instigated, interestingly, at the pope's "request") criticizing the Vatican Bank's protocols for managing suspicious customer transactions.[9] It rated the Holy See as noncompliant or partially compliant on seven out of sixteen essential criteria. The report stated that the "Vatican [Bank]'s rules for customer due diligence, wire transfers and suspicious transaction reporting were insufficient" by basic international standards, and it concluded that the ASIF lacked the legal authority and independence needed to supervise and sanction Vatican financial institutions.[10]

All this was a huge embarrassment for the Holy See, an institution that was supposed to be a beacon of human morality and that was already experiencing substantial outrage for its mishandling of child sex abuse by Catholic priests. Even some of its most faithful were openly questioning the church's "raw deal," as it became apparent that senior clerics at the highest levels in the Vatican had known and

covered up heinous illegal actions—in some cases, even being implicated themselves in child abuse; in other cases, simply transferring
accused priests to other jurisdictions where they could offend anew.

Then, just a few months after the critical Moneyval report, during
the 2012 Christmas season, the Bank of Italy officially suspended the
use of credit and debit cards in Vatican City amid concerns that the
Vatican Bank had not yet complied with global banking rules. It was
a crippling financial blow because the shops and museums inside the
Vatican—reportedly, some 120 point-of-sale terminals—all relied on
this digital banking system, and their revenues accounted for a large
proportion of the church's operating income.[11] The move effectively
rendered the Vatican a cash-only society during the height of the pil-
grim and tourist season. "If you wanted to go to the museums, you
couldn't book tickets online," remarked a Vatican official.[12]

At around the same time, several top Vatican Bank officials, including President Gotti Tedeschi, a layperson, suddenly quit or were fired,
fueling further speculation about possible financial improprieties in
the church. Then, Italian government investigators made accusations
that a senior church prelate had abused the secrecy of his Vatican
Bank account to run a cross-border money-smuggling side business
for rich clients. Out of frustration with these events, a number of
international banks froze the correspondent accounts they maintained
for the Vatican. Now, employees and clerics who kept their accounts
at the Vatican Bank could not even wire money to other banks, and
they could only obtain cash from the Vatican Bank's offices.[13]

Faced with this crisis, Pope Benedict finally looked outside the
Vatican for someone who could figure a way out of the mess, and in
November 2012, shortly before his surprise abdication, appointed a
Swiss financial lawyer, René Brülhart, as director of the ASIF. Before
long, Benedict had sequestered himself in retirement in a monastery
within the Vatican walls, and his successor, Pope Francis, became
Brülhart's boss. Reportedly then, the new powers in the church gave
Brülhart a seemingly simple instruction: he was to extract the Vati-
can Bank from the embarrassment of being frozen out of the global

banking system but without bringing the church into disrepute. Put bluntly, if there were any truth to the concerns that the Vatican Bank was enabling criminal activity, that had to be stopped, of course, but quietly.

Brülhart had considerable expertise in financial governance. He had made his name by helping reform the banking sector in the small nation of Liechtenstein, which, like the Vatican, had been previously blacklisted for not complying with global standards to prevent money laundering. He had also earned a reputation for financial forensics, when he helped uncover the Siemens scandal that involved bribery of government officials, and he had even helped trace and return Saddam Hussein's private jet to Iraq's new government in 2005. These achievements had won him the respect of his peers and gave him international credibility.[14]

In terms of our power framework, it is easy to see that, in principle, Brülhart potentially had a considerable amount of rational power, by virtue of his experience in dealing with regulatory reform. But, the rational power that might have carried some weight in Liechtenstein was of limited value in his new setting, given that the key people he would have to motivate—senior clerics in the Catholic Church—saw themselves as answerable to God rather to some rules of legal logic laid out by the US and EU banking systems. Likewise, he had almost no emotive power, as his dashing personality and charismatic style meant little to his new audience, even if he were a Catholic. And, as a complete outsider to the Vatican—and Italy as a whole, he had almost no reciprocal power—neither the transactional kind nor the relational kind. In theory, as director of the ASIF, he did have coercive power to compel the Vatican Bank to comply with European, US, and other international regulations, by virtue of having been directly appointed by the Pope, whose word was law in the Vatican, which was in essence an absolute monarchy.

Brülhart's mandate was to do whatever was necessary to bring the Vatican Bank into compliance with financial regulations. But he also had a mandate not to bring the church, already sapped by scandal and outrage, into further disrepute. Therein lay his problem. There was already a great deal of evidence suggesting that the bank was involved in questionable financial dealings and that some of these dealings involved senior Vatican officials. In early 2012, Pope Benedict XVI's personal butler had been arrested for leaking confidential letters and documents to Italian journalists. These "Vatileaks" documents had revealed that Vatican officials who had tried to stop corruption were either sidelined or removed from office. They had also fed long-standing suspicions about possible money laundering involving the Mafia.

The fallout from the Vatileaks scandal further complicated the already fraught relationship between clergy and finance professionals in the Vatican Bank. In May 2012, President Tedeschi was removed in a unanimous vote by the board of the Vatican Bank. Tedeschi was accused of personal and professional failings, including spending only two days a week in the office. But the leaked documents suggested a different likely reason for his dismissal.[15] When another bank, JPMorgan Chase, requested information from the IOR on certain transactions, Tedeschi had been supportive, even as others within the Vatican were not. The *New Yorker* quoted Tedeschi as asking in a board meeting, "Why shouldn't we share our records? As if to say, 'We have nothing to hide, right?'"[16] Soon, he was gone.

Not all the opposition to compliance was rooted in a desire to cover up questionable dealings. The Vatican Bank was founded in part precisely because it provided some measure of financial safety and independence to the church's operations abroad, and the bank's ability to operate beyond the reach of global financial regulations at times enabled it to advance the church's humanitarian mission in critical ways. For example, during the Cold War, Pope John Paul II used the bank to circumvent national restrictions to finance the Polish Solidarity movement.[17] Similarly, the bank gave financial support to anti-communist groups in many parts of the world including Nicaragua, Honduras, and Cuba.[18] And the bank's extra-judicial status also allegedly helped finance anti-Nazi resistance during World

War II. Unfortunately, it was not always easy to set clear boundaries between these moral "unreported" dealings and more questionable ones. Nor was it likely that Brülhart, a mere layman, could effect any change in Vatican culture around financial transactions. Successive popes had failed in this endeavor, and it is still rumored that Pope John Paul I was poisoned by the Mafia in order to prevent him from instituting an enquiry into the management of church finances.[19]

With all this context, Brülhart's formal coercive power was itself then severely limited. What about his influence options? The prevailing culture in the Vatican Bank, which Brülhart could not feasibly change, generally supported the opacity around financial dealings that he was struggling to dispel, which meant that he could not leverage any shared beliefs. Operating through others was also unfeasible because he was himself the agent of the pope, and no one in the organization would have been prepared to act as his agent, given his limited coercive power. But what he could do, it turned out, was set an agenda.

In a series of press conferences, Brülhart gave specific undertakings that the Vatican would bring its financial processes into compliance with international norms, focusing on the specific shortcomings highlighted in the 2012 Moneyval report. He undertook, for example, to provide international regulators with details of Vatican Bank client accounts by a certain date. By giving these press conferences, and later publishing annual reports, Brülhart remained within the terms of his mandate—it was certainly not an embarrassment for the Vatican to commit to respecting international banking norms, and Brülhart certainly had the mandate to make such commitments as the designated Vatican regulator for the Vatican Bank. What the commitments did do, however, was place responsibility for creating embarrassment for the church on the shoulders of those Vatican Bank clients whose actions were forcing the bank into noncompliance. If any account holdings eventually submitted to regulators attracted the attention of regulators and police, then responsibility for those accounts would lie squarely with the account holders in question.

Brülhart had found a workable solution to get the Vatican Bank back into the international system without embarrassing the church. In effect, his public commitments in press conferences forced any bad actors in the Vatican Bank to either clean up their act or take their bad business elsewhere. Brülhart's press conferences were refreshingly candid (and his annual reports were accessible and thorough), even when progress was modest: "I'm not here today to say that everything is great and perfect," he was reported admitting to journalists in May 2013.[20] The move made it clear to the bank's shady counterparties that the Vatican would, going forward, undertake financial transparency by the book and would throw anyone, no matter how important, to the wolves (i.e., US prosecutors) if they did not comply within global financial rules.

The gambit worked, and by 2014, even Moneyval acknowledged the progress that the Vatican Bank, now more fully embracing global banking rules, had made. Subsequently, the Board of European Payments Council formally admitted the Vatican into the Single Euro Payments Area, a decision that made cross-border electronic euro payments to and from the Holy See as seamless as domestic money transfers. In 2014, Pope Francis promoted René Brülhart from director to president of the ASIF, in effect making him the Vatican's central bank governor.[21] This apparently was the highest position in the Vatican to which a layperson had ever been appointed.

Weighing the Risks

In different ways, the examples we have studied in this and in previous chapters illustrate how unenviable the role of the leader is in organizations navigating challenges in the age of outrage. To begin with, as I cautioned at the outset of this book, there is almost never a complete solution. The best outcome a leader can realistically hope for is *some* progress.

In some cases, the organizational leader may not even be able to do that. What's striking about the Met example discussed in chapter 3 is

that the police commissioner, Cressida Dick, had plenty of organizational power of all kinds. She had considerable coercive power, given
her position atop a command hierarchy, although, as with OUH's
Meghana Pandit, exercising such coercive power in pursuit of changing organizational culture would be ill-advised. She also had reams
of reciprocal power—at least of the relational kind—by virtue of her
long career in the Met, and likewise some measure of rational and
emotive power. Indeed, Dick was, by many accounts, hugely popular
within the force, and when she left the commissioner role in 2022,
there was reportedly widespread dismay across the police ranks.[22] But
even with all this power, her scope for exercising it was limited. The
Met already suffered from a shortage of police officers, and her negotiating position with rank-and-file officers was constrained. Addi-
tionally, she was herself part of the problem: to some activists, she
was seen as a betrayer of liberal values that as a gay woman she was
expected to harbor personally; and had she chosen a more activist
agenda, to some police officers in the Met she would have been seen
as betraying traditional policing values (something of which, ironically, a white-male police leader would be less suspect). The bottom
line was that any leader risked losing the trust of her police force if
she were to try push for aggressive reform, which limited the leader's
ability to leverage her power.

In terms of channeling power, because Dick's crisis was a culture
problem, any influence would have to come through agenda-setting
or through the exercise of coercive power—either directly by herself
or through agents. With the coercive route off the table as unsustainable, agenda-setting was potentially the only channel through which
she could exercise power. But culture change was already top of the
agenda for the Met; there was little that she could do that might
be perceived as making it a more important priority. She was faced,
therefore, with a choice between acceding to demands in order to
placate the Met's critics—at least for the moment—and label the force
as institutionally racist, and protecting the transformation she had
begun by publicly defending her officers from the immediate outrage.

She might also have calculated that to accede to activists' demands might only increase their expectations for change, planting the scenes for future confrontations with both sides that she would not be able to calm. One option might simply have been to suspend stop-and-search pending further review, but that would have deprived the Met's rank-and-file police force of what they saw as a valuable crime-fighting tool, potentially increasing violence and inviting the wrath of other citizens of London.

Whatever decision she made was, of course, a gamble, and with every gamble there are risks. By rejecting the label of institutional racism and defending stop-and-search, Dick only increased the perception among some segments of the population that she herself was part of the problem. By doing that, she set herself up to be used as a potential scapegoat by her political masters—the mayor of London and the home secretary—in the event that another crisis erupted over the Met's policing culture. This duly happened in the wake of the rape and murder of a young woman, Sarah Everard, by a serving Met officer. The horrific scandal—and police handling of subsequent protests—exacerbated the already intense criticism of police culture and the Met's seeming inability to change, ultimately resulting in Dick's resignation. Whatever the extenuating circumstances, too many scandals had happened on her watch, even as the Met culture might have been slowly improving.

René Brülhart also paid for his decisions in the Vatican Bank crisis of 2013. Unlike Dick, he did succeed in solving the immediate problem—the bank's exclusion from the international banking system, and he was able to do this without a greater embarrassment for the Vatican. He was duly rewarded with a promotion, as noted earlier, which, on paper, increased his coercive power. But what perhaps was unknown at the time was the relational power of those within the Vatican whom he "inconvenienced" through his reforms: those agents would live to fight back another day, as the Vatican is unlikely to be the sort of place where lay Swiss lawyers can forever hold sway.

In 2022, Brülhart was, to the surprise of many including myself, put on trial in a Vatican court for permitting the processing of a corrupt transaction, in 2018, on behalf of the Vatican's Secretariat of State, for which he apparently acted as a paid financial adviser in addition to his role as head of the ASIF. The transaction related to the €350 million purchase of a luxury property in the West End of London, for which the secretariat, it was later determined, overpaid by an estimated 33 percent. It emerged from the investigation that Cardinal Angelo Becciu, at the time one of the most senior clerics at the Vatican and a personal friend of Pope Francis, had helped both to arrange the deal and to obtain approval from the secretariat (where he served as assistant secretary until 2018) for the transmission of funds to various parties associated with the deal. The charges against Becciu were of self-dealing and kickbacks, but the charges against Brülhart were of negligence in his governance role. At his trial, Brülhart pointed out that he had no real authority over the transaction, because, he argued, it had been approved and encouraged at the highest level in the Vatican—implicating both the Cardinal Secretary of State and the Pope himself. Becciu's involvement in this and other scandals resulted in his defrocking and demotion. But Brülhart's legal exposure continues, and given his implication of Francis, it is unlikely that any Vatican court will offer a definitive conclusion while the current Pope is in office.

Whatever the rights and wrongs of the case, it is quite plausible to see how Brülhart's entanglement with this scandal allows the clergy to discredit Brülhart's prior reforms at the Vatican Bank. Some of them might well see the trial as a comeuppance for the professional outsider who had the audacity to disrupt the long-standing independence and extralegal status of the Vatican Bank. Certainly, in his efforts to bring the Vatican back into the international system, Brülhart would have made enemies, who would probably be only too pleased to have a less capable financial overseer. With the benefit of hindsight, Brülhart might conclude that his one mistake was to have stayed on at the Holy See after bringing the Vatican Bank back into compliance with international norms.

Both the Met case and the Vatican case demonstrate how decisions in these crises can expose leaders to serious risks. So why did OUH's Meghana Pandit emerge stronger from her crisis, while these other leaders were weakened (Pandit is now the CEO of OUH, promoted from CMO). Part of the answer in Dick's case is simply that her transformation was advancing too slowly. For the Met, accusations of racism were on a collision course with accusations of not protecting the general public from criminal activity. Two sets of values that should not be at odds with each other had become so, which meant that the transformation challenge Dick faced was much greater. Moreover, as Dick herself pointed out to me, there is something about policing that is quite distinct from other contexts for leadership, being, as it is, "in the middle of society's disputes, often at the worst of times." Policing "is high impact, high profile, and always contested," she explained. Viewed in this light, it seems plausible that Dick's priority could have been to protect the process, however slow, and if necessary, to be available as a scapegoat in order to facilitate progress for her successor. (On this point, it is worth noting that her successor as commissioner also eschewed the label of institutional racism.) This illustrates both the fact that the decision-maker is part of the problem and the likelihood, by extension, that the leader may have to be sacrificed in order for progress to continue.

What differentiated Pandit from Brülhart was rather different. Brülhart never had a mandate, let alone the power, to change the Vatican's culture—arguably, not even the Pope has that kind of power. Brülhart's crisis response, therefore, needed to be far more bounded. As events later proved, his fix was less a solution to the Vatican's cultural problems around corruption than a clever short-term settlement to address an embarrassment. With that fix in place, there was little else for Brülhart to do than leave. Pandit's problem-solving, by contrast, had a broader mandate and was deeply rooted in her vision of the future of OUH, one that advanced both patients' welfare and medical innovation. She was, in effect, trying to both solve the immediate problem and at the same time create the conditions such that her response to the first power-channel question—can I exercise my powers through shared beliefs?—would be yes. Let's look at that in more detail.

Leading from the Future for the Present

As noted earlier, by delegating her decision to the surgeons questioning the government directive, Pandit was signaling that she trusted them to make the right decision—and that whatever their decision was, she would accept it as such. She was, therefore, potentially committing to defying the government's order, if that was where their decision went. By placing this trust in their hands, Pandit was leaning in both to a vision of their better selves and to her vision of a patient-centric hospital in which doctors and nurses work together to make on-the-ground decisions that fully reflect the organization's values. This was the OUH she had set out to build through her 2019 culture shifts. And in the OUH culture she aspired to, she would never have to order doctors to act in accordance with the organization's values. They would just know that is how the place works. By turning over decision rights to the surgeons, she was acting as if that future was already present.

At the time, some of her advisers thought she was crazy to do this. This was not the time for culture-transformation experiments, they argued. It was a time for making hard command decisions that saved patients' lives. As I described earlier, this sentiment is often echoed when I teach the case. Her reply, when students ask what she thought of that: if we are not able to live the culture during a pandemic crisis, then what is the value of that culture anyway?

In addition, and we'll look at this issue further in the next chapter, it is impossible for any single leader to consistently make the right decisions. In a healthy organization with the right culture, you should have many people making the decisions, which means you have many more people bringing their judgment and information to bear. This reduces risk. Organizations that live or die by one person's judgment will inevitably fail. It was for these reasons that she chose to delegate her power.

Listening to these explanations, I was struck by the similarities of her arguments to some of the ideas of the celebrated Harvard academic Fritz Roethlisberger, one of the pioneers of modern management thinking, who published, with William John Dickson, the first comprehensive findings of the famous Hawthorne experiments. In an essay published nearly six decades ago, Roethlisberger advised managers that "most people think of the future as the ends and the present as the means, whereas, in fact, the present is the ends and the future the means."[23] I was led to this quote by Wiley Souba, a former cancer surgeon who now teaches leadership at Dartmouth College's Tuck School in New Hampshire. Souba wrote an intriguing essay of his own on the concept of "hittability," inspired by an interview with baseball great Ted Williams.[24] What was it, he asked himself, that made even the most implausibly challenging pitches hittable to some players and not to others? By extension, what was it that made the wickedest leadership challenges similarly hittable to some leaders but not others.

A large part of the answer, Souba argued, was that exceptional leaders apply a vision of the future, per Roethlisberger, to define how to resolve a present seemingly unsolvable problem. Souba was focusing on the challenge of health-care reform in the context of the US Affordable Care Act, and he was advocating that the right approach to thinking about health-care reform was to root decisions made today in a vision of what health care should look like in some future world with greater social justice.

Souba believed that "the future is the *means* by which you change your behavior in the present (*ends*)." His approach was rooted in the art of building an aspirational narrative (through his actions) that itself could shape the present, which makes that future all the more probable. This was precisely the dynamic at play in Pandit's decision-making at OUH—she used her vision of the future to inform her decision in the present, seizing an opportunity to increase the chances of realizing that future. And by seeing the challenge that way, it became a home-run opportunity rather than an unplayable ball. Incidentally, Pandit herself was unaware of Roethlisberger's and Souba's work, but arrived at the same place, indicating the strength of the idea as a feature of great leaders.

In contrast to Pandit, neither René Brülhart nor Cressida Dick appeared to leverage a compelling future vision to inform how they would use their decision-making power. In fairness to both, perhaps neither really could, given their circumstances. In Dick's case, her long-term plan was certainly to ensure that racial (and gender) bias would not inform policing decisions, and a large part of this was to be achieved through recruitment, training, and outreach.[25] But she was not seen to be creating a compelling public narrative around her vision. As part of such a narrative, she could, perhaps, have accelerated reform by conceding the activists' point and admitting that the Met was institutionally racist and suspending stop-and-search until it was clear that on-the-ground decisions would be demonstrably less biased. The review set up in the wake of the Everard murder certainly revealed profound flaws in police practice that the Met had done little to improve. And, in the end, the Met was publicly described as institutionally racist, the label that Dick had been so reluctant to accept.

Brülhart's position was different: Although a Vatican functionary, he is perhaps best seen as a hired gun, with a very specific task, that he ably fulfilled. His solution was very circumscribed, not informed by a compelling vision of a future culture that was out of his remit in any event. In baseball terms, he was able to make sure that the Vatican Bank could at least be walked to first base, keeping the Vatican in the game, but he never did have the authority to swing for the fences and deliver a home run for Vatican culture change. That can only be done by successive popes making hard decisions, including some that embarrass the church in the short run.

Of course, what defines leadership cannot be reduced to one feature. As in any discipline, mastery in leadership requires many skills and much experience. What Ted Williams saw as hittable evolved as he practiced and as he watched and rewatched films of his own and other hitters' swings, learning how the ball moved from pitcher to hitter. All this enabled him to identify seventy-seven different strike zones, and he calculated his average for each one. Leadership is the same; your next challenges are more likely to be hittable if you've faced—and studied—many challenges before. But the ability to use the future as the frame is one bit that really seems to matter, and it is by framing an outrage crisis as an opportunity to lean into a better future that a leader can start to bring their organization out of the crisis stronger than it was before.

My final observation on deploying power in this age of outrage is to remind people of my caveat at the beginning of this book, which is that (for all the talk of home runs) few solutions to crises are as successful as Pandit's approach to the threatened surgeons' strike. As the Met example illustrates, some responses to crisis, by even the most experienced leaders, will fail, even when they are working to deliver a better future. And even when leaders do leverage an inspiring future vision, there may be further unexpected events and revelations, or the leader may simply make a bad judgment call. And for this reason, leaders and organizations need to develop the ability to pick themselves up, dust themselves off, and be ready to start again. For the abiding quality of enduring leaders and organizations is not the absence of failures but that they can bounce back from setbacks—an ability, like the others described in this book, that they can practice and develop, as we'll see in the next chapter.

Chapter 6

Building Organizational and Personal Resilience

In a May 2021 interview with *Bloomberg Businessweek*, even as the world was still trying to make sense of Covid-19, a psychology professor at Texas A&M, Anthony Klotz, predicted the coming of a "Great Resignation."[1] He was right. In the following few months, driven largely by millennial and Gen Z workers, America and large parts of the world experienced worker resignations at higher-than-usual rates, especially given the high unemployment and continuing economic uncertainty of the time. A PwC survey in August 2021 reported that 65 percent of US workers were "looking for a new job."[2]

The Covid-19 pandemic—and peoples' desires to reassess pressures on them in the wake of abrupt shifts in the nature of work—was given as a main reason for the Great Resignation. Although workforce retention rates have now recovered to pre-pandemic levels, the upheaval caused by those months of actual and pondered job shifts likely imposed a substantial cost on both individual businesses and the economy as a whole. The pandemic catalyzed people's anxieties about the drivers of outrage and, in many cases, heightened that outrage—putting more pressure on themselves in their roles as both citizen-consumers and employee-providers. Organizations, it turned out, were not nearly as robust as they had thought, and they had underinvested in building the capabilities of their people to withstand the (invariable) upheavals that are likely to come our way in this age.

Indeed, the emotional hazards of navigating organizations through these times are amply evident from the various case studies covered. Simply working through the four steps of the framework discussed thus far can be fairly demanding on both managers and, as we see from the case of the OUH surgeons, their teams as well. There is only so much one can do, and one must be ready for the next assault. This means that both leader and the organization must invest in building resilience, organizationally and individually.

This brings us to the last step of the age of outrage framework—building organizational and personal resilience. While presented as a final step, leaders must invest in building resilience throughout the entire process of responding to and managing outrage because, as mentioned earlier, each step can take its toll on people.

Before exploring how to build resilience, it's important to understand what characterizes it. Broadly speaking, resilience can be defined as the ability to withstand and recover from negative shocks. Critically, this definition assumes that the resilient organization will experience unexpected shocks, and sometimes those shocks can even be the outcome of poor prior decisions. Building resilience, therefore, is not an exercise in preventing or even anticipating adverse shocks but rather building the capacity for intelligent failure that enables risk-taking, learning, and growth, in full knowledge that shocks will occur. This is not to say that trying to predict and forestall shocks isn't important, but rather that resilience is what you need for events that you haven't predicted.

A resilient organization (or system) is characterized by the delegation of authority: by situating decision-making close to ground realities, the organization both improves the informativeness of its decisions and diversifies its thinking and, as a consequence, can endure and even thrive amid negative shocks. Further, with many people making potentially different decisions in a crisis, the organization can experiment its way out of that crisis. Investing in resilience, therefore, entails creating organizations in which leaders can delegate authority to individuals who have the capacity to make decisions and the confidence to fail as it happens, and who can themselves absorb and adapt to external shocks.

In this chapter I'll discuss what that involves. Unlike the previous four steps, investing in resilience is not a specific process; rather it is a set of disciplines that the organization should engage in as part of everyday activities. Some of the disciplines are managerial in nature—investments in the creation of an adaptive, learning organization—while others are practices engaged in by individuals seeking to develop their personal resilience. I'll begin by looking at the different ways leaders can build organizational resilience before turning to what's involved in creating personal resilience. (See figure 6-1 for a graphic presentation of the elements involved in this final step of the framework.)

Create Relational Contracts

As I noted in the last chapter, in an ideal world, power is exercised implicitly through an organization's culture. In the OUH case, for example, when the crisis over surgery hit, Meghana Pandit was in the process of creating a culture in which frontline decision-makers—including the surgeons—would make the kind of decisions that exemplified the organization's commitments to patient safety and teamwork. The gamble she took in delegating the decision on whether or not to comply with government orders on elective procedures to her surgeons was that she did not know whether the surgeons knew when it was or was not acceptable to violate a government order (on elective surgeries or otherwise). In turn, for the surgeons to receive this decision-making authority from Pandit was risky because they did not know whether they could trust Pandit if they made a decision that was at odds with her own view. On both sides, therefore, there was a problem of *clarity* on what should be done. There was also a

FIGURE 6-1

Building organizational and personal resilience

This chart summarizes the elements making up the final of the four framework processes (see figure 1-1).

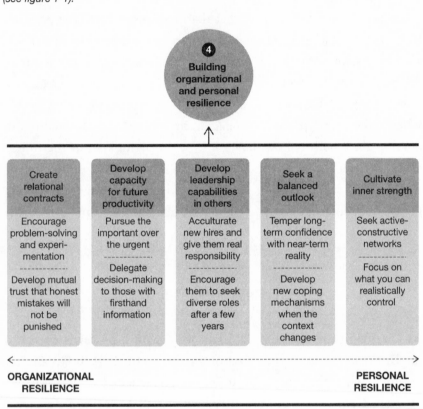

Create relational contracts	Develop capacity for future productivity	Develop leadership capabilities in others	Seek a balanced outlook	Cultivate inner strength
Encourage problem-solving and experimentation	Pursue the important over the urgent	Acculturate new hires and give them real responsibility	Temper long-term confidence with near-term reality	Seek active-constructive networks
Develop mutual trust that honest mistakes will not be punished	Delegate decision-making to those with firsthand information	Encourage them to seek diverse roles after a few years	Develop new coping mechanisms when the context changes	Focus on what you can realistically control

←--→

ORGANIZATIONAL RESILIENCE   **PERSONAL RESILIENCE**

problem of *credibility* for each side: employees could not be sure that they would not be exposed to negative consequences if they made what turned out to be a poor decision, while the chief medical officer could not be sure that the employees would not make a decision in their own rather than the organization's interests.

Part of why they had this challenge of clarity and credibility is because OUH was only a year into its cultural transformation. In effect, Pandit and her team had not yet been able to establish what economists call a "relational contract."[3] That term may sound wonky, but the underlying idea is the essence of trust-building in a managerial relationship. Relational contracts are powerful implicit understandings between parties on both the motivations that will guide each side's decision-making and the reactions from each side to decisions made by the other. The "contract," in effect, provides both sides with greater clarity and credibility in decision-making. Relational contracts are how organizational leaders can channel power through shared beliefs—and building and sustaining them is the holy grail of organizational resilience.

Toyota is one company that exemplifies relational contracts. One of the best-known features of the famous Toyota Production System (TPS) is the Andon cord, which is instrumental to Toyota's reputation for balancing reliability and cost. Workers on the Toyota assembly line are encouraged to pull the Andon cord (which illuminates a lantern) when they notice a possible manufacturing defect on the line, effectively stopping the entire production process at great expense.

There are no explicit rules on when to pull the cord and when not to—pull the cord too often and costs will rise; pull it too seldom and reliability will fall. If it were possible to specify such rules, then the cord itself would be unnecessary, and low-cost reliability would not be as elusive as it is. Instead, line workers and management have built an implicit understanding that the former will not frivolously pull the cord and the latter will not punish the former if indeed they pulled (or did not pull) the cord in error. Both sides are motivated by Toyota's famed reliability-at-cost culture, and they are inspired to act by trust in each other.

Other car companies have tried for years to copy the Toyota system, knowing, on paper, what it entails. But they have not succeeded. A classic example is Toyota's US competitor, General Motors. As Case Western's Susan Helper and Harvard's Rebecca Henderson describe in their 2014 article in the *Journal of Economic Perspectives*, in the 1980s the US automaker, finding itself consistently outcompeted on cost and productivity by Toyota and other Japanese companies, attempted to introduce TPS practices.[4] The company initially created a joint venture called New United Motor Manufacturing, Inc. (NUMMI) in 1984 with Toyota itself, in which the Japanese partner managed the operations of GM's Fremont plant in California, which had long been one of GM's least productive plants, known for fractious worker relations. As part of that joint venture, Toyota rehired, and retrained, almost the entire (unionized) workforce and was able to achieve the productivity and quality levels of its Japanese plants.

Despite this experience and easy access to Toyota's methods, GM struggled to transfer the success to its other plants. As Helper and Henderson observed: "They appeared to have believed that the essence of Toyota's advantage lay in tools like the fixtures designed to change stamping dies rapidly, or in the use of 'just in time' inventory systems, rather than in the management practices that made it possible to develop and deploy these techniques." Jeff Liker, an academic who advised GM for many years, captured this in a 2010 interview for *This American Life*: "One of the GM managers was ordered, from a very senior level—(it) came from a vice president—to make a GM plant look like NUMMI. And he said, 'I want you to go there with cameras and take a picture of every square inch. And whatever you take a picture of; I want it to look like that in our plant. There should be no excuse for why we're different than NUMMI, why our quality is lower, why our productivity isn't as high, because you're going to copy everything you see.'"[5]

The problem was that the TPS could not be reduced to a set of physical processes. It was predicated on delegation of tremendous responsibility to frontline employees who would make the best decisions they could, given the information available to them. Workers and managers understood the values and processes driving decision-making: workers could safely believe that they would not be penalized for a mistake in pulling (or not pulling) the Andon cord, and managers could safely rely on workers to make decisions in the group interest. In other words, the TPS would only work properly in the presence of strong relational contracts—credibility and clarity.

These were conspicuously absent at GM. Steven Bera, a GM executive who worked at NUMMI and a number of other plants, observed (again in *This American Life*) that "there was no change in the culture. Workers and managers continued their old antagonistic ways. In some of the factories where they installed the Andon cord, workers got yelled at when they pulled it."[6] Many managers believed that workers were not interested in process improvement and would pull the Andon cord simply to get a break. When workers did volunteer their suggestions for improvement, they were ignored. In a separate study, Susan Helper noted that at one New Jersey parts plant, workers were trained in statistical process control and encouraged to contribute ideas. They responded positively, submitting many suggestions and even tracking key quality metrics. But "management had not assigned anyone to respond to the suggestions or examine the data the workers had carefully collected." Inevitably, the workers "reverted to past patterns, feeling betrayed and much less interested in participating in future experiments."[7]

Neither side had clarity around values and norms driving the decision to embrace TPS at GM. And neither side had credibility with the other.

The purpose of TPS at Toyota is learning for improvement, or as described by Steven Spear in the *Harvard Business Review*, one of scientific experimentation. This requires a commitment to accuracy and detail, on which is then built the trust between managers and the managed. In "Learning to Lead at Toyota," Spear describes the training one experienced US automaker manager received at Toyota prior to taking a position at a Toyota plant in Kentucky.[8] Managers at most companies might propose an improvement along the following lines: if we move the parts rack closer to the assembler, we can expect to reduce the throughput time by a few seconds. But, as Spear observes, "in the eyes of a Toyota manager . . . such a result would indicate that the manager didn't fully understand the work that he was trying to improve. Why hadn't he been more specific about how far he was going to move the rack? And how many seconds did he *expect* to save?

Four? If the actual savings is six seconds, that's cause for celebration—but also for additional inquiry. Why was there a two-second difference? With the explicit precision . . . the discrepancy would prompt a deeper investigation into how a process worked and, perhaps more important, how a particular person studied and improved the process."

With the manager's commitment to accuracy, then comes Toyota's license to the manager to experiment. Ditto with the workers. The TPS, therefore, is constantly evolving and adapting as new information comes in from experiments, and managers serve to enable change at layers below them through a relational contract rather than impose change upon them. This is very different from GM's command-and-control structure that transactionalized employees. But, as the NUMMI joint venture case shows, it is possible for leaders to create relational contracts with workers if managers really understand and commit genuinely to the values the relationship is predicated on. And it can be done quite quickly.

This is what Meghana Pandit did when she delegated her decision-making power to the OUH surgeons. She offered them a relational contract by accepting that she would take responsibility for their decision. She made a credible commitment that they would not be held responsible. She also made it clear that she implicitly believed that they would not frivolously pull their equivalent of the Andon cord (just because they wanted to escape from the anxiety of the pandemic). This expression of faith in their desire to do the right thing, motivated by a shared commitment to the Hippocratic Oath, in turn made it more likely that they would respond in kind—reinforcing the relational contract she offered.

Develop Capacity for Future Productivity

Beyond enabling intelligent failure through relational contracts, the task of organizational resilience requires enhancing *future* productivity, even through a crisis (or an age of outrage where organizations are under constant fire). As Lewis Carroll reminds us in *Through the Looking-Glass, and What Alice Found There,* "Now, here, you see, it takes all the running you can do, to keep in the same place. If you want to get somewhere else, you must run at least twice as fast as that!"[9]

From the long laundry list of to-dos in March 2020 that Pandit had to consider alongside the possible surgeons' revolt, she chose as her foremost priority, "driving the cultural change." At first glance, that might seem absurd: Why focus on the intangible when there are so many tangible tasks to deliver?

Stephen Covey provides an elegant answer to this question.[10] Drawing on a distinction popularly attributed to President Eisenhower, Covey notes how leaders often conflate the *urgent* with the *important*. There are always lots of "urgent" issues on a manager's plate, especially in a crisis (e.g., dealing with the angry surgeons' threatened revolt). Responding to these issues can very quickly become all-consuming, and for many leaders there is also something satisfying about "putting out fires." But the reality is that the more managers focus on firefighting, the less time they have to focus on fire prevention, and the more fires they will have to put out tomorrow. Important decisions that don't appear as urgent today, and therefore get put off, then often end up becoming more important and urgent in the future.

Given this unsustainable dynamic, leaders in a crisis, like Pandit, who was receiving requests for decisions at the rate of about two hundred emails an hour, need to rethink what they spend their time on. To begin with, the importance or urgency of a given decision is not always correlated to the organizational status of the decision-maker. As we have already seen, in a resilient organization, many important and urgent decisions are delegated to people closer in touch with ground realities, who are often better informed than decision-makers higher up in the chain.

Pandit knew that she would never have the personal capacity to address the interminable stream of "urgent and important" decisions that would come her way through a pandemic of indeterminate length. So, she decided to prioritize the certainly important but not apparently urgent decision to continue with building a culture of patient safety, management trust, and intelligent risk-taking by delegating the certainly urgent and apparently important decision about how to respond to the government's requirement to continue with elective surgeries. By doing so, she calculated that she would help the organization become more capable of making sensible decisions independently and expeditiously—and thus more productive in the future.

Also playing into this decision, of course, was Pandit's implicit awareness that in a crisis, an organization and leader should lean into their aspirations rather than defer them, a point I made in the last chapter. In Pandit's vision of the future, she would not have had to make a decision on elective surgeries, and, in her estimation, the risk to the organization of making the decision herself—derailment of the cultural transformation—was greater than the risk of the surgeons making the wrong decision.

I cannot emphasize enough how difficult it is for leaders to make the right calls in judging which decisions are important and urgent for them. Managers usually have a predisposition to make decisions—and they rise in the organization by making quick decisions often. The result, of course, is that when they reach the top, they may struggle to adjust to the realization that they should not, in fact, be making a lot of decisions, but rather making it possible for other people to make those decisions. We come back to Eisenhower, who observed that a president should only make those decisions that only a president could make and that good presidents create structures in which only such decisions are brought to them. Eisenhower is said to have advised the younger John Kennedy, his successor, on his accession: "There are no easy matters that will ever come to you as President. If they are easy, they will be settled at a lower level."[11] Pandit sought to exemplify this principle. She declined to make a decision that she knew other people could make and thereby fostered an organization in which more people were able to take decisions in her place.

But this approach does present organizations with a conundrum. They need to develop employees into leaders capable of having good judgment around hard calls. Let's turn to look at how that can be done.

Develop Leadership Capabilities Everywhere in the Organization

There's voluminous literature on the topic of good leadership judgment, but one short essay that bears reading is Isaiah Berlin's 1996 piece in the *New York Review of Books* titled "On Political Judgment." The article is a sprawling sweep of arguments on what makes leaders like Bismarck and George Washington just so. Although the article focuses largely on leadership judgment on the geopolitical stage, its core thesis applies to any form of managerial judgment, which Berlin defines as "a highly developed discrimination of what matters from the rest" in a given situation.[12] In the article, Berlin speaks to the value of a scientific approach to decision-making, an approach that helps the decision-maker narrow the set of options on what can be done in a given knotty situation. But, in the end, he argues that making a decision needs something well beyond the science—*this*, he says, is judgment, and it is developed from plenty of practice.

The bottom line to Berlin's argument is that you cannot build great judgment in someone without exposing them repeatedly to the task of making hard decisions. This is the essence of the case method of teaching and learning that I acquired as a young professor at Harvard Business School and expanded into Oxford's Blavatnik School of Government. In the case method, students are taught the art of leadership through good judgment by having them work their way through dozens of thorny problems.

Outside the university context, an organization that does this at scale in the real world, and has successfully done this over generations, is the US Attorney's Office for the Southern District of New York (SDNY), about which I coauthored a case study for the Blavatnik School at Oxford.[13] Let us take a quick look at its curious culture of excellence.

Although its salaries are largely uncompetitive relative to private-sector offerings for top legal recruits in New York City, the SDNY consistently attracts entry-level candidates of the very highest caliber: graduates of top law schools who have had the opportunity to clerk for the United States' senior federal judges. The SDNY is equally well known for the quality of its senior legal staff, who often leave lucrative outside opportunities to take on its low-paying management jobs. In this recruiting, the SDNY benefits, to be sure, from its history as the oldest federal jurisdiction in the country—the SDNY Federal Court was "the first to sit under the US Constitution," preceding the creation of even the US Supreme Court. SDNY also benefits from the importance of New York City to the global economy, which has resulted in the SDNY US Attorney's Office being frequently involved in landmark trials. But, importantly, the office is also known for a cult-like emphasis on "doing the right thing" and for its fierce political independence. This is combined with giving recruits radically immersive responsibilities.

Early on in their careers, the newly recruited assistant US attorneys (AUSAs) at the SDNY are given the remarkable, and some would argue risky, opportunity to work independently on complex cases and to be in the courtroom often. Reflecting on her time at SDNY, former AUSA Bonnie Jonas explained: "As a young prosecutor you were entrusted with a tremendous amount of responsibility that junior lawyers are rarely given at law firms."[14] She added, "My experience is that other government agencies do not give new lawyers the same degree of responsibility."[15] David Kennedy, the Civil Rights Division co-chief at the SDNY, concurred, "I am one of the people who interviews applicants for AUSA positions, and I am constantly amazed at how attorneys I interview have had so few litigation opportunities. Applicants often proudly claim that in their years at the firm they took or defended a few depositions, had an oral argument, or wrote an appeal brief, all things we do about once a month."[16]

This immersive, high-stakes work experience is further enhanced by the complexity and diversity of the caseload and the quality of the defense counsels whom SDNY prosecutors can expect to face.[17] As former SDNY US Attorney Robert Fiske points out, "The SDNY tries cases in the public domain every single day. Its civil division has some of the most important cases in the country. In my four years as US Attorney, five cases that our Civil Division handled went to the US Supreme Court because the issues were so important. Young lawyers get the opportunity to work on precedent-setting cases against some of the best lawyers in New York. This is great experience. The kind of responsibility you get at the SDNY at a young age is unmatched."[18]

To reduce the risks of giving young AUSAs such responsibilities, the office looks beyond the résumés. As Mary Jo White, the first woman US attorney of the SDNY (1993–2002), comments: "All the candidates are spectacular on paper. The key question is how will they deal with the power they get at such a young age? Will it go to their head? Everything you do at the SDNY matters a lot."[19] Bonnie Jonas, who held a range of supervisory positions after being an AUSA, agreed: "Coming from big law firms, assistants go from no power to so much. There has to be a sense of responsibility that comes with the ability to take people's liberty away. . . . The office needs to screen for those who simply want power, to notch convictions, versus those who are truly interested in public service and want to give back. It has to vet for people who have an ethos of contributing to something bigger than themselves."[20] Put very simply, what the SDNY does is delegate responsibility as much as it can, while managing the risk through carefully recruiting people who fit its "do the right thing" culture—the relational contract is made visibly up front.

What's further interesting about this situation is that, having given AUSAs such an education, the SDNY has historically discouraged them from staying with the organization too long, in sharp contrast to many other government agencies, where the typical employee tends to be a careerist. A study that traced the careers of 152 AUSAs employed at the SDNY beginning in 2001 found that within a decade, more than 60 percent had moved to the private sector, a majority of whom had become partners at private law firms. The study's author, David Zaring, a professor at the University of Pennsylvania's Wharton School, reflected, "The story of a job in the SDNY is largely a story of a revolving door into private practice—not to business, and not to academia, but to law firms, with a minority remaining in the government."[21] He added that "my guess is that a gig in the Southern District is the greatest path to wealth maximization in the federal government that there is."[22] The SDNY's securities division, which oversaw prosecution of many financial crimes, was referred to as its "departure lounge," an allusion to the fact that experience in this department was of particular interest to private law firms.[23] So, while the SDNY cannot pay its new recruits competitively (being as they are on government pay scales), it does create a flourishing path for their eventual financial success. This, it seemingly does, without having the revolving door corrupt its public mission, by sustaining a strong relational contract.

At the same time, however, the SDNY often recruits back former AUSAs for senior managerial positions, after they have had a successful career outside the organization, preferably in the private sector. In fact, private-sector experience is considered to be a rite of passage for the most coveted senior positions at the SDNY. Insiders explained that the US attorney was traditionally someone who served as an AUSA at the SDNY, but then established themselves in the wider legal profession. Once appointed, the new leader typically reaches back into the pool of SDNY senior alumni to fill key positions on their executive staff, like the chief of the criminal division and the chief counsel position. Jonas explained, "The most senior jobs at the SDNY are typically reserved for those who have left. This is different from other district offices where the top positions go to insiders."[24] Others return to public service in different senior positions. Former SDNY prosecutors have become judges of the US Supreme Court and the US Court of Appeals for the Second Circuit (the federal appellate court with jurisdiction over New York), heads of agencies such as the FBI and the Securities and Exchange Commission, members of Congress, cabinet secretaries, the mayor of New York City, and the governor of New York State.[25]

This example suggests an interesting model for organizations looking to seed leadership judgment everywhere in their ranks and to ensure that they have a robust pipeline of potential senior leaders who can come in with a strong understanding of the relevant culture. The SDNY's talent strategy seems to have been (implicitly) built on Isaiah Berlin's ideal that leadership judgment is forged by repeatedly exposing individuals to the task of making hard decisions. By recruiting very bright AUSAs who already have good cultural fit with the organization early in their careers, they build strong relational contracts by offering them considerable decision-making authority in return for a commitment that those decisions reflect the SDNY's values. The experience with SDNY offers the AUSAs a springboard into highly profitable private-sector positions at organizations that value both the experience and the culture that the SDNY has instilled in the AUSAs. It also means that when the SDNY recruits back its alumni, they can walk back into the relational contracts, while bringing with them their new experiences—and they very likely won't be returning simply because they need the money. This last factor contributes to the organization's fierce independence from Washington politics: regardless of who is president, they tend to fear their own prosecutors at SDNY.

Of course, being a leader is not just about being a good decision-maker. As important is their ability to motivate their people. In some situations, that may require the ability to credibly communicate an appealing vision of the future, to which the team will want to aspire. But in crisis and divisive situations, such as those I have been describing in this book, an effective leader needs to take a more nuanced approach, balancing the need to provide hope of a successful outcome with a realistic acceptance of the difficulties confronting the organization. This brings me to the next element of resilience.

Seek a Balanced Outlook

One of the most common responses of people in leadership positions to a crisis (of outrage or otherwise) is denial that the crisis is, in fact, occurring. OUH's Pandit described to me an experience she had when on a conference call with a number of other organizational leaders during the Covid-19 pandemic. She shared with this group that the pandemic was causing her sleepless nights from worrying whether her hospital would run out of oxygen for ventilators and, in fact, whether the broader measures they were introducing to manage the response to the pandemic were in fact working.

She expected to hear peer leaders express similar emotions. Instead, her confession encountered a stony silence. In part, this reaction reflects a fear, common among many leaders, of not being seen to cope or have the answers in the face of a crisis, which strikes at the identity of executives who have succeeded because they "have all the answers." The fear is often rationalized by a perceived necessity to provide hope to and hide weakness from their teams. If senior executives confess to losing sleep, the argument goes, then how much confidence can their followers be expected to have of a positive outcome? In short, many leaders are biased toward a projection of optimism, even in the face of clearly adverse conditions that in no way merit optimism.

The risk with this approach is that when followers perceive that the optimism is simply unrealistic, they lose faith in the leader's judgment, thereby upending what the leader had been hoping to achieve.

What Pandit was doing was admitting that she was tired. What she saw was how much other people were fooling themselves into thinking that they were more resilient than they actually were. Many in that room must have felt tired, but they were afraid to admit it because that might suggest that they were not cut out to be good leaders. They might even have been questioning Pandit's leadership qualities because of her admission of tiredness. Of course, that conclusion is quite wrong. Resilience begins with realism about your own vulnerabilities. People who are tired are more likely to make poor decisions. So, if tiredness is your problem, good leaders admit it, so that they can get additional advice from people whose judgment they trust.

Many leaders emphasize the importance of optimism in crisis situations. But an optimistic outlook has its limits, illustrated by what Jim Collins has dubbed the Stockdale Paradox, for the famous US admiral who had endured a long and brutal experience as a POW in the hands of the Vietcong in the late 1960s.[26] Early in his incarceration, Stockdale was struck by the optimism of many of his fellow POWs that they would be quickly liberated. Many of these optimists did not make it out of the Vietcong prison alive, which Stockdale suspected was in part a result of the disappointment they experienced when they were not freed by the time they had expected to be. They died, he said, from "a broken heart" when their hope was extinguished.

Stockdale himself took a different approach. He tempered his belief that he would ultimately be released with realistic regular assessments of the proximate chances of such liberation. There were periods when liberation seemed a long time coming, and so he had to prepare himself for a long and harsh imprisonment. There were also periods when liberation seemed more likely, and he had to prepare accordingly. Applied to crisis situations such as the pandemic, Stockdale's lesson is that leaders should maintain confidence in long-term success but acknowledge and regularly reappraise whatever are the realities of the immediate circumstances.

But how does such an "idealist without illusions" (to quote President Kennedy) cope in practice? The answer, suggest Harvard's Boris Groysberg and Robin Abrahams, is getting up and fighting each day, quoting Stockdale in *A Vietnam Experience*, by being "the persistent practitioner of endurance."[27] Stockdale continues, "The game of physical intimidation was not won or lost in one grand showdown. The hero of us all was the plucky little guy who made them start all over every day." Groysberg and Abrahams also cite the psychologist John Leach, who quoted the remarks of a shipwreck survivor who wrote during the fifteenth day on his life raft, "My mood follows the sun. The light of each day makes me optimistic that I might last another forty. But the darkness of each night makes me realize that, if any one thing goes wrong, I will not survive." As Leach puts it, once a person accepts the unwanted and hostile new circumstances as "real," the survivor "becomes someone again."[28] It is only when they reach this stage that they can help others through the process.

Part of the daily struggle involves reinventing how you cope with stress. In crisis situations, people frequently lose their intrinsic coping mechanisms, which can be understood as regular habits, such as treating yourself to a weekly lunch with your best friend, that bring predictability and comfort to your life.[29] These coping mechanisms help make you resilient to adverse events. But imagine for a moment that your best friend moves away—then that lunch is no longer possible. And in the pandemic context, in which Pandit and other hospital CMOs were working, people were deprived of many of their comforting routines. As Groysberg and Abrahams observed, "The services and businesses that facilitated our lives—childcare, dry cleaning, the coffee shop on the way to work, gyms, housecleaners—[were] shuttered or more difficult to access. Masks [had to] be found and worn and cleaned. Simple conversations require[d] managing new technologies and protocols. Even walking down the street require[d] a level of hypervigilance not required in even the most dangerous neighborhood."

My pandemic experience as director of the Oxford MPP program provided me with an illustration of the importance of creating new coping mechanisms. One of the worst privations of the lockdown was the absence of social contact. As it happened, one of the students in the cohort first affected by the pandemic in March 2020 was a computer programmer. He created an app that randomly paired people for one-on-one outside walks, the only form of social contact permitted under the rules in the UK at the time. The advantage of this meant that people just had to sign up to get a walking partner—they didn't have to take the initiative to reach out and make an individual arrangement—which created anxiety (would the invitation be accepted?) or obligation (I don't want to go on a walk with this person, but I have to). By volunteering to be put into this system, they accepted the deal. Many of the students signed up—and the walks became a central part of each participant's day and new intrinsic coping mechanism.

If, like my MPP students, a group facing a collective crisis has developed a strong sense of community—that is, it has strong relational contracts between its members—confronting the new reality can be a group effort. When the UK went into lockdown in March 2020, we were only a few days away from the course's examination period, contemplating the very real possibility that an Oxford degree program would not be able to hold examinations. Ostensibly, this is something that had not happened before in the university's nine-hundred-year history—a period that covered multiple civil wars and several deadly plagues. To figure out a way through this challenge, I took the question to the students.

I reminded them of our shared objectives for the long term but also of the need to enable people to express their doubts and fears. Because we wanted to build a community committed to public service, we had a responsibility to stakeholders—we owed it both to those who come here and work hard and to the people that we purport to serve, that the people who leave here from this program will have the quality of mind and the certification that comes from having a graduate degree at Oxford University. But we also had to accept that we faced a crisis that could easily (and even legitimately) compromise our ability to meet those obligations fairly.

The challenge facing us as members of this community was to come up with a way in which we could fairly assess people, given the circumstances, and in the understanding that while not everyone might agree with our conclusion, we could all accept it because we would have had robust conversation about it. We had this conversation on a Zoom call; there were about 130 people involved. It lasted almost four hours because everyone was very anxious and wanted to be heard. At the beginning, people took very different positions. Some said that we should suspend exams for the year completely and give everyone the degree, but others were vehemently opposed—they felt that would signal that they had not really earned their degree. Feeding into these differences was that the pandemic had not hit people equally. Some students had families and were living in lockdown, sharing a two-room apartment with a partner and two kids, while others were living alone in sprawling Victorian dorm rooms.

Eventually we reached an understanding. In a normal year, every student would have had to take four exams in a week. For this year, we required that the students took a minimum of two exams. If they wished to take three or four, they could do so, but only two graded exams were required. What we had done in that conversation was to come together as a community and recognize both that we had a critical common objective that we couldn't abandon—we had to provide a degree that was seen as genuinely earned—and that we couldn't fairly stick to our traditional process, given that we had all been differently affected by the pandemic. There were people in the program who could not achieve the results that they normally would have gotten because of how the pandemic had hit them. The agreement we reached struck us as a fair one—achieving our overall obligation to provide a degree that people could have faith in, while recognizing the effects of the extraordinary circumstances we were working in. In the end, a substantial majority of students took at least three exams, with many taking all four. The remaining students ended up taking the minimum required of two papers. Crucially, because of our robust communal discussions, students generally accepted the outcomes as legitimate.

Culture can, of course, also blind people to reality. Recall the case of the Maggi Noodles crisis in India. The situation was aggravated by Nestlé's Swiss culture, which had made the company very confident that the government's testing procedures rather than any failings on the company's part were responsible for the findings. In these situations, leaders need to administer a reality shock. Nestlé did this by replacing the local CEO as prime decision-maker with Wan Ling Martello, then senior vice president for Asia Pacific, as I describe in my case study.[30]

Martello's first act as leader was to call a town hall meeting, much like the Zoom call that I held with my MPP participants. This allowed the Nestlé team to both reaffirm its shared values and, at the same time, develop a better and shared understanding of the reality that its strategy of blaming regulators simply wasn't working. The real issue was not about whether the lab tests were fair or not but about Nestlé's relationships with Indian stakeholders—whether regulators or consumers could trust the company to do the right thing. Reflecting on takeaways, Nestlé CEO Paul Bulcke said: "The skills that are needed to manage something like this, you can't write down. You have to be in the scene and empathize with constituents, but you should also be able to step back and take perspective. What guided me through the episode . . . [was] . . . the fact that we've been in India over a hundred years now, and I want us to be in the country a hundred years from now."[31]

The town hall helped Nestlé's local managers agree on the reality of their crisis. Then, they could move from thinking that Nestlé was the greatest food company in the world and therefore could do no wrong to thinking that Nestlé was the greatest food company in the world and therefore should fix the problem. Similarly, on the Oxford MPP, the whole group agreed that Oxford should always be the preeminent school for public leadership education, adhering to the highest standards of quality and integrity, but also recognized that achieving those standards needed a different approach for different individuals from what one would expect in normal conditions.

Cultivate an Inner Strength

Do you recall the knowledge structures that I discussed in chapter 2, when addressing how to "turn down the temperature"? When we experience adverse events, we can sometimes develop *myths* about the causes of that adversity, attributing it to what we see as our structural weaknesses: in effect, the knowledge structures from our lived experiences implicitly forestall our ability to overcome the adverse events. This trap that we fall into is called "learned helplessness," a concept nicely summed up in a 2011 *Harvard Business Review* article by University of Pennsylvania psychology professor Martin Seligman.[32] For instance, being laid off from work is a profoundly traumatic event to many, which can result in seeding knowledge structures around negative self-worth, so that when such an individual subsequently experiences another challenging work environment, they attribute it to their own failings and are unable to address the challenges.

Surmounting learned helplessness involves acknowledging the erroneous logic of our knowledge structures so that people reach a more balanced sense of what they can or cannot do. Doing this usually requires external support, drawing on what experts call "active-constructive relationships." Commissioner Dick of the London Metropolitan Police noted this in a coda on her case study, in emphasizing the indispensability of "a community of trusted friends" when managing in the age of outrage. In her case, this circle consisted of people she had known for a long time and had reason to trust because she had relied on their judgment before. What's more, some of these trusted friends were not from her immediate professional world. While they might face equivalent challenges, they did not face her challenges and were, therefore, more dispassionate in analyzing and parsing the challenges the Met faced. Finally, she tended to consult the people in this circle on a confidential basis—the feedback she got was for her ears alone.

Dick's "trusted friends" are the sort of circle every leader needs to cultivate to avoid learned helplessness and maintain resilience in the face of the relentless obloquy, in Dick's case, from politicians, activists, and the media. Regardless of where one stands on whether she had the right approach to leading the Met through the age of outrage, she did maintain her own resilience and, for the most part, the confidence of her force, no mean accomplishment in the years of crisis that she had to handle.

Even as we overcome learned helplessness, resilience also entails identifying and setting aside that which you truly cannot control about an adverse situation, so as to avoid being consumed by destructive emotions. In the words of Epictetus, a Stoic from antiquity: "The chief task in life is simply this: to identify and separate matters so that I can say clearly to myself which are externals not under my control, and which have to do with the choices I actually control." And so it is that the final component of resilience comes from classical Stoicism.[33] I was drawn to this philosophy by the many protagonists in my case studies, as I noticed that successful managers in the age of outrage are often closeted or even openly practicing Stoics.[34] Admiral Stockdale himself was often cited as a Stoic.

Stoicism is often misunderstood as advocating a "diffident emotionlessness" in the face of both pleasure and pain. But to Stoics, the objective is not to deny emotions but rather to avoid pathological, destructive emotions. As with other classical Greek philosophies, the ancient Stoics held that the purpose of human life is to exemplify the cardinal virtues of justice, temperance, courage, and wisdom. They saw "good" only in actions that advanced these virtues, just as they saw "bad" in actions that detracted from them. Everything in between—actions that neither elevated nor diminished the classical virtues or circumstances that were beyond the individual's control—they called "things indifferent," and their objective was to avoid becoming consumed by the seemingly ubiquitous distractions of things indifferent, identifying and ignoring them as they presented themselves. They focused only on (a) what they could control and (b) what would add to their virtue (to be pursued) or diminish it (to be removed or avoided). Stoicism, therefore, is very much a practice in which the individual cultivates an awareness both of the self and of the environment in order to improve their virtues.

A good example of a leader taking a stoic approach to handling an ongoing conflictual situation is Chris Liddell, who served as White House deputy chief of staff in the administration of President Donald Trump and who was broadly credited for managing the eventual handover of the White House to the incoming Biden administration, quietly and safely, behind the scenes.

Regardless of one's politics, it is widely acknowledged that for its four years, the Trump administration was somewhat chaotic, largely due to its unpredictable leader. The 2020 election, which handed Joe Biden a victory, ended in extreme controversy, with Trump falsely alleging massive electoral fraud, and the formal confirmation of the result by the US Congress on January 6, 2021, being marred by a violent insurrection. In this context, it is hard to imagine that a Trump White House official could even begin to cooperate with the Biden team.

Liddell was not the stereotypical Trump official. He was one of the few senior staffers who was not a family member and yet who stayed the course of Trump's four years in office. A citizen of both the United States and New Zealand, Liddell had served as a senior executive at a number of major corporations, including a stint as CEO at Carter Holt Harvey, a leading timber and building supplies group in Australia and New Zealand, along with positions at Microsoft (CFO), International Paper (CFO), and General Motors (vice chairman, where he was credited with helping the company reemerge from bankruptcy). The offer to join the Trump team had come as a surprise to Liddell. Although he had had experience with the Mitt Romney campaign (in Romney's run against President Obama's reelection in 2012), where he had put together a transition plan in the event of Romney's victory, and was a fiscal conservative, he did not identify with Trump's specific brand of politics. But he also felt that it was an honor and a responsibility to serve in government—the choice to accept the position, therefore, was consistent with Stoic decision-making criteria. Liddell openly credits Stoicism for his decision-making.

As described in an article, "The Trump Official Who Did the Right Thing," by David Marchick, a former director of the nonpartisan Partnership for Public Service's Center for Presidential Transition, Liddell's role in effecting an orderly transition from Trump to Biden was pivotal.[35] Sorely tempted to resign in protest at various points in the closing months of Trump's presidency, including especially after January 6, Liddell worked more or less undercover, at the risk of being summarily dismissed by Trump at any time. The risks were not just professional: a Trump official seen as a "traitor" risked being personally targeted by the president's more extreme supporters, as Vice President Pence's experience on January 6 vividly illustrated.

Liddell started preparing for what he initially thought would be a Trump second term in January 2020, almost a whole year before the November elections, working with Marchick's help. Marchick pointed out early on that Liddell needed also to plan for a Trump loss. During the lead-up to the election, Liddell was able to work more or less openly, and Marchick commented that preelection transition planning was the most organized and efficient part of the White House. Throughout the process, Liddell communicated through Marchick with the Biden transition team, in order to avoid attracting the anger of Trump loyalists. Within the White House, he kept a low profile—avoiding the Oval Office in case Trump asked him what he was doing on the transition. As Chris Whipple reported in his *Vanity Fair* article on the transition, "He confided in just a few trusted colleagues: Robert O'Brien, the national security adviser; Matt Pottinger, his deputy; and Pat Cipollone, the White House counsel."[36]

After the election result, and in the wake of the January 6 insurrection, Liddell was urged by family and friends to resign. But he didn't, eventually concluding that it was his duty to ensure as effective a transition as he could deliver. As Marchick noted, "History will judge the roles of those close to Trump, and when it does, Chris should be applauded for staying. He tried to create order amid chaos and pushed for the faithful implementation of the Presidential Transition Act. He was the direct liaison with the Biden team once the formal transition began. As chaotic and dangerous as the roughly 75 days between the election and the inauguration were, I shudder to think what would have happened had Chris not been there."

Liddell's decision to remain in that highly combustible situation was motivated by a Stoic mindset. His behavior illustrates two general advantages associated with stoicism. The first is his ability to ignore "things indifferent" and focus on what was or could be in his span of control. It would have been easy for Liddell to have thrown up his hands in despair and walked away in protest. But that would only have made a bad situation worse. In Liddell's own words: "When outrage is all around you, it is hard to separate 'signal from noise'. . . . In my case the noise was the outrage around January 6th, but the signal was completing a successful transition." Importantly, Liddell's stoic mindset meant that he did not see his work on the transition as disobeying President Trump. He noted to me, "In my case, I always saw that I was serving both the president and the country. If I couldn't be true to both, then I should leave. The case for serving the country was clear—a successful transition was critical. But I also never believed I was doing something that wasn't in the interest of the president. He could contest the election results—that was a totally different issue [a 'thing indifferent' that Liddell couldn't control]—but having lost that legal case, I believed a successful transition was ultimately in his interests as well."[37]

The second advantage to Liddell's stoicism is seen in Marchick's comment on how measured and discreet Liddell was in his communications to all sides involved in the transition. This reflects what the Stoic philosopher Epictetus called a "dialectical sophistication," that is, a moderated tone and an economy of words in communication that avoids being misinterpreted. This quality reduces the likelihood of triggering or inflaming destructive emotions in the people with whom a leader must negotiate to get the job done in an age of outrage.

• • •

The organizational and personal disciplines that form this concluding step in our age of outrage framework collectively represent critical investments that a leader must make to sustain resilience. This was sorely missing in many organizations during the recent pandemic, precipitating the Great Resignation. The stoic disciplines I just described, for example, enable individuals to see past their "scripts" in aggression situations and make them less likely to trigger aversive scripts in others. The cultivation of strong relational contracts also helps individuals in a group find the common ground necessary to identify solutions and further moderates the influence of negative personal scripts. And organizations with leadership models that widely delegate decision-making will be better placed to have people in position who can deal with outrage and crisis situations. Put differently, stoic-minded leaders with strong personal support networks, working in the context of strong relational contracts, appear better placed to diffuse and manage situations of high emotion and are more likely to make better judgments on crisis matters. In an age of outrage, organizations that invest in developing such people stand a far better chance of navigating the crises they will inevitably face.

Let us conclude the book by examining what this observation means for how we should think about leadership more generally in the twenty-first century. In the following chapter, we will switch gears from the practical, problem-solving approach we have taken thus far to consider the implications of our age-of-outrage framework for what it means to be a leader.

Chapter 7

How to Lead in a Polarized World

Shortly after I came to Oxford and took over the administration of the MPP program, I became interested in "transformational leadership," and I cofounded a fellowship for very senior leaders on this phenomenon.[1] In fact, some of the protagonists we have met thus far—including President Duque of Colombia and Chris Liddell of the White House—are alumni of this fellowship. Other fellows include Phuthuma Nhleko and Afzal Abdul Rahim who, respectively, established some of the largest technology businesses in Sub-Saharan Africa and Southeast Asia. What I think all of us have in common is a sense that the conventional understanding of leadership from the last half-century needs updating for the challenges of our current age. My objective in this final part of the book is to provoke reflection on where to find the leadership instinct needed for our times. I will argue that rather than assume that it is somehow boldly ordained by some top-down vision, the leadership instinct most appropriate for the age of outrage emerges incrementally from the bottom up, as a result of active listening and deep humility, especially from those in positions of power.

Leadership as a Noble Lie

Throughout most of human history, the dominant leadership paradigm across civilizations has been one that presents the leader as a virtuous person who brings followers together in pursuit of a well-articulated and inspiring goal. In Western canon, this is a model that, like many other constructs in political philosophy, is rooted in the works of Plato, who argued in *The Republic* that for a prosperous society to emerge and be sustained, it should be led by highly educated guardians or philosopher kings.

The argument for this form of leadership is that ordinary people are not necessarily virtuous, in so far as being wise, courageous, or just, and therefore will not always make virtuous decisions. In order for society to be generally virtuous, therefore, guardrails on people's behavior and processes for justly resolving disagreements are required. The leaders charged with such responsibilities should, therefore, themselves be among the most virtuous in society.

Plato recognized that a major problem with this arrangement was one of consent. For the system to work, members of the society needed to generally agree on who the leaders should be, and his solution to this conundrum was the famous "noble lie," sometimes known as the Parable of the Metals.[2] He proposed that for a just society to work, all members had to agree or be convinced that they were born with an inherent personality, the characteristics of which were presented as metals. Some were base—iron and brass; others more noble—gold and silver. The nobler metals corresponded to the higher virtues—wisdom and courage, for instance—and the other metals to lower virtues, such as endurance.

The mix of metals in the soul determined the person's social potential—whether they should be farmers, artisans, or leaders. As the inherent personality of each individual became clear, their education and training should be adapted accordingly.

It's easy to see the faults in this deterministic narrative (see Huxley's *Brave New World*, for instance), but to be fair, Plato did concede that virtues were not necessarily inherited—a leader's child might well turn out to have a laborer's personality. And it is perhaps because he recognized that the narrative was a construct rather than a confirmable truth that he referred to it as a lie or "myth" (depending on one's reading of the original Greek).

Whatever the faults in Plato's version of it, this concept that a foundational narrative is necessary for achieving collective harmony has proved remarkably enduring, and to some extent, this is the result of the influence of that other great classical philosopher, Aristotle, Plato's pupil, who took the idea somewhat further. Aristotle took a less predestinarian view of decisions, recognizing that in a strictly deterministic world, it is impossible to praise or condemn any person's "decision" because the actor has no agency, a view that is difficult to square with value-based ethics. Roger Martin and Tony Golsby-Smith remind us that he thus made a clear distinction between the natural world in which outcomes are predetermined or inevitable ("things cannot be other than they are") and a human world in which people's choices make a difference ("things can be other than they are").[3] In the *Rhetoric*, Aristotle describes how a leader can create such a narrative by combining logos (the proponent's reasoning) with pathos (an appeal to the listener's emotions) and ethos (the narrator's authority), a construct known as the rhetorical triangle. (Readers may also note the connection of this triangle to three of the forms of power we explored in chapter 5: rational, emotive, and coercive—although, interestingly, not reciprocal power.)

But is this model—combining virtuous, strong leadership with a compelling but probably fictitious foundational narrative on which people can rally or at least agree—sustainable in our age of outrage? Even in cases where we have seen leaders in this book use narratives to deliver on their objectives (e.g., Duque of Colombia or Pandit of OUH), these have not been Aristotelian clarion calls, but rather circumscribed, action-led efforts that draw and build on reciprocal power of the relational kind. And so, if it is not the classical philosopher king with his noble lie that will lead us through the age of outrage, what alternative model might we put in its place?

To answer these questions, I'll begin by looking at the noble lies or
foundation myths that have underpinned the growth and prosperity
of two important, and very different, democracies: the United States
and Turkey. I'll identify the inherent contradictions embedded in
these narratives and show how the phenomena (the outrage drivers)
I identified in chapter 1 are destructively laying these contradictions
bare. As these narratives collapse, charismatic leaders are taking the
opportunity to advance exclusionary agendas that appeal to specific
groups and interests, but that limit many others, reinforcing a sense of
division and contributing to social fragmentation.

I'll then describe an alternative model of leadership that also has as
long a history in some respects and argue that, in combination with
the management system I have been describing, it may offer a surer
pathway to organizational and social stability than searching for a
new noble lie. Let's begin by examining one of the most compelling
and powerful noble lies of modern times.

The noble myth of American exceptionalism

The American founding fathers, notably Thomas Jefferson, were
deeply motivated by the ancient Greeks. Jefferson, the intellectual
driver of the country's founding myth, created the narrative that
underlies the American identity, which is that in contrast to all other
nations before it—except perhaps Classical Athens—the United States
is a nation defined by a set of republican ideals rather than a common
heritage, ethnicity, or the power of a ruling elite or monarch. The
justification for seceding from the British monarchy was founded on
three basic axioms. The key extract from the Declaration of Independence is worth considering in full:[4]

> We hold these truths to be self-evident, that all men are cre-
> ated equal, that they are endowed by their Creator with certain
> unalienable Rights, that among these are Life, Liberty and the
> pursuit of Happiness.—That to secure these rights, Governments
> are instituted among Men, deriving their just powers from the

consent of the governed, —That whenever any Form of Government becomes destructive of these ends, it is the Right of the People to alter or to abolish it, and to institute new Government, laying its foundation on such principles and organizing its powers in such form, as to them shall seem most likely to effect their Safety and Happiness. Prudence, indeed, will dictate that Governments long established should not be changed for light and transient causes; and accordingly all experience hath shewn, that mankind are more disposed to suffer, while evils are sufferable, than to right themselves by abolishing the forms to which they are accustomed. But when a long train of abuses and usurpations, pursuing invariably the same Object evinces a design to reduce them under absolute Despotism, it is their right, it is their duty, to throw off such Government, and to provide new Guards for their future security.

My reading of this preamble is that Jefferson was embarking on the creation of a noble lie, the elegant, logical structuring of his argument reflecting the philosopher he was. But the self-evidence of the first and most fundamental claim would have been questionable even at that time. Thomas Jefferson himself was a not inconsiderable slave-owner, and the hypocrisy of basing the American revolution on the rights of man when so much of its prosperity—like that of Classical Athens—was based on the institution of slavery has haunted the legitimacy of the myth to the present day, a point I'll be coming to shortly.

But it is important to realize the purpose of Jefferson's declaration—which was to provide a justification for independence—a narrative that would rally and motivate the colonists of all the thirteen original states to break with the British monarchy, an institution that still commanded the loyalty of many on the American shores. The narrative around justice and freedom performed that function—appealing to (and stoking) the sense of colonists everywhere that they were being abused and exploited by the British government. It is significant that Jefferson singled out the British king as his target—even though he would undoubtedly have known that the king's power in Britain, even in the eighteenth century, was limited (so he is here creating another fiction). But to paint the king as a classical tyrant preventing the citizens from enjoying their inalienable rights was a compelling message and provided colonists with a clearly identifiable common enemy. Just like Plato's parable of the metals, Jefferson's story was full of holes. And equally like Plato, Jefferson, ostensibly, could think of no better way to motivate America's colonists to break away from Britain than to create a fiction that they would all buy into.

Although an idealized fiction, Jefferson's narrative has deeply informed the creation and evolution of the US Constitution, which sets out how the country's guardians will be chosen and establishes the limits in which they will operate. Jefferson saw government essentially as an act of delegation by citizens to other citizens that they judged capable and wise to regulate the country's economy, defense, relations with other countries, and disputes, within a set of hard-to-change guardrails that limited the leaders' ability to abuse their delegated powers. The constitution identifies the basic inalienable rights, the basic offices of government, and the means of selecting government.

In so many ways, Jefferson's achievement was remarkable. The society his narrative has helped to create has been, in many respects, a model for the world of economic and social progress—a "City Upon a Hill." The principles of Jefferson's declaration, and the constitution that embodies them, empowered the entrepreneurialism that characterizes the US economy, and which has remained at the core of the US identity for most of its history: that any person can come to America and thrive if they have the will and wit to work hard and well—the idea known as the American Dream. It was that idea that attracted generations of immigrants from Europe during America's first century to make this new world their home, because the opportunities that America's openness provided were far greater than what could be found in a Europe governed by monarchies and elites exploiting tribal differences in pursuit of greater power for those elites.

To be sure, the countries of nineteenth-century Europe were economically dynamic too—the Industrial Revolution started there—but the primary beneficiaries of Europe's economic transformation were people who had inherited their wealth. And while jobs in manufacturing represented an alternative to rural poverty and starvation, most people moving to work in the mills and mines simply found themselves trapped in a different poverty. Unsurprisingly they found the American Dream a compelling proposition—and although few people might have fully realized the dream, enough did for the dream to remain a realistic aspiration.

In many ways, you could argue that Jefferson's America was the poster child for the Enlightenment spirit that he embodied. The Enlightenment was of course a European movement, and one particularly espoused by the newly emerging bourgeois classes whose wealth derived from commerce. Underpinning the movement was the idea that the world was knowable through philosophical and scientific inquiry—the more you knew, the better you became (more virtuous in the classical sense). This idea, once again, is by no means a self-evident truth, attractive though it may be as a motivation. There are many important aspects of life that were not knowable then and still are not. More to the point, as the famous Austrian philosopher and mathematician Kurt Gödel formally demonstrated in his incompleteness theorems, formal knowledge never can be complete, which makes the Enlightenment itself a noble lie, and an intuitive understanding of the limits of formal knowledge led, in time, to the rise of Romanticism.

Nevertheless, the movement fueled economic progress and encouraged a culture of meritocracy, and it is not surprising, therefore, that it led people to question the social order, which was seen as obstructing individuals' right to improve themselves. Indeed, the French Revolution that followed the American was also led by people who espoused many of the same values as the American Founding Fathers. But the French experiment turned out very differently, reflecting important contextual differences. In France, the revolution completely toppled those institutions and elites that were seen by the revolution's Enlightenment leaders as the "other." But this success threatened the security of the kingdoms and empires surrounding France, which fueled conflict and ultimately led to the creation of a militaristic imperial regime dominated by France's most successful general, Napoleon Bonaparte.

In contrast, America's revolution did not pose an existential threat to the institutions of British government nor the elites that dominated it. And as Britain started counting the costs of maintaining its rule in America, it soon found richer imperial opportunities elsewhere in the East and, in reasonably short order, became embroiled in what was arguably one of the first global wars with the new Napoleonic France. The newly independent citizens of the United States were left to explore and develop the vast resources of their huge continent-nation.

That, at any rate, is one version of the story. But the lies behind the noble myth provide the potential for a very different reading of US history. The first and most obvious problem is slavery, sometimes described as America's original sin. The contradiction of a state politically founded on the rights of man relying heavily on the institution of slavery to deliver prosperity led to an inevitable confrontation between the abolitionist northern states, gradually emerging as a global manufacturing powerhouse, and the agrarian pro-slavery southern states. In some respects, this struggle mirrored the contest taking place in Europe from the late eighteenth century between supporters of the traditional *Ancien Régime* (the monarchy, clergy, and nobility) and a middle class growing on the back of an industrial revolution. The rivalry between the two camps in the United States led, ultimately, to the bloody conflict of the American Civil War.

The rights of individuals won that struggle, but the conflict has remained unresolved and continues to flare up in the United States. And, moreover, the rights of individuals did not prevail in the other conflicts defining the birth and growth of America. As the country expanded, white Americans progressively occupied more and more territories that had largely been annexed by force from the people already there: native Americans. The insatiable appetite of the new republic for land, much like its mother country across the sea, meant the continued dispossessing of Indigenous populations, through war, through disease, and through disruption of their way of life. The equal right of men (and, only latterly, women) to life, liberty, and the pursuit of happiness did not, it seem, apply to the peoples labeled, derogatively, as "Red Indians."

Slavery and the genocide of native populations present a narrative of American exceptionalism that stands in sharp contrast to the high school stories celebrating the exploits of American pioneers such as Meriwether Lewis and William Clark, who explored the territories acquired by the United States in the Louisiana Purchase of 1803 on a commission from the third US President, one Thomas Jefferson.

What emerges from this analysis is that one of the defining noble myths of the modern period was founded, on the one hand, on principles that were, at best, selectively applied and at worst, deliberately false and, on the other hand, by the identification of "others" who served to supply, at best, a resource to be exploited and, at worst, a common enemy to a self-identified group of people engaged in the project of building their own nation. Although the flawed narrative has contributed greatly to the development of the modern United States, that development has come at great cost to the people who have, at various points of the country's history, been deemed not to count as human, let alone as members of a republic founded on the inalienable human rights.[5]

Sadly, that conclusion can be reached for almost any foundational narrative in human history, suggesting that practical applications of the Platonic ideal of the noble lie are ultimately doomed to fail. Let's look at another example.

Turkey's modern state

It's often sobering to realize that many readers today had grandparents who lived at a time when a dowager empress ruled China, Nicolas II was tsar of all the Russias, and a sultan known as Abdul the Damned resided in the Topkapi Palace in Istanbul. Absolute monarchy was still seen as a legitimate system of government little more than a century ago, and many countries still retain the vestiges of these regimes, including many liberal democracies in Europe: Britain, Spain, and the Netherlands among them, along with Denmark, Sweden, and Norway.

In general, the difference between countries that retain a monarchy and those who don't is largely down to whether the country in question has gradually evolved a democratic system to limit the monarchy or whether the monarchy was suddenly and forcibly deposed. In China, Russia, and Turkey, the transition was achieved rapidly, through a revolution, each of which came with its own founding narrative. One of the most interesting of these new narratives is that of Turkey.

Although the process of liberalization in the Ottoman Empire started as early as 1839, with the Edict of Gülhane, "new" Turkey was largely the product of one man's vision. This is in contrast to America, which was a collective effort: the principal intellectual contributor to the American myth, Thomas Jefferson, was not the undisputed leader of the country's revolution, and many of his views were widely contested by rivals who at times prevailed. Mustafa Kemal Atatürk, however, effectively stood alone in his moment.[6] Born in modern-day Thessaloniki, he had been one of the Ottoman Empire's most successful military leaders, largely responsible for the defeat of the Allied forces in the Gallipoli campaign. After the eventual Allied victory in World War I, the central Ottoman territory that makes up modern-day Turkey went through a period of violence and revolution, with the dominant ethnic Turkic groups turning against minorities, notably the Armenians in Anatolia and the Greek communities on the Mediterranean coast. During this period, Atatürk led the Turkish national movement, which successfully resisted an attempt by Allied powers—operating largely through ethnic Greek and Armenian movements—to partition the country. He established a new government in the present-day Turkish capital of Ankara and formally abolished the Ottoman Empire, dethroning the last sultan, and proclaimed a Turkish republic in its place.

Atatürk had a vision of the new Turkey as a modern, secular nation-state, in contrast to the multinational Ottoman caliphate that it replaced. It would be peopled by an educated citizenry that pursued economic and social progress, and the goal was to create a nation that could compete on level terms with modern European economies. It was also to be primarily a Turkish republic—Atatürk had been part of a movement that looked in particular to Germany for inspiration as to what a modern state should resemble. His experience as a soldier had also reinforced his belief in technology and strong leadership, and he wanted to free the new Turkey from what he saw as the dead hand of religious conservatism. This ethnic, secular nationalism was very much a feature of politics in late nineteenth- and early twentieth-century Europe and, in the aftermath of World War I, took on prominence as the multicultural Austro-Hungarian Empire—the heir of the pre-Napoleonic Holy Roman Empire—was dismantled, on the grounds that distinct peoples deserved a right to self-determination.

In pursuit of this vision, Atatürk expressly founded his new nation on a set of principles, which he referred to as the six arrows, that were somewhat akin to Jefferson's basic formulation.[7] The first of these principles, *republicanism*, states that the new Turkey is a republic as opposed to a monarchy or any other sort of regime. Officially, Turkey is a relatively democratic republic, with laws passed by a popularly elected parliament of which the chief government officers would be members, and whose head of state would be an elected president with veto and similar powers. The power of governments must be limited by a constitution protecting individual rights and is subject to independent judicial review.

This all sounds very attractive, but historically the institutions of the state have not been as democratic as the constitution suggests. Atatürk served as the country's president from the republic's creation in 1923 until his death in 1938. He also made the country a one-party state during his tenure—a legal opposition emerged only twice and each time briefly, and it was not until 1945 that the country became a multiparty polity. Since then, the country has experienced three military coups (1960, 1971, and 1980), and an unsuccessfully attempted civil coup, suppressed by the current president. The political reality of Turkey clearly does not reflect what its politics should be like in theory, which legitimizes insurgents who seek to change that system.

Atatürk's following three principles were aimed at distancing the new republic from the traditions and institutions of the Ottoman Empire. The second principle of *populism* sought to ground the new republic in its citizenry. Sovereignty in the new republic was to be vested in its people, expressed through their votes. It would not rest with a divinely delegated, hereditary monarch. This was reinforced by Atatürk's third principle of *laicism*, an import from French political thought, which expressly separates state and religion. Education, in particular, was taken out of the hands of the Muslim clergy, and a national school curriculum was imposed. Laicism also took aim at eliminating religious distinctions between citizens. Under Ottoman rule, people's religious affiliations and social ranks were communicated through dress and headgear, but, under the new republic, these distinctions were banned outside places of worship. The fourth principle of *reformism* expressly conferred on the state the right to dismantle social traditions and to create new ones.

Perhaps the most contentious of Atatürk's principles is the fifth: *nationalism*. Through this principle, Atatürk sought to create a unifying national identity—a concept ultimately deriving from Rousseau's notion of the social contract.[8] According to Rousseau, a sovereign people engaged in a contract with a government to administer and steer a nation. As long as the government did not enslave the people or remove basic rights, and enjoyed the general support of the people, the government was legitimate. In Atatürk's view, for such a contract to work effectively, the sovereign people needed to have a clear sense of identity. Keenly aware of the role that ethnic and religious divisions had played in the decline of the Ottoman Empire, Atatürk sought to create a new shared identity for his new republic: they would all be Turkish, and this was defined by "the natural and historical facts which effected the establishment of the Turkish nation," which were "(a) unity in political existence, (b) unity in language, (c) unity in homeland, (d) unity in race and origin, (e) to be historically related and (f) to be morally related."[9]

Officially, none of this meant that a Turkish citizen had to be an ethnic Turk, and it is far from clear that Atatürk himself conflated the two. But he was certainly no supporter of other ethnic identities in the public sphere: "Within the political and social unity of today's Turkish nation, there are citizens and co-nationals who have been incited to think of themselves as Kurds, Circassians, Laz, or Bosnians. But these erroneous appellations—the product of past periods of tyranny—have brought nothing but sorrow to individual members of the nation."[10] Atatürk's position may have been an attempt to have his cake and eat it. He recognized that ethnicity is a major element in cultural identity, and his concept of Turkishness meant that he could keep an ethnic connection while offering a way in for non-ethnic citizens.

Whatever Atatürk's own position, many of his supporters did conflate civil and ethnic identities, and the modern Turkish state was forged largely in the fires of ethnic conflict between Muslim Turks and the Christian Greek and Armenian minorities. The new capital of Turkey was moved from historic Istanbul, the seat of Ottoman rule for centuries, to a small city in central Anatolia, the Turkic homeland, modern-day Ankara. And although Atatürk was himself born in modern-day Greece, it is worth observing that some biographers trace his ancestors to Turkic Anatolia. Indeed, the principle of nationalism is arguably Turkey's equivalent of America's original sin, and its ramifications continue to fester, most notably in the relationship between the state and Turkey's Kurdish and other minorities.

Atatürk's final principle, *statism*, essentially positions the state as a major economic agent, regulating business activities and investing directly where private enterprise was unwilling or unable to get involved—notably in large infrastructure projects or the development of heavy industries such as coal and steel. Atatürk himself supported private enterprise and encouraged equity participation in state-owned enterprises. The motivation behind this principle was twofold. The country needed large-scale investment to get back on its feet, and Atatürk's modernizing agenda needed the mobilization of capital and resources to invest in infrastructure and manufacturing industries that could make the new Turkey economically self-reliant.

Atatürk's exercise in nation-building a century ago was an impressive achievement for any time period—the Turkey he created out of the rubble of the Ottoman Empire remains an enviable society for much of the world today. And in many ways, Atatürk exemplifies an Aristotelian model of leadership, someone who creates a new reality that was not a determined outcome through the application of logos, pathos, and ethos—force of argument, emotional appeal, and personal authority.

But, as I have already argued, many of the new nation's founding principles rang hollow from the start; the supposed liberal democracy was also a one-party state for most of its existence, and it was led, almost dictatorially, by its founding father for the first fifteen years of its existence. Politics since the introduction of a multiparty system have been punctuated by military coups, usually motivated, paradoxically, by fears on the part of the army about the growing popularity of religious conservatism. The problem with this dynamic, of course, is that each military intervention in the workings of Turkish democracy only serves to undermine the principle of republicanism itself—how self-evident is the proposition that Turkey is a democratic republic when the military intervenes to protect the democracy from the (conservative religious) will of its people? This contradiction is aggravated by the inherent othering that is built into the remaining central propositions, which appear to deliberately exclude religion from public life and appear to present identification with non-Turkic ethnicities (and faiths) as illegitimate. Like Jefferson's narrative of America, and in very similar ways, Turkey's foundation myth contains contradictions and tensions that may ultimately prove its undoing.

Certainly, Turkey is, like America, in the eye of the perfect storm of outrage drivers that I described in the first chapter. In common with the rest of the world, Turkish citizens face the prospect of reduced economic growth, the environmental consequences of a warming planet, and the threat to jobs posed by technology. They also feel a sense of exclusion from economic gains, justified by the fact that Turkey's income is highly concentrated. Over 47 percent of household income is concentrated in the highest-earning fifth of households—a number that more closely resembles Sub-Saharan Africa than Europe or the United States.[11] What's more, this proportion is only slightly less than it was forty-five years ago, so it is reasonable enough for Turkish citizens to suspect that they are getting a raw deal. Added to this, they have experienced multiple rebuffs in their attempts to join the European Union, ironically largely out of European concerns for Turkey's Muslimness. But it is the third driver of outrage that is especially salient in Turkey's case: ideologies of othering.

The Turkish state, as I suggested earlier, was founded on a rejection of the idea that religion had an important role in public life. Atatürk saw it as the enemy of progress but recognized that it played a large role in personal identity, which was why he tried to create a new national identity in his founding principles. But the embrace of a secular identity was never completed. Ethnic Turks seemed to somehow be more equal than others, as many Kurds would testify. Adding fuel to these existing fires are the migrations resulting from conflicts in Iraq and Syria, which have introduced new "others." Meanwhile Atatürk's rejection of religion as a driver of public policy has itself been thrown into reverse. This is perhaps best reflected in the electoral appeal of Turkey's current president, Recep Tayyip Erdoğan, who has spent over two decades occupying some of the nation's highest offices.

In some ways, Erdoğan cannot be more different from Atatürk— where Atatürk was motivated by building secular institutions that would last well beyond his lifetime, Erdoğan's governance approaches are more rooted in traditional values. Whereas Atatürk established Turkey's first democratic political party, Erdoğan was famously quoted as saying: "Democracy is like a tram. You ride it until you arrive at your destination, then you step off."[12] But, seen another way, Erdoğan, who hails from a religiously conservative tradition, is a version of Atatürk, forged for this age of outrage—a charismatic leader preaching a new gospel, this time presenting traditional values as an antidote to a secular Turkey's woes. Although Erdoğan did borrow from and extend on Atatürk's playbook, especially in economic and foreign policies in his first years in power, he departed from Atatürk's belief that religious conservatism is the source of a country's backwardness. To the contrary, the Freedom and Justice party he founded aligns itself with Muslim values, though it does not explicitly press a religious agenda. (Erdoğan himself was briefly imprisoned and banned from politics for "inciting religious hatred after reciting a poem" comparing "mosques to barracks and the faithful to an army."[13]) By appealing to religious conservatives, the new party and its leader have gained consistent support from about 50 percent of voters, with the remainder largely splintered between secularists and ethnic minorities. Erdoğan has exploited his positional power to pursue an increasingly personality-driven style of governance, one that pedestals him as the strongman savior of his country, much as Atatürk did himself, but one with new narratives of exclusion.

Toward a Radical Moderation of Leadership in an Age of Outrage

To me, the conflicted stories of America and Turkey illustrate the limitations of the traditional Platonic community-building narrative and the Aristotelian leadership model. The conclusion I draw from this analysis is that we should perhaps try a fundamentally different approach, one that is better suited to the fragmented, angry postmodern context in which we live, and I submit that the system outlined in this book points the way to such an approach, one more suited to what is increasingly being recognized as a post–truth society in which ideas and even facts are subjectively determined.

This relativism is not entirely new. Thinkers and writers have long been skeptical of the kinds of absolutes in which politicians, in particular, are prone to dealing. The Irish poet William Butler Yeats, for example, observed that "the best lack all conviction, while the worst/ Are filled with a passionate intensity."[14] And, as the forces that we have considered in chapter 1 unfold, the conflict of narratives is only intensifying, with each person or group clinging more strongly to their own. A popular talk show host invites a disaffected duchess to share "your truth." A president of the United States claims, in defiance of photographic evidence to the contrary, that his inauguration was better attended than his predecessor's. In this environment, it is hard to imagine that the traditional model for leading large but increasingly diverse social communities—the heroic leader and noble lie—is any longer workable for achieving social harmony and collective progress at scale. The flaws that seem inherent in the kinds of foundation myths that the model requires are intensified in an age of outrage, and their sustainability is compromised, as new protagonists—from the alternative right and from the left-wing woke movement—exploit the contradictions and seek to replace hitherto established truths with their and their followers' truths. If Meghan Markle can have her truth, why can Donald Trump not have his, and vice versa?[15] And, in light of the violence and othering in which the Founding Fathers indulged, criticism by establishmentarians of these disruptive outsider tactics rings hollow.

Given the vastly more complicated relationship we seem to be having with truth, the system I have laid out in this book may offer a more suitable model for leadership. It replaces the classical model of establishing and proselytizing agreed truths with an incremental, bottom-up process for negotiating consensus across scripts. As such, it acknowledges rather than challenges the validity of narratives that may reflect people's lived experiences. It leads protagonists to agreements that enable multiple perspectives to coexist, at least in the near term until more enduring understandings of reality can emerge.

To the extent leaders using such a system engage in narratives to drive outcomes, they do so via their own actions, not via rhetoric. And, perhaps most importantly, such an approach reduces the potential for othering (and therefore violence).

As I have described throughout the book, one feature of this approach is that it is never complete. It does not seek to produce a specific set of hard-to-change principles as an outcome. The only principles involved are norms of engagement—any agreement negotiated through engagement may be renegotiated through more engagement—enabling an organization or community to adapt to changing environments. It's an approach that may also have promise at a societal and even a global level. It is perhaps not a coincidence that countries that have an approach most like this one—in which nearly all government is provided by carefully negotiated and renegotiated coalitions, such as those in Scandinavia—are also known for their relative social stability.

For the system to work, however, we need to recalibrate our idea of effective leadership, in particular to demand a quality that few leaders traditionally regarded as successful typically exhibit, and one about which we may have mixed feelings. The type of leadership I am talking about here is not a new—certainly not to students of leadership. The author Jim Collins, for example, has advanced a theory that, in general, the most sustainable type of leadership is what he calls "Level Five Leadership," described in a *Harvard Business Review* article.[16] It is the presence of Level Five leaders that makes the difference between good and great organizations.

Collins's theory of leadership rests on a hierarchy of capabilities, in which the quality of leadership is defined by the person's abilities. The basic ability (Level 1) expected of any leader is personal competence. Leadership skills improve, however, if the manager can work in a team (Level 2). The next step up is the ability to organize and direct a team toward a common goal (Level 3, the competent manager). Then, in addition to these previous capabilities, an effective leader (Level 4) "catalyzes vigorous pursuit of a clear and compelling vision

. . . [and] . . . stimulates the group to high performance standards." At the top of this hierarchy, however, is the Level 5 executive, whose distinguishing quality is "a paradoxical combination of personal humility plus professional will."

In many respects, the Collins model is broadly consistent with Daniel Goleman's theory (which also has five components of leadership): that leaders excel through their emotional skills. The ability to be personally competent, to work in and organize teams, through to motivating them in a common goal would all require the kind of emotional skills that Goleman describes: self-awareness, empathy for others, self-motivation, the ability to inspire others, and, crucially, self-restraint—the five components of emotional intelligence.[17] Goleman's psychology-based theory has also been hugely important in the field of business leadership and has helped structure many leadership-development programs.

This brings me to what I find particularly interesting in both Jim Collins's and Daniel Goleman's models, which is that a differentiating feature of great leaders ("humility" and "self-restraint," respectively) is closely related to "temperance," which is one of the four classical Greek virtues (the others being wisdom, justice, and courage). Personal competence and the ability to read and motivate people to a clear and compelling goal are important qualities in a leader. But the fact that Collins and Goleman both eventually prize a version of temperance is especially noteworthy for this age of outrage. This is a skill that requires leaders to know when to hold back from advancing their *own* goals and principles.

Of course, the idea that temperance is a necessary characteristic of great leadership long predates Jim Collins and Daniel Goleman. Even Plato and Aristotle would have agreed that a leader should be temperate. And indeed, "humility" is a virtue in many established religions, including Christianity and Islam. But perhaps the most poetic exemplar of the need for temperance in leadership can be found in one of William Shakespeare's lesser-known plays, which is nevertheless one of my favorites for a class on leadership development.

Coriolanus and the perils of intemperance

Coriolanus tells the apocryphal story of the scion of a grand patrician family in the early Roman Republic.[18] The protagonist, so named for his exemplary victory on behalf of Rome against the nearby city of Corioli, is feted by peers for his unwavering courage and his commitment to unvarnished truthfulness. To them, his status as a war hero all but guarantees him the republic's top job: the consulship of Rome.

But among Rome's plebeians, Coriolanus has a different reputation: one of a senator who sought to deny them subsidized imported grain during a famine. His decision in that matter was not wholly arbitrary: he was motivated by his observation that the famine itself was due to the plebeians striking from farmwork in protest of the wealth of the ruling class. Their protest should not go unpunished, he reckoned, so he insisted that they work for the imported grain for which his fellow nobles had paid. His position on this issue then risks derailing the campaign to elect him consul. He is urged by his fellow patricians to soften his stance on the grain, but he proudly refuses to do so (begging the pardon of his peers) and argues that the long-term cost of yielding to the plebeians outweighs any short-term gain:[19]

> "Now, as I live, I will. My nobler friends,
> I crave their pardons:
> For the mutable, rank-scented many, let them
> Regard me as I do not flatter, and
> Therein behold themselves: I say again,
> In soothing them, we nourish 'gainst our senate
> The cockle of rebellion . . . "

Coriolanus's hard stand eventually enables his plebeian enemies to force him into exile. Angered at this insult to his dignity, he forges an alliance with Rome's enemies, the Volscii, whom he had so resoundingly defeated at Corioli, and leads their army to take Rome. He is only dissuaded from taking his homeland city by force through the intercession of his mother, who convinces him to broker a peace treaty between Rome and the Volscians. But the Volscian leaders he had approached for support in his campaign on Rome conspire to have him assassinated in retribution for failing to deliver on his promise to lead them to victory against the Eternal City.

In classical Greek tragedy, a hero's downfall is usually the result of "hamartia" or error, a concept discussed most famously by Aristotle in his *Poetics*.[20] The term is broad, encompassing errors of judgment, errors arising from ignorance, or errors triggered by character flaws. In *Coriolanus*, which in some ways is the most classical of Shakespeare's tragedies, both in terms of content and in terms of its writing, I would argue that the hero's "error" stems from his lack of that cardinal classical virtue for this age of outrage, as shown in his *intemperate* reaction to opposition from the plebeians and to his consequent exile.

If you describe Coriolanus's personality in terms of the classical virtues, it is evident that he has the courage of his convictions; he will fight for what he believes to be right. He also displays an analytical wisdom, in that he considers the longer-term social costs of the plebeians' protest of patrician wealth, and he is just in that he makes reasoned arguments for the rights of those who have paid for the grain—he does not reach a conclusion purely on his own emotions. And, in terms of classical virtues, in an aristocratic society like Rome or Tudor England, a leader's belief in his innate superiority would not be regarded as biased, but rather as the natural order. What Coriolanus does manifestly lack though is temperance: he holds to his convictions to the point of hubris or overweening pride. He is not willing to stand down until his mother convinces him to do so, by reminding him that the offense to his personal virtue should not blind him to his obligation to country and family. The price he eventually pays for his lack of temperance is his own death at the hands of the Volscians. Had he been willing to forge a consensus with the plebeian leaders in the first place, he would not have needed to leave Rome, and even if he had been exiled, a man with a more temperate personality would not have been so offended by the plebeians' reaction that he would conspire with Rome's mortal enemies.

How to Lead in a Polarized World

This cautionary tale brings me back to my earlier discussion of the Stoics, in the previous chapter. I argued there that stoicism provided a valuable mindset for leaders experiencing adversity. To be stoic, in fact, is almost synonymous with being resilient. In common with most classical schools of thought, Stoics are virtue ethicists—they believe in cultivating the cardinal virtues and to applying them in making decisions. So far, this is consistent with Coriolanus's philosophy. But where Coriolanus seeks to bring the world in line with his virtues, stoics accept that there are people and outcomes that they cannot fully control or change, and they accept, in general, that they must live with that as best they can, making decisions that necessarily involve accommodating to unchangeable realities. As Epictetus explained, a virtuous stoic will be "sick and yet happy, in peril and yet happy, dying and yet happy, in exile and happy, in disgrace and happy."[21] It is because stoics understand that they cannot control everything that they make resilient leaders. And it is when leaders are resilient that they can really have sustainable impact.

Of course, the boundary between what a leader can or cannot change will vary—one can be too accommodating as well as too inflexible in actions and decisions—but what I believe you can conclude about leadership from the story of Coriolanus is this: a leader must temper their personal convictions if the pursuit of those convictions places a strain on the leader's obligations to those for whom they lead. Why? Because, as Jan Potačka summarizes Socrates, the privilege of leadership is that it is "better to undergo injustice than to commit it."[22] Or, as one of my more-radical activist MPP students said to me when she was elected class representative, "I suppose I must act differently now."

I must stress that temperance is not the same as compromise. A compromise is a deal, a decision to abandon a prior belief in order to attain a goal. Temperance, in contrast, does not imply a shift in beliefs but rather a willingness to create space for other beliefs to coexist and for new shared beliefs to emerge. Temperance, therefore, is not a decision, as compromise is; rather, it is a state of mind that allows a leader to entertain even strong beliefs while accepting that fulfilling those beliefs is not always within the leader's gift. Indeed, holding well-defined beliefs is often an important quality for becoming a leader because leaders who are not perceived as having clear convictions are often distrusted. President Bill Clinton, for example, was often seen as an opportunist, and this sometimes made it difficult for other politicians and many voters to trust him. Tempering a belief is not the same as giving it up. No one has ever suggested that Nelson Mandela or Yitzhak Rabin lacked convictions. Yet they were critically able at the right moment to temper the beliefs of a lifetime in order to move their communities to a better place.

Many constituencies are touched by a leader's decisions. Some of these constituencies are aligned with the leader's beliefs and others are not. If you only want to lead those who are already aligned with your beliefs, you do not need the virtue of temperance. That may work for a time—as it did for Coriolanus—but you will inevitably find that a lack of temperance will lead to conflict, and in our modern, post-truth world, the road there will be short. Temperance, in other words, is the virtue that makes leadership work in the age of outrage.

For an example of a leader who was able to make space for beliefs other than her own, let me go back to a case study I introduced at the end of the first chapter. Maria Helena Guimarães de Castro, executive secretary at the Ministry of Education in Brazil, was the leader of the working group charged with drafting the national core curriculum when it faced its existential threat from the Evangelical Caucus. A sociologist, teacher, and professor of political science, with a distinguished career in education policy spanning several decades,

Castro was a member of one of Brazil's largest political parties, the liberal Brazilian Social Democratic Party (PSDB). During the last PSDB administration (of President Fernando Henrique Cardoso, 1995–2002), Castro had worked in the Ministry of Education as the president of the National Institute of Educational Studies and Research, as well as briefly as interim minister in 2001. She had also been involved in local education administration, having served as municipal secretary of education in Campinas, as well as state secretary of education in both the Federal District and São Paulo. A committed advocate of curriculum standards, Castro had worked to implement a common curriculum for the entire state network in São Paulo, one of the largest school systems in the whole of Latin America, serving millions of students.[23]

The process for coming up with the nationwide core curriculum had been protracted. It had kicked off in 2013, as I described in chapter 2, as a series of discussions hosted at Yale University and including, among others, Education Ministry officials and representatives of the teachers unions. As a result of those meetings, a multistakeholder working group, considered to be broadly representative of the various strands of national opinion, was tasked to produce the common core. All parties to the group committed to abide by whatever draft they approved, which meant that the draft presented to the National Council of Education, after rounds of public and legislative input, would be the promulgated draft. Unsurprisingly, discussions and negotiations were intense. A first working draft was submitted for political review in 2015, and a second in 2016, before the group settled on a final draft in 2017. During this time frame, the country confronted two presidential impeachments, one of which was successful, further straining relationships within the working group. In fact, Castro herself had assumed the group's top role in 2016, as part of administration changes after President Rousseff was removed from office and replaced by President Temer.

Throughout all this, Castro and her leadership predecessors successfully managed negotiations and accommodations across the stakeholders to engineer drafts that all members of the diverse group agreed made space for their views. Castro would not have succeeded in this task had she not gone into it with an acceptance that some of her own long-held beliefs and ideals would have to be tempered to make room for those of other people. At the same time, none of the stakeholders could be in any doubt about her commitment to nation-wide education reform, given her decades of commitment to that cause and her achievements in pursuit of it.

As I have described earlier, at the zero hour, the newly empow-ered cross-party Evangelical Caucus of Brazil's Congress had threatened to derail the entire reform unless clauses relating to the protection of gender identity and sexuality were removed. In the face of this definitive threat to years of work, Castro took it upon herself—exercising her prerogative as the group leader—to remove the clauses from the draft, thereby preserving the reform. She did not undertake this lightly, describing it as one of the hardest judg-ment calls of her career. The clauses in question had been agreed to in the process. And, as a fully paid-up member of the teaching and learning community, she herself was a staunch supporter of embed-ding the principles of nondiscrimination in the classroom. "As far back as 2009, when I was in São Paulo, we had allowed students to use pronouns and given names of their choice, regardless of [legal] gender," she said to me.[24] While with the São Paulo schools, she had also criticized the "pedagogical fragmentation" that she witnessed there, which had largely resulted, in her view, on the one hand from attempts in rural communities to make school curricula reflect tradi-tional Catholic values at the expense of critical thinking, and on the other from the desire of liberal-minded teachers in urban commu-nities to advance progressive values. Her ambition in supporting this reform was to create an enlightened and globally competitive society that did not allow social exclusion on grounds of race, gender, or sexual orientation.

Yet she also recognized that her allies were not the only stakehold-ers in education reform. Given the increased power of the Evangelical lobby and the number of people who shared its views, space needed to be made for their beliefs, even if that meant tempering some of her own. She recognized, of course, that she would draw friendly fire for this decision. "What made this decision difficult: my own group—the group behind the writing of the reforms—was very angry about it," she noted. The immediate reaction of the left-leaning teachers union was also sharply critical of her decision. The teachers were already outraged by what they saw as the illegitimate impeachment of the left-wing President Rousseff, and with this decision, they were now furious, Castro told me. But she understood—as Socrates had counseled—that it was better that she suffer the injustice of their accusations of betrayal than that she commit the greater injustice of sinking the education reform that Brazil so badly needed and which would—still despite the excision of the specific clauses—advance a greater good. This was not a leader who abandoned her beliefs; this was one who tempered them where necessary to create space for the cherished beliefs of others. The space she created would not fit any one group perfectly, but all, more or less, could live in it. She reflected: "In the document, we had to change some words, but we left some phrases that gave space for different interpretations. I think Brazilian schools understood what they could still do."[25] That, in an age of outrage, is progress, even if partial.[26]

This, I submit, is a leadership model that will work better for our divided times. In contrast to traditional leadership, what we might call *temperate leadership* does not involve the imposition of a questionable unifying narrative—a noble lie—that is built on excluding important stakeholders. Instead, it seeks to navigate across different lived realities and agendas, achieving not a final resolution but an evolving accommodation. For this reason, it is a model that is well adapted to the management system outlined in this book, which is itself rooted in our empirical-based understanding of behavioral and social dynamics. The inherent sustainability of temperate leadership is becoming an increasingly attractive quality in an increasingly unstable and conflictual political environment: we need leaders to provide stability rather than introduce yet more volatility through unyieldingness. To be sure, temperate leaders will have all the capabilities and virtues that traditional leaders have—courage, smarts, and empathy, to name a few—but they can be distinguished by this one cardinal virtue of temperance.

Or, as the late Tina Turner memorably put it: "We don't need another hero."

Coda

As I was putting the finishing touches on this book, Claudine Gay, a respected academic consensus-builder, suddenly resigned from the presidency of Harvard. Appointed less than two hundred days prior, with the expectation that she would lead America's oldest university for at least a decade, Gay's tenure was the shortest of the university's thirty leaders over nearly four hundred years. Gay's downfall was catalyzed by controversial testimony she made before the US Congress on antisemitism and free speech in academia. Her words, lawyerly and terse, were easy to interpret as unreasonable. Opponents of many types emerged swiftly, surfacing concerns about not just her leadership judgment but even her scholarly integrity, and soon she had to go. A similar fate had just months earlier befallen Bob Chapek's tenure as Disney's CEO, in the wake of the "Don't Say Gay" matter.

Alas, the age of outrage is here to stay, and leaders are on precariously thin ice as they navigate ever-narrower channels between increasingly divided and agitated polities. The playbook for leadership in this moment has to be urgently updated if we wish to avoid losing all our experienced players to outraged assaults. Indeed, the wiser ones among us may simply opt out of formal leadership roles, wary as they should be of devastating personal destruction.

We cannot, of course, afford that outcome. In the twelve months around the publication of this book, about half of the world's populations have been engaged in elections to pick their political leaders. These are the individuals who will be called to manage the moment: to address our fears for the future, the lingering resentments over past raw deals, and the growing exclusionary instincts of many who have embraced the us-versus-them mindset. Already in the context of the US elections, deepfake AI videos and pictures are being channeled through social media and other targeted platforms to confuse and potentially manipulate voters. Some of these tactics are being driven by political operatives within America often without the knowledge of the candidates themselves, some by foreign agents seeking to undermine the democratic process. Regardless, the candidates who emerge victorious from this process will have to cope with the fallout of an election that will likely be viewed by a significant segment of society as illegitimate. Then, there are the companies whose brands are being co-opted into deepfake imagery and whose platforms are (sometimes unwittingly) enabling this process: these companies and their leaders too must brace themselves for forthcoming outrage. If we are to avoid catastrophic violence in resolving the anxieties and divisions that the elections and their aftermaths will surface, our newly (re)empowered leaders will need a new approach.

That is what I hope from the framework herein. Even amid the torrent of dismay and churn, there are glimmers of successful approaches to managing in the age of outrage. The many protagonists we have encountered in this book each offer, even if in limited measure, a sense of what you can achieve simply by keeping the book's two core axioms in mind—don't try to address the whole problem, and admit and accept that you will be seen as part of the problem. With that perspective comes their sense of temperance; their equanimity that enables them to be personally resilient while also seeding it in others around them; their judicious use of reciprocal power in ways that renew it; their circumscription in what can be done, so that it is done right and sustainably; and above all, their active listening via trusted channels so that they may cut through the cacophony and nail down what really matters in a crisis.

All this is the new discipline of leadership in the age of outrage, toward which this book I hope is a clear step.

Notes

Preface

1. See, for example, Carl Quintanilla, "A Look inside the 'West Point' of Capitalism," NBC News, July 31, 2008, https://www.nbcnews.com/id/wbna25950947.

2. See, for example, Case Collection: Blavatnik School of Government, Case Centre, https://www.thecasecentre.org/caseCollection/BlavatnikSchool.

Chapter 1

1. See, for example, "Disney and Florida's Parental Rights in Education Act," Wikipedia, https://en.wikipedia.org/wiki/Disney_and_Florida%27s_Parental_Rights_in_Education_Act.

2. See, for example, "Climate Plans Remain Insufficient: More Ambitious Action Needed Now," press release, United Nations Climate Change, October 26, 2022, https://unfccc.int/news/climate-plans-remain-insufficient-more-ambitious-action-needed-now.

3. See Jacob Poushter, Moira Fagan, and Sneha Gubbala, "Climate Change Remains Top Global Threat across 19-Country Survey," Pew Research Center, August 31, 2022, https://www.pewresearch.org/global/2022/08/31/climate-change-remains-top-global-threat-across-19-country-survey/.

4. See L. Lebreton et al., "Evidence That the Great Pacific Garbage Patch Is Rapidly Accumulating Plastic," *Scientific Reports* 8 (March 22, 2018), https://www.nature.com/articles/s41598-018-22939-w.

5. See Carl Benedikt Frey et al., "Technology at Work v2.0," Citi GPS: Global Perspectives & Solutions, January 2016, https://www.oxfordmartin.ox.ac.uk/downloads/reports/Citi_GPS_Technology_Work_2.pdf.

6. See Michael Olenick and Peter Zemsky, "Can GenAI Do Strategy?," hbr.org, November 24, 2023, https://hbr.org/2023/11/can-genai-do-strategy.

7. See, for example, Michael Grothaus, "Elon Musk Says 'Humans Are Underrated' after His Robots Slow Model 3 Production," *Fast Company*, April 16, 2018, https://www.fastcompany.com/40559386/elon-musk-says-humans-are-underrated-after-his-robots-slow-model-3-production.

8. See, for example, Mike Seymour et al., "AI with a Human Face," *Harvard Business Review*, March–April 2023.

9. See, for example, "French Supermarket Workers Protest against Automated Checkout Stations," *Independent*, August 29, 2019, https://wol.iza.org/news/french-supermarket-workers-protest-against-automated-checkout-stations.

10. See, for example, Alice Gibbs, "Welcome to the First Ever McDonald's Where You're Served by Robots—in Texas," *Newsweek*, December 22, 2022, https://www.newsweek.com/first-ever-mcdonalds-served-robots-texas-1769116.

11. See, for example, "2022 Revision of World Population Prospects," United Nations, https://population.un.org/wpp/DataQuery/; and Edward Price, "By 2050, a Quarter of the World's People Will Be African—This Will Shape Our Future," *Guardian*, January 20, 2022, https://www.theguardian.com/global-development/2022/jan/20/by-2050-a-quarter-of-the-worlds-people-will-be-african-this-will-shape-our-future.

12. See, for example, "Demography Is Not Destiny," *Financial Times*, August 8, 2022, https://www.ft.com/content/e04ba005-a913-4362-8434-dae488220310.

13. See OECD, "The Future of Work: OECD Employment Outlook 2019," https://www.oecd.org/employment/Employment-Outlook-2019-Highlight-EN.pdf.

14. See Fund for Peace, "Fragile States Index Annual Report 2022," https://fragilestatesindex.org/wp-content/uploads/2022/07/22-FSI-Report-Final.pdf.

15. See, for example, Casey Bond, "Consumer Debt Just Hit a Collective $17 Trillion. Here's What to Know If You're Struggling," *Fortune Recommends*, May 16, 2023, https://fortune.com/recommends/credit-cards/consumer-debt-just-hit-a-collective-17-trillion/.

16. See Karthik Ramanna, "Should America Still Believe in Free Markets?," *American Interest*, July 6, 2020, https://www.the-american-interest.com/2020/07/06/should-america-still-believe-in-free-markets/.

17. See Anne Case and Angus Deaton, "Rising Morbidity and Mortality in Midlife among White Non-Hispanic Americans in the 21st Century," *PNAS* 112, no. 49 (2015), https://www.pnas.org/doi/10.1073/pnas.1518393112.

18. See Anne Case and Angus Deaton, "Life Expectancy in Adulthood Is Falling for Those without a BA Degree, but as Education Gaps Have Widened, Racial Gaps Have Narrowed," *PNAS* 118, no. 11 (2021), https://www.pnas.org/doi/10.1073/pnas.2024777118.

19. See, for example, Clive Crook, "Beyond Belief," *Atlantic*, October 2007, https://www.theatlantic.com/magazine/archive/2007/10/beyond-belief/306172/.

20. See İrem Güçeri, Clare Leaver, and Oenone Kubie, "Tax Reform in Colombia: A Moment for 'Greatness, Consensus and Solidarity'?," case 222-0040-1 (Oxford, UK: Blavatnik School of Government, University of Oxford, 2023), https://www.thecasecentre.org/products/view?id=185640.

21. See also, "The Clash of Civilizations," *Foreign Affairs* 72, no. 3 (1993), by the same author for the original articulation of this idea.

22. See, for example, Paul W. Farris and Eric A. Gregg, "Harley-Davidson: Building a Brand through Consumer Engagement," case UVA-M-0698 (Charlottesville, VA: Darden Business Publishing, 2002), https://www.thecasecentre.org/products/view?id=94340.

23. See, for example, David Burkus, "Why McKinsey & Company's Alumni Network Is Crucial to Its Success," *Forbes*, July 5, 2016, https://www.forbes.com/sites /davidburkus/2016/07/05/why-mckinsey-companys-alumni-network-is-crucial-to-its -success/.

24. See, for example, Amy Fleming, "Why Social Media Makes Us So Angry, and What You Can Do About It," *BBC Science Focus Magazine*, April 2, 2020, https://www .sciencefocus.com/the-human-body/why-social-media-makes-us-so-angry-and-what -you-can-do-about-it.

25. See, for example, Fernando P. Santos, Yphtach Lelkes, and Simon A. Levin, "Link Recommendation Algorithms and Dynamics of Polarization in Online Social Networks," *PNAS* 118, no. 50 (2021), https://www.pnas.org/doi/10.1073/pnas .2102141118.

26. See, for example, Greg Blackburn and Erica Scharrer, "Video Game Playing and Beliefs about Masculinity among Male and Female Emerging Adults," *Sex Roles* 80 (2019), https://doi.org/10.1007/s11199-018-0934-4.

27. See, for example, Lisa Mascaro, "GOP Torn as Greene Speaks to Far Right Amid 'Putin!' Chants," Associated Press, March 1, 2022, https://apnews.com/article /russia-ukraine-marjorie-taylor-greene-race-and-ethnicity-europe-mitch-mcconnell -6dd6985db085537fcb103c0d022ac775.

28. See Anna Petherick, Karthik Ramanna, and Oenone Kubie, "Education Reform in Brazil: An Enduring Coalition?," case 223-0075-1 (Oxford, UK: Blavatnik School of Government, University of Oxford, 2023), https://www.thecasecentre.org/products /view?id=193842.

Chapter 2

1. See, for example, https://en.wikipedia.org/wiki/Facebook%E2%80%93 Cambridge_Analytica_data_scandal.

2. See, for example, Manuela Tobias, "Comparing Facebook Data Use by Obama, Cambridge Analytica," Politifact, March 22, 2018, https://www.politifact.com /factchecks/2018/mar/22/meghan-mccain/comparing-facebook-data-use-obama -cambridge-analyt/.

3. See Craig Anderson and Brad Bushman, "Human Aggression," *Annual Review of Psychology* 53, no. 1 (2002), https://doi.org/10.1146/annurev.psych.53.100901.135231.

4. Alan Bandura's work on "moral disengagement" provides a conceptual understanding of this subject. For a managerial overview, see, for example, Sandra J. Sucher and Celia Moore, "Ethical Analysis: Moral Disengagement," Background Note 612-043 (Boston: Harvard Business School, 2011), https://www.hbs.edu/faculty/Pages/item .aspx?num=41039.

5. The ancient historian Herodotus claimed, ostensibly apocryphally, that Persians took important decisions twice—once drunk and once sober. See https://en.wikipedia .org/wiki/In_vino_veritas.

6. See, for example, Carolos Sanchis et al., "Effects of Caffeine Intake and Exercise Intensity on Executive and Arousal Vigilance," *Scientific Reports* 10, no. 8393 (2020), https://www.ncbi.nlm.nih.gov/pmc/articles/PMC7242431/.

7. See Anderson and Bushman, "Human Aggression."

8. See, for example, Anil Seth, *Being You: A New Science of Consciousness* (London: Faber and Faber, 2021).

9. See, for example, "Perception as Controlled Hallucination, a Conversation with Andy Clark," *Edge*, June 6, 2019, https://www.edge.org/conversation/andy_clark -perception-as-controlled-hallucination.

10. See Anderson and Bushman, "Human Aggression."

11. See, for example, Adam Tomison, "Intergenerational Transmission of Maltreatment," policy and practice paper, Child Family Community Australia, Australian Institute of Family Studies, June 1996, https://aifs.gov.au/resources/policy -and-practice-papers/intergenerational-transmission-maltreatment.

12. See Anna Petherick, Karthik Ramanna, and Oenone Kubie, "Education Reform in Brazil: An Enduring Coalition?," case 223-0075-1 (Oxford, UK: Blavatnik School of Government, University of Oxford, 2023), https://www.thecasecentre.org/products /view?id=193842.

13. See Petherick et al., "Education Reform in Brazil: An Enduring Coalition?"

14. See Karthik Ramanna, Thomas Simpson, and Sarah McAra, "Priscilla Ankut at the Kaduna State Peace Commission," case 423-0007-1 (Oxford, UK: Blavatnik School of Government, University of Oxford, 2023), https://www.thecasecentre.org/products /view?id=189067.

15. See, for example, Desmond Tutu, "Truth and Reconciliation Commission, South Africa," *Britannica*, December 20, 2023, https://www.britannica.com/topic /Truth-and-Reconciliation-Commission-South-Africa.

16. See, for example, https://en.wikipedia.org/wiki/Article_19.

17. See, for example, Oversight Board, "Ensuring Respect for Free Expression, through Independent Judgment," https://www.oversightboard.com; and https:// en.wikipedia.org/wiki/Oversight_Board_(Meta).

18. See https://en.wikipedia.org/wiki/Social_Science_One.

Chapter 3

1. See Christopher Stone, Karthik Ramanna, and Sarah McAra, "Stop & Search in London in the Summer of Covid," case 221-0040-1 (Oxford, UK: Blavatnik School of Government, University of Oxford, 2021), https://www.thecasecentre.org/products /view?id=178278. The descriptions that follow are quoted and paraphrased from the case study.

2. See, for example, Peter Walker and Severin Carrell, "Follow Rules to Avoid Second National Lockdown, Warns Boris Johnson," *Guardian*, July 31, 2020, https:// www.theguardian.com/world/2020/jul/31/coronavirus-boris-johnson-postpones -latest-round-of-lockdown-easing.

3. The Stephen Lawrence Inquiry: Report of an Inquiry by Sir William Macpherson of Cluny, quoted from Stone et al., "Stop & Search in London in the Summer of Covid."

4. The Stephen Lawrence Inquiry: Report of an Inquiry by Sir William Macpherson of Cluny, quoted from Stone et al., "Stop & Search in London in the Summer of Covid."

5. "Reading the Riots," *Guardian* and London School of Economics and Political Science, 2011, http://eprints.lse.ac.uk/46297/1/Reading%20the%20riots%28published%29 .pdf, quoted from Stone et al., "Stop & Search in London in the Summer of Covid."

6. Quoted and paraphrased from Stone et al., "Stop & Search in London in the Summer of Covid."

7. Quoted and paraphrased from Stone et al., "Stop & Search in London in the Summer of Covid."

8. "Inclusion and Diversity Strategy 2017–2021," Metropolitan Police Service, https://www.met.police.uk/SysSiteAssets/foi-media/metropolitan-police/policies /inclusion-strategy-2017-2021.pdf.

9. See, for example, Aaron Walawalkar, "Black Lives Matter Activists Call for Met Commissioner to Step Down," *Guardian*, September 12, 2020, https://www .theguardian.com/world/2020/sep/12/black-lives-matter-activists-call-for-met -commissioner-to-step-down.

10. Tom Ambrose, "Met Officers 'Feared Sarah Everard Vigil Had Become Anti-Police Protest,'" *Guardian*, June 7, 2022, https://www.theguardian.com/uk-news/2022 /jun/07/met-officers-feared-sarah-everard-vigil-had-become-anti-police-protest.

11. This refers to Sir Robert Peel, who was a leading British statesman between the 1820s and 1840s, serving as home secretary and later prime minister. Peel founded the Metropolitan Police and is considered the "father of modern British policing." Peel is credited with instructing the new force to remain civilian (rather than military) in nature and to always police by consent of the people. See, for example, https:// en.wikipedia.org/wiki/Robert_Peel.

12. Quoted and paraphrased from Stone et al., "Stop & Search in London in the Summer of Covid."

13. See, for example: "George Mitchell: Building Peace in Northern Ireland," United States Institute of Peace, video, 2011, https://www.usip.org/public-education -new/george-mitchell-building-peace-northern-ireland.

14. I have experimented with taking the opposite approach—getting straight to the question of what the Met commissioner should do about the outrage. In these situations, people complain about not being given space to speak about their experience.

15. See, for example, https://en.wikipedia.org/wiki/Rotherham_child_sexual _exploitation_scandal.

16. See "Details of Tax Revenue—Columbia," OECD.Stat, https://stats.oecd.org /Index.aspx?DataSetCode=LAC_REVCOL.

Chapter 4

1. See Karthik Ramanna and Radhika Kak, "The Maggi Noodle Safety Crisis in India (A)," case 116-013 (Boston: Harvard Business School, 2016), https://www.hbs .edu/faculty/Pages/item.aspx?num=50443.

2. See, for example, Simon Chapman, "The Rule of Rescue," The Conversation, March 26, 2015, https://theconversation.com/the-rule-of-rescue-39371.

3. See, for example, https://en.wikipedia.org/wiki/Noblesse_oblige.

4. In the case of the Disney situation, even if one argues that the company is not directly responsible for the blowup over "Don't Say Gay," its prior commitments as an LGBT+ friendly company behooved it to act.

5. See Richard S. Tedlow and Wendy Smith, "James Burke: A Career in American Business (A)," case 389-177 (Boston: Harvard Business School, 1989), https://www.hbs.edu/faculty/Pages/item.aspx?num=11501.

6. See Lisa Girion, "Johnson & Johnson Knew for Decades That Asbestos Lurked in Its Baby Powder," Reuters, December 14, 2018, https://www.reuters.com/investigates/special-report/johnsonandjohnson-cancer/; and https://en.wikipedia.org/wiki/Johnson_%26_Johnson.

7. See, for example, Kenya Evelyn, "Amazon Fires New York Worker Who Led Strike over Coronavirus Concerns," Guardian, March 31, 2020, https://www.theguardian.com/us-news/2020/mar/31/amazon-strike-worker-fired-organizing-walkout-chris-smallls.

8. See, for example, Karen Weise and Noam Scheiber, "Amazon Abruptly Fires Senior Managers Tied to Unionized Warehouse," New York Times, May 6, 2022, https://www.nytimes.com/2022/05/06/technology/amazon-fires-managers-union-staten-island.html.

9. See, for example, Keith Zhai and Fanny Potkin, "At Alibaba's Lazada, Coronavirus Measures Become the Latest Culture Conflict," Reuters, March 23, 2020, https://www.reuters.com/article/idUSKBN21A3V5/.

10. See, for example, Chengyi Lin, "In the Face of Lockdown, China's E-Commerce Giants Deliver," hbr.org, April 1, 2020, https://hbr.org/2020/04/in-the-face-of-lockdown-chinas-e-commerce-giants-deliver.

11. See, for example, Lulu Yilun Chen, "Alibaba's Jack Ma Sends Boxes of Coronavirus Test Kits and Masks to U.S.," Time, March 16, 2020, https://time.com/5803791/jack-ma-alibaba-coronavirus/.

12. See Karthik Ramanna, Jérôme Lenhardt, and Marc Homsy, "IKEA in Saudi Arabia (A)," case 116-015 (Boston: Harvard Business School, 2016), https://www.hbs.edu/faculty/Pages/item.aspx?num=50214.

13. See "IKEA Criticized for Airbrushing Women out of Saudi Catalogue," The Telegraph, October 1, 2012, quoted from Karthik Ramanna, Jérôme Lenhardt, and Marc Homsy, "IKEA in Saudi Arabia (A)," case 116-015 (Boston: Harvard Business School, 2016), https://www.hbs.edu/faculty/Pages/item.aspx?num=50214.

14. See Anna Ringstrom, "Swedes Slam IKEA for Its Female-Free Saudi Catalogue," Reuters, October 2, 2012, quoted from Karthik Ramanna, Jérôme Lenhardt, and Marc Homsy, "IKEA in Saudi Arabia (A)," case 116-015 (Boston: Harvard Business School, 2016), https://www.hbs.edu/faculty/Pages/item.aspx?num=50214.

15. See David Eskander and Mohamed Kotaiba Abdul Al, "Does IKEA Culture Apply Abroad?," February 5, 2010, quoted from Karthik Ramanna, Jérôme Lenhardt, and Marc Homsy, "IKEA in Saudi Arabia (A)," case 116-015 (Boston: Harvard Business School, 2016), https://www.hbs.edu/faculty/Pages/item.aspx?num=50214.

16. See Joe Sterling, "Images of Women Shelved in IKEA's Saudi Catalog," CNN, October 10, 2012, quoted from Karthik Ramanna, Jérôme Lenhardt, and Marc Homsy,

"IKEA in Saudi Arabia (A)," case 116-015 (Boston: Harvard Business School, 2016), https://www.hbs.edu/faculty/Pages/item.aspx?num=50214.

17. See Ardi Kolah, "Why Culture Matters and How Brands Get This So Wrong!" LinkedIn Pulse, May 1, 2014, quoted from Karthik Ramanna, Jérôme Lenhardt, and Marc Homsy, "IKEA in Saudi Arabia (A)," case 116-015 (Boston: Harvard Business School, 2016), https://www.hbs.edu/faculty/Pages/item.aspx?num=50214.

18. See Karthik Ramanna, "Dylan Pierce at Peninsula Industries," case 115-024 (Boston: Harvard Business School, 2014), https://www.hbs.edu/faculty/Pages/item.aspx?num=48324.

Chapter 5

1. See Karthik Ramanna and Sarah McAra, "Covid-19 at Oxford University Hospitals: Sustaining Morale on the Eve of a Crisis," case 321-0062-1 (Oxford, UK: Blavatnik School of Government, University of Oxford, 2020), https://www.thecasecentre.org/products/view?id=175090; see Karthik Ramanna and Vidhya Murthuram, "Of Faith and Fortunes: Reforming the Vatican's Finances," case 321-0219-1 (Oxford, UK: Blavatnik School of Government, University of Oxford, 2021), https://www.thecasecentre.org/products/view?id=178266.

2. See, for example, Kathleen L. McGinn and Eizabeth Long Lingo, "Power and Influence: Achieving Your Objectives in Organizations," background note 801-425 (Boston: Harvard Business School, 2001), https://www.hbs.edu/faculty/Pages/item.aspx?num=28031.

3. See, for example, https://en.wikipedia.org/wiki/Upayas_(diplomacy).

4. See, for example, Dr. Larry Goodson, "Kautilya—Noon Time Lecture," US Army War College, n.d., https://www.youtube.com/watch?v=7fKrLdRVkGw.

5. See Ramanna and McAra, "Covid-19 at Oxford University Hospitals."

6. See, for example, McGinn and Lingo, "Power and Influence: Achieving Your Objectives in Organizations."

7. See Ramanna and Murthuram, "Of Faith and Fortunes: Reforming the Vatican's Finances."

8. See, for example, https://en.wikipedia.org/wiki?curid=57141.

9. See, for example, Council of Europe, "The Holy See to Be Evaluated by the Council of Europe's Anti Money Laundering and Terrorist Financing Evaluation Body," press release, April 7, 2011, https://rm.coe.int/168071d40f.

10. "The Holy See (Including the Vatican City State)," Mutual Evaluation Report, Committee of Experts on the Evaluation of Anti-money Laundering Measures and the Financing of Terrorism (Moneyval), July 4, 2012, quoted from Ramanna and Murthuram, "Of Faith and Fortunes: Reforming the Vatican's Finances."

11. See "The Holy See (Including the Vatican City State)," Mutual Evaluation Report, p. 32.

12. "The Holy See (Including the Vatican City State)," Mutual Evaluation Report.

13. Quoted and paraphrased from "The Holy See (Including the Vatican City State)," Mutual Evaluation Report.

14. Quoted and paraphrased from "The Holy See (Including the Vatican City State)," Mutual Evaluation Report.

15. Quoted and paraphrased from "The Holy See (Including the Vatican City State)," Mutual Evaluation Report.

16. Alexander Stille, "Holy Orders," *New Yorker*, September 14, 2015, quoted from "The Holy See (Including the Vatican City State)," Mutual Evaluation Report.

17. The Polish Solidarity movement of the 1980s helped spread nonviolent, anti-communist ideas in Eastern Europe, eventually contributing to the fall of communism there.

18. Thomas J. Reese, *Inside the Vatican: The Politics and Organization of the Catholic Church* (Cambridge, MA: Harvard University Press, 1996), quoted from "The Holy See (Including the Vatican City State)," Mutual Evaluation Report.

19. See, for example, https://en.wikipedia.org/wiki/Pope_John_Paul_I _conspiracy_theories.

20. See, for example, Nicole Winfield, "Vatican Releases 1st Report of Financial Watchdog," *San Diego Union-Tribune*, May 22, 2013, https://www .sandiegouniontribune.com/sdut-vatican-releases-1st-report-of-financial-watchdog-2013may22-story.html; and Financial Intelligence Authority, Annual Report 2013, Vatican City State, https://www.aif.va/eng/pdf/AIF%20Report%202013%20ENG.pdf.

21. The appointment of non-clerics to ASIF leadership roles appears to have been in response to pressures from Moneyval. See, for instance, Council of Europe, "Anti-money Laundering and Combating the Financing of Terrorism, The Holy See," Mutual Evaluation Report, p. 147, http://rm.coe.int/mutual-evaluation-report-anti -money-laundering-and-combating-the-finan/16807160fa.

22. See, for example, Rebecca Speare-Cole, "Cressida Dick: Critics Delighted and Supporters Saddened as Met Commissioner Resigns," *Standard*, February 11, 2022, https://www.standard.co.uk/news/london/cressida-dick-critics-supporters-met -comissioner-resigns-b981984.html.

23. See Fritz Roethlisberger, "The Secret of Success," in *Man-in-Organization: Essays of F.J. Roethlisberger* (Cambridge, MA: Belknap Press of Harvard University Press, 1968).

24. See Wiley Souba, "Hittability: The Leader's Edge," *Academic Medicine* 92, no. 4 (2017), https://doi.org/10.1097/acm.0000000000001498.

25. In 2021, the year after the anti-policing protests described in chapter 3, the Met under Dick released a detailed strategy and action plan to improve inclusion, diversity, and engagement. That plan was still in effect in 2024, as of this writing.

Chapter 6

1. See Arianne Cohen, "How to Quit Your Job in the Great Post-Pandemic Resignation Boom," *Bloomberg*, May 10, 2021, https://www.bloomberg.com/news /articles/2021-05-10/quit-your-job-how-to-resign-after-covid-pandemic.

2. See PwC, "PwC Pulse Survey: Next in Work," n.d., https://www.pwc.com/us /en/library/pulse-survey/future-of-work.html.

3. See, for example, Robert Gibbons and Rebecca Henderson, "Relational Contracts and Organizational Capabilities," *Organization Science* 23, no. 5 (2012), https://doi.org/10.1287/orsc.1110.0715.

4. See Susan Helper and Rebecca Henderson, "Management Practices, Relational Contracts, and the Decline of General Motors," *Journal of Economic Perspectives* 28, no. 1 (2014), https://pubs.aeaweb.org/doi/pdfplus/10.1257/jep.28.1.49.

5. See "NUMMI," *This American Life*, March 26, 2020, https://www .thisamericanlife.org/403/nummi-2010. Quoted from Helper and Henderson, "Management Practices, Relational Contracts, and the Decline of General Motors."

6. See "NUMMI," *This American Life*. Quoted from Helper and Henderson, "Management Practices, Relational Contracts, and the Decline of General Motors."

7. See Helper and Henderson, "Management Practices, Relational Contracts, and the Decline of General Motors."

8. See Steven Spear, "Learning to Lead at Toyota," *Harvard Business Review*, May 2004.

9. See, for example, Lewis Carroll, *Through the Looking-Glass, and What Alice Found There*, https://www.gutenberg.org/files/12/12-h/12-h.htm.

10. See Stephen Covey, *The Seven Habits of Highly Effective People* (New York: Free Press, 1989).

11. See, for example, "After Two Years—A Conversation with the President," Television and Radio interview, American Presidency Project, December 17, 1962, https://www.presidency.ucsb.edu/documents/television-and-radio-interview-after -two-years-conversation-with-the-president.

12. See Isaiah Berlin, "On Political Judgment," *New York Review*, October 3, 1996, https://www.nybooks.com/articles/1996/10/03/on-political-judgment/.

13. See Karthik Ramanna and Radhika Kak, "A Model Public-Service Organisation? The US Attorney's Office for the Southern District of New York," case 421-0061-5 (Oxford, UK: Blavatnik School of Government, University of Oxford, 2019), https://www.thecasecentre.org/products/view?id=178260.

14. "Law and Order with Pallas Global CEO Bonnie Jonas," *GenHERation*, November 14, 2017, quoted from Ramanna and Kak, "A Model Public-Service Organisation?"

15. Interview with Bonnie Jonas, quoted from Ramanna and Kak, "A Model Public-Service Organisation?"

16. "Public Interest Careers," Career Development Office, Yale Law School, August 2019, quoted from Ramanna and Kak, "A Model Public-Service Organisation?"

17. Quoted and paraphrased from Ramanna and Kak, "A Model Public-Service Organisation?"

18. Interview with Robert Fiske, quoted from Ramanna and Kak, "A Model Public-Service Organisation?"

19. Interview with Mary Jo White, quoted from Ramanna and Kak, "A Model Public-Service Organisation?"

20. Interview with Bonnie Jonas, quoted from Ramanna and Kak, "A Model Public-Service Organisation?"

21. David Zaring, "Against Being against the Revolving Door," *University of Illinois Law Review* 2 (2013), quoted from Ramanna and Kak, "A Model Public-Service Organisation?"

22. David Zaring, "The Southern District of New York Offers Riches," *The Conglomerate*, August 16, 2010, quoted from Ramanna and Kak, "A Model Public-Service Organisation?"

23. Nicholas Lemann, "Street Cop," *New Yorker,* November 3, 2013, quoted from Ramanna and Kak, "A Model Public-Service Organisation?"

24. Interview with Bonnie Jonas, quoted from Ramanna and Kak, "A Model Public-Service Organisation?"

25. Quoted and paraphrased from Ramanna and Kak, "A Model Public-Service Organisation?"

26. See, for example, Jim Collins, "The Stockdale Paradox," n.d., https://www.jimcollins.com/concepts/Stockdale-Concept.html.

27. See Boris Groysberg and Robin Abrahams, "What the Stockdale Paradox Tells Us about Crisis Leadership," HBS Working Knowledge, August 17, 2020, https://hbswk.hbs.edu/item/what-the-stockdale-paradox-tells-us-about-crisis-leadership; see James Bond Stockdale, *A Vietnam Experience: Ten Years of Reflection* (Stanford, CA: Hoover Institution Press, 1984), https://www.hoover.org/research/vietnam-experience-ten-years-reflection.

28. See John Leach, "Survival Psychology: The Won't to Live," *The Psychologist,* January 22, 2011, https://www.bps.org.uk/psychologist/survival-psychology-wont-live.

29. See Groysberg and Abrahams, "What the Stockdale Paradox Tells Us about Crisis Leadership."

30. See Karthik Ramanna and Radhika Kak, "The Maggi Noodle Safety Crisis in India (B)," case supplement 116-014 (Boston: Harvard Business School, 2016), https://www.hbs.edu/faculty/Pages/item.aspx?num=50444.

31. See Karthik Ramanna and Radhika Kak, "The Maggi Noodle Safety Crisis in India (C)," case supplement 116-038 (Boston: Harvard Business School, 2016), https://www.hbs.edu/faculty/Pages/item.aspx?num=50446.

32. See Martin E.P. Seligman, "Building Resilience," *Harvard Business Review,* April 2011, https://hbr.org/2011/04/building-resilience.

33. For an excellent overview, see, for example, Brad Inwood, *Stoicism: A Very Short Introduction* (Oxford, UK: Oxford University Press, 2018), https://academic.oup.com/book/380.

34. See, for example, "What Is Stoicism? A Definition and 9 Stoic Exercises to Get You Started," Daily Stoic, n.d., https://dailystoic.com/what-is-stoicism-a-definition-3-stoic-exercises-to-get-you-started/, an excellent website to which I was directed by one of my case protagonists.

35. See David Marchick, "The Trump Official Who Did the Right Thing," *Washington Monthly,* October 7, 2022, https://washingtonmonthly.com/2022/10/07/the-trump-official-who-did-the-right-thing/.

36. See Chris Whipple, "Exclusive: Inside the S---tshow That Was the Trump-Biden Transition," *Vanity Fair,* October 12, 2022, https://www.vanityfair.com/news/2022/10/exclusive-inside-the-shtshow-that-was-the-trump-biden-transition.

37. Email correspondence with Chris Liddell, 2023.

Chapter 7

1. See Transformational Leadership Fellows, Blavatnik School of Government, University of Oxford, https://www.bsg.ox.ac.uk/transformational-leadership-fellows.

2. See, for example, https://en.wikipedia.org/wiki/Noble_lie.

3. See, for example, Roger L. Martin and Tony Golsby-Smith, "Management Is Much More Than a Science," *Harvard Business Review*, September–October 2017.

4. See, for example, Declaration of Independence: A Transcription, National Archives, https://www.archives.gov/founding-docs/declaration-transcript.

5. For an overview on this complex issue see, for example, the following resources from the Smithsonian: "Reconstructing Citizenship," National Museum of African American History and Culture, https://nmaahc.si.edu/explore/exhibitions /reconstruction/citizenship.

6. See https://en.wikipedia.org/wiki/Mustafa_Kemal_Atatürk.

7. This discussion draws and quotes from https://en.wikipedia.org/wiki/Kemalism.

8. See, for example, https://en.wikipedia.org/wiki/The_Social_Contract.

9. See Derya Bayir (2013), "Minorities and Nationalism in Turkish Law," p. 110, quoted from https://en.wikipedia.org/wiki/Kemalism.

10. See Andrew Mango, *Atatürk and the Kurds*, Middle Eastern Studies 35, no 4 (1999): 20, quoted from https://en.wikipedia.org/wiki/Kemalism.

11. See Fazıl Kayıkçı, "Course of Income Inequality in Turkey," *Theoretical Economics Letters* 9, no. 6 (2019), https://doi.org/10.4236/tel.2019.96131.

12. See, for example, Jenny White, "Democracy Is Like a Tram," Turkey Institute, July 14, 2016, https://www.turkeyinstitute.org.uk/commentary/democracy-like-tram/.

13. Quoted from https://en.wikipedia.org/wiki?curid=376619.

14. See, for example, William Butler Yeats, "The Second Coming," Poetry Foundation, https://www.poetryfoundation.org/poems/43290/the-second-coming.

15. See, for example, Meagan Fredette, "The Most Shocking Moments from Meghan Markle's Oprah Interview," *W Magazine*, March 8, 2021, https://www .wmagazine.com/culture/meghan-markle-oprah-interview-shocking-revelations; see, for example, https://en.wikipedia.org/wiki/Alternative_facts.

16. See Jim Collins, "Level 5 Leadership: The Triumph of Humility and Fierce Resolve," *Harvard Business Review*, January 2001.

17. See Daniel Goleman, "What Makes a Leader?," *Harvard Business Review*, January 2004.

18. For an excellent introduction, see Marjorie Garber, *Shakespeare After All* (New York: Pantheon, 2004).

19. See, for example, https://shakespeare.mit.edu/coriolanus/full.html.

20. See, for example, https://en.wikipedia.org/wiki/Hamartia.

21. Quoted from https://en.wikipedia.org/wiki/Stoicism.

22. See Marijke Doms, "Spiritual Leadership and Dissidence: Roger Scruton and Jan Patočka on Care for the Soul in the Modern Era," Academia, https://www.academia .edu/37221995/Spiritual_Leadership_and_Dissidence_Roger_Scruton_and_Jan _Patočka_on_Care_for_the_Soul_in_the_Modern_Era.

23. Quoted and paraphrased from Anna Petherick, Karthik Ramanna, and Oenone Kubie, "Education Reform in Brazil: An Enduring Coalition?," case 223-0075-1 (Oxford, UK: Blavatnik School of Government, University of Oxford, 2023), https:// www.thecasecentre.org/products/view?id=193842.

24. Email correspondence with Maria Helena Guimarães de Castro, 2024.

25. Quoted and paraphrased from email correspondence and conversations with Maria Helena Guimarães de Castro, 2024.

26. The common core curriculum was eventually adopted in 2018, and by 2020, it began to be implemented by various local education boards, albeit with difficulty due to the Covid-19 pandemic. In 2023, however, with a change in government, the core curriculum was once again under attack.

Index

republicanism, 177–178
resilience, xviii, 3, 4, 139–165, 196
　balanced outlook and, 153–159
　definition of, 140
　future productivity capacity and,
　　146–149
　inner strength and, 159–164
　leadership development and, 149–153
　relational contracts and, 141–146
　stoicism and, 187
　the uncontrollable and, 161–164
responsibility, capability asymmetries
　　and, 91, 95
Rhetoric (Aristotle), 169
rhetorical triangle, 169
Ricardo, David, 18
Roethlisberger, Fritz, 136
Romanticism, 173
Romney, Mitt, 162
Rousseau, John, 178–179
Rousseff, Dilma, 47, 190, 192
rule of rescue, 91
Rusbridger, Alan, 53

Sajó, András, 53
Samuelson, Paul, 18
self-awareness, 48–49, 185
self-motivation, 185
self-worth, 12–14, 37, 160
Seligman, Martin, 160
Seth, Anil, 41
Shakespeare, William, 185–186
Siemens, 127
Simpson, Thomas, 50
Single Euro Payments Area, 130
situation appraisals, 41–43
slavery, American exceptionalism and,
　　171, 174–175
social contract, 95–96, 178–179
　capabilities asymmetries and, 91, 92–93
　faith in in India, 17
social media, xiii–xiv, 6
　election meddling and, 33–34
　othering and, 22, 24–26

social grouping and, 27–28
　turning down the temperature and,
　　52–53
social norms, 37
social prestige of occupations, 13–14
social responsibility, 105–106
Social Science One, 53
Socrates, 188, 192
solutions
　incompleteness of, 28–30, 78
　weighing the risks and, 130–135
Souba, Wiley, 136–137
South Africa, 52
span of control, 164
Spear, Steven, 145–146
special interests, 20–21
stakeholders
　catalytic roles of, 64
　expectations of, 82, 83, 92–93, 98–109
　in making sense of the moment, 73–75
　organizational response and, 81
　platform for making sense of the
　　moment with, 62–65
Starbucks, 102
statism, 179–180
Stockdale, James, xviii, 155–156, 161
Stockdale Paradox, 154
stoicism, 161–164, 188
Stone, Chris, 56
stop-and-search policies. *see* London
　　Metropolitan Police
sustainability, of temperate leadership,
　　192–193
systemic factors, 83

tactics, 3, 4
taxi drivers, 8–9
tax reform, 19–21
TD Bank, ix
technology. *see also* social media
　education, demography, and, 10–11
　fear for the future and, 8–10
　jobs and, 8–10
　othering and, 22

Acknowledgments

As we leaned back on the wicker porch chairs overlooking the lush rosewood forest at our vacation retreat in Coorg, Jon said to me, "Tell me a story." But then, he quickly added, "And not about the age of outrage." I had apparently subjected him to so many oral drafts of this manuscript that he had had enough!

Life is unpredictable, especially in our deeply polarized times, but the comfort of having someone in your corner, who is always rooting for you (and is almost always willing to hear you profess on), certainly makes the ups more pleasurable and the downs less distressing. Jon, my husband, is that someone for me—and it is to him that I am most grateful.

● ● ●

This book would simply not have been possible without David Champion, my boundlessly curious and creative editor on numerous pieces in the *Harvard Business Review*. I first sent David an 11,000-word essay on the topic of "Managing in the Age of Outrage" in the summer of 2022. He carefully read every word of it, and then he said, "It is too long and too short." David had immediately determined that the essay could be the basis for both a feature article in *Harvard Business Review* (about 5,000 words) and a book for HBR Press (about 70,000 words). The article was published in January 2023, and with David's artful editorship (nay, his coauthorship!), here is the book.

With David playing more the role of co-adventurer on this project, Kevin Evers took on the role of commissioning this piece for HBR Press. Thereafter, Melinda Merino—the Press's master architect—became the book's editor in chief. Melinda has that rare eye for immediately seeing the forest from the trees—zooming into any detail that needs to be developed so that the whole narrative holds together more aesthetically and compellingly. Thanks largely to her, and the anonymous readers, the book is now in a form in which I hope it can be of some help in this divided world. At the Press, many thanks are also due to Macaulay Campbell, Victoria Desmond, Jane Gebhart, and Cheyenne Paterson.

I have never encountered anyone who is not the product of at least some mentors, and two people in particular have stewarded my development from a quantitative economist to a student and teacher of leadership. Rebecca Henderson, who herself made that journey some years before me, taught me to think at once like both a generalist and a specialist. She has since carefully (and very generously, given her own schedule) read nearly everything I have written in this area, including a draft of this book, on which she made numerous, spot-on suggestions for improvement. And SP Kothari, who has served as an intellectual sounding board and sparring partner over the years, has unreservedly helped me sharpen my ideas to the high standards of academic rigor without losing sight of their usefulness to practical problem-solving.

This book emerges from three communities, to whom it really must be credited. The first are the protagonists and supporters of the various case studies that feature herein. Priscilla Ankut, René Brülhart, Maria Helena Guimarães de Castro, Cressida Dick, Iván Duque, Chris Liddell, Meghana Pandit, "Dylan Pierce," and many others, have given their precious time to help me and my case teams build out some of their most difficult moments as leaders into lessons for the next generation. Many of these individuals also thoughtfully reacted to drafts of this manuscript, allowing me to more clearly capture the emotions that animated those crucial decision points. My connections to some of these individuals are the result of bold investments in leadership education by an associated community of supporters, who include Jamie Cooper, Michael Feigelson, Dabesaki Mac-Ikemenjima, Shankar Maruwada, Denis Mizne, and Hilary Pennington.

The second community to thank are my coauthors on those case studies—the professional case writers and faculty colleagues who plunged into some fairly controversial subject areas with me. While at Harvard, I worked variously with Esel Çekin, Vincent Dessain, Marc Homsy, Radhika Kak, Carin Knoop, Jerome Lenhardt, Anjali Raina, and Rachna Tahilyani on the Nestlé, IKEA, and Dylan Pierce case studies. The rest of the case studies in this book were the product of the Oxford Case Centre on Public Leadership, which I established upon arriving here. Vidhya Muthuram, our first employee at the centre, helped me put together the Vatican case. Thereafter, we were joined by Sarah McAra, who now serves as the centre's associate director. Sarah has been the engine of my productivity at Oxford, and as my coauthor on so many projects. She, together with Oenone Kubie, JP Caleiro, Sarah Gulick, Zuzana Hlavkova, and Radhika Kak, were variously the driving forces on the Brazil education, Colombia tax, Kaduna peace, Met Police, Oxford Hospitals, and Southern District case studies. My faculty coauthors on the cases were İrem Güçeri and Clare Leaver (Colombia), Anna Petherick (Brazil), Thomas Simpson (Kaduna), and Chris Stone (Met).

And the third community is, of course, my students from the Oxford MPP who bravely took a course with me on leadership in the age of outrage, even before I had a conceptual structure to offer—just on the basis of my promise of some potentially interesting stories. We have learned collectively through this experience—and it is from this learning that I hope you are building all the "unlikely coalitions" that this world sorely needs today.

Joe Badaracco and Sandra Sucher, together with the wider teaching group for the HBS Leadership & Corporate Accountability course (including Doug Anderson, David Fubini, Lina Goldberg, Richard Hamermesh, Paul Healy, Nien-hê Hsieh, Robert Kaplan, Joshua Margolis, Henry McGee, Nitin Nohria, Clayton Rose, and Derek

Van Beaver), contributed immeasurably to my development as a leadership scholar and to associated concepts such as identifying capability asymmetries.

Here at Oxford, my foremost thanks are to Ngaire Woods—unquestionably, one of the most inspiring higher-ed leaders in the world today—who took a bet on me to direct the fledgling MPP program of her creation. Helen Barnard, Helen Belcher, Daniel Cioccoloni, Fred Davis, Richenda Gambles, Joely Gibbens, Natasha Forrest, Zoe Hart, Jackie Liu, Tom Rigault, Tom Simpson, Charlotte Smith, Dan Snape, Huei-Chun Su, Alan Tipping, Anda Trifan, Adam Webster, Sarah Wilkin, Anne Wynne, and Ruosi Zhang—among many, many others—were my companions on that leadership experience, sometimes through very dark moments dealing with very distraught students and colleagues in the depths of Covid-19.

Others who have shaped the ideas in this book include Craig Anderson and Brad Bushman (authors of the GAM framework), Timon Forster (my research assistant on the quantitative analysis underlying chapter 1), Dutch Leonard (who "red teamed" early versions of my framework), and Anette Mikes (whose instincts as a sociologist bring new nuance to my "economist's brain"). Thanks also to Karan Bilimoria, Koushik Chatterjee, Sophie Linden, Ifueko Omoigui Okauru, Jonathan Wolff, Gamze Yücaoğlu, and Sarah Zaidi. Bob Kaplan, with whom I am now deeply involved in building a global accounting system for carbon emissions and removals, first introduced me to Wiley Souba's framework on "hittability." But, more importantly, Bob—together with Krishna Palepu—taught me, as a freshman faculty member at Harvard, to combine the scientific method with commonsense inductive reasoning to engage in potentially transformative "action research," which has since been my preferred method of scholarship.

My otherwise chaotic schedule—which involves juggling across multiple responsibilities from teaching, to advising, to managing, to finding quiet time for scholarly reflection and writing—has been tamed by the unperturbable Dee Murphy. Thanks further to "Sarge," whose unfailingly reliable chauffeuring, notwithstanding my habitual tardiness, got me on time for countless flights and meetings with the protagonists and experts from whom this book draws.

• • •

A note on citations: this book is not referenced like an academic tome, using instead the HBR Press citation approach. The core of the book draws from two of my articles and from ten coauthored case studies. The case studies themselves have many citations to primary and secondary sources, but not all those citations are in the book. Direct quotations to others' work are cited as such, but quotations from my authored or coauthored work are not generally used—instead, the original publication is noted in the text. In situations where I have relied on primary sources for this book (e.g., email correspondence with protagonists beyond the underlying cases), I have noted those in the endnotes or text. And, where I have relied on general experience and knowledge, I have cited a comprehensive resource (such as Wikipedia), which was used for fact checking and further referencing.

As with my previous book, this one represents the consolidation of about a decade of experience. That book was, in part, a diagnosis of the drivers of outrage—related to arguments on capitalism's "raw deal" presented in chapter 1. This one, hopefully more helpfully, is focused on solutions to the outrage. As is likely to be the case with such an undertaking, there are many others beyond those listed earlier to whom much thanks are due. Most notably omitted from the list are my many friends and family in Oxford, Cambridge, and around the world who helped Jon and me stay "resilient" through the pandemic, over Zoom cocktails, bone-chilling winter walks through the English and New England countrysides, and the like.

Finally, to my parents, to Jon's, and to our sisters, who shower us with love, thank you! And to our niece and nephew, who represent the future for which we must build a better world, I dedicate this book.

About the Author

KARTHIK RAMANNA is a professor of Business and Public Policy at the University of Oxford's Blavatnik School of Government, where he's served as director of one of the world's most experientially diverse leadership programs. A senior adviser to the United States' Public Company Accounting Oversight Board, he was previously a professor and the Marvin Bower Fellow at Harvard Business School. Ramanna's scholarship examines how leaders in business and public service build trust with stakeholders and has won numerous awards, including the *Harvard Business Review* McKinsey Award for "groundbreaking management thinking," the *Journal of Accounting and Economics* Best Paper Prize, and the international Case Centre's outstanding case-writer prize, dubbed by the *Financial Times* as "the business school Oscars."

(Disclaimer: The views expressed in this work are solely those of the author and do not necessarily represent the views of the PCAOB Board, individual board members, or staff of the PCAOB.)